D0844770

Emergency Department Treatment
of the Psychiatric Patient

Emergency Department Treatment of the Psychiatric Patient

Policy Issues and Legal Requirements

Susan Stefan

UNIVERSITY PRESS

2006

OXFORD
UNIVERSITY PRESS

Oxford University Press, Inc., publishes works that further
Oxford University's objective of excellence
in research, scholarship, and education.

Oxford   New York
Auckland   Cape Town   Dar es Salaam   Hong Kong   Karachi
Kuala Lumpur   Madrid   Melbourne   Mexico City   Nairobi
New Delhi   Shanghai   Taipei   Toronto

With offices in
Argentina   Austria   Brazil   Chile   Czech Republic   France   Greece
Guatemala   Hungary   Italy   Japan   Poland   Portugal   Singapore
South Korea   Switzerland   Thailand   Turkey   Ukraine   Vietnam

Published by Oxford University Press, Inc.
198 Madison Avenue, New York, New York 10016

www.oup.com

Oxford is a registered trademark of Oxford University Press

Library of Congress Cataloging-in-Publication Data
Stefan, Susan.
Emergency department treatment of the psychiatric patient : policy issues
and legal requirements / Susan Stefan.
p.   cm.—(American Psychology-Law Society series)
ISBN-13: 978-0-19-518929-2
ISBN-10: 0-19-518929-9
1. Psychiatric emergencies. 2. Hospitals—Emergency service. 3. Crisis intervention
(Mental health services). 4. Mental health laws—United States. I. Title II. Series.
[DNLM: 1. Emergency Services, Psychiatric—legislation & jurisprudence—United States.
2. Emergency Service, Hospital—standards—United States. 3. Mentally Disabled Persons—United States.
4. Patient Rights—United States. 5. Attitude of Health Personnel—United States. 6. Quality of Health
Care—standards—United States.   WM 33 AA1 S816e 2006]
RC480.5.S667   2006
362.2'2—dc22   2005020674

9 8 7 6 5 4 3 2 1

Printed in the United States of America
on acid-free paper

To my crisis intervention team, my respite services, my experts in de-escalation, and my providers of shelter, refuge, and support in the community—otherwise known as

my mother, Gabrielle Stefan
my husband, Wes Daniels
and my best friend, Jamie Elmer

Series Foreword

Ronald Roesch, Series Editor

This book series is sponsored by the American Psychology-Law Society (APLS). APLS is an interdisciplinary organization devoted to scholarship, practice, and public service in psychology and law. Its goals include advancing the contributions of psychology to the understanding of law and legal institutions through basic and applied research; promoting the education of psychologists in matters of law and the education of legal personnel in matters of psychology; and informing the psychological and legal communities and the general public of current research, educational, and service activities in the field of psychology and law. APLS membership includes psychologists from the academic research and clinical practice communities as well as members of the legal community. Research and practice is represented in both the civil and criminal legal arenas. APLS has chosen Oxford University Press as a strategic partner because of its commitment to scholarship, quality, and the international dissemination of ideas. These strengths will help APLS reach our goal of educating the psychology and legal professions and the general public about important developments in psychology and law. The focus of the book series reflects the diversity of the field of psychology and law as we will publish books on a broad range of topics.

Susan Stefan's book focuses on an increasingly important problem that has in part resulted from the changes that have taken place in the mental health system in the past several decades. Although the reorientation of mental health treatment from the institution to the community is a welcome change, it has thrust upon emergency departments a variety of roles for which they are ill-suited. Emergency department staff members now often serve as the gate-keepers for inpatient beds, the crisis management providers that most communities still lack, and the basic health care safety net when Medicaid budgets are trimmed or doctors' schedules are too busy. For many people with serious psychiatric disabilities—and, even more importantly, for care providers, police, and family members—emergency departments are the solution when the health care system is inadequate, too complex to navigate, or has refused requests for assistance. Thus, hospital emergency departments become the answer to a wide range of problems they were never intended to solve.

How have emergency departments dealt with these changes? Stefan provides a critical analysis of the problems faced in emergency rooms, from the perspective of both emergency department patients and the professionals who treat them. She also examines statutory and case law, which provides the context for both the current situation as well as the changes that need to be made if we are to improve the quality of care of persons in the community who experience mental health problems. Overall, she finds that those labeled as "psychiatric patients" are all too often treated by emergency room personnel with impatience and even hostility. Stefan concludes the book with a clear set of recommendations for changing the manner in which emergency departments deal with patients who have mental health problems. Importantly, she also discusses community-based alternatives to emergency rooms for those with mental health problems, such as family foster homes, crisis hostels, mobile treatment units, and home companion programs.

Preface

This book began with the tears of devastated women as they told me about their experiences in emergency departments (EDs). These women lived in different states, in large cities, small towns, and rural areas. They had gone to EDs for help with depression, anxiety, or other serious psychiatric problems and were told they had to take off all their clothes. Many of these women had harrowing histories of childhood sexual abuse and were terrified. Others didn't understand why seeking help for a psychiatric crisis meant they had to take their clothes off. Some who initially refused to remove their clothing were held down and stripped by security guards and restrained by their wrists and ankles to the gurney if they struggled. By the time they had been at the ED for a few hours, they were in much worse emotional condition than when they arrived. Some of these women just wanted to tell their stories. Others wanted to fight back, but they had no idea what remedies were available to them. Indeed, there was no book, Web site, or other resource to which I could refer them.

I spoke to ED nurses, clinicians, and administrators about these complaints and others relating to the treatment of people with psychiatric disabilities. While some ED staff were defensive and hostile, most were genuinely troubled by what they perceived to be irresolvable conflicts between safety concerns, liability issues, time constraints, crowded spaces, and the needs of people in psychiatric crisis for time, comfort, listening, and caring. They, too, had questions about how to achieve better practices within inevitable constraints inherent in ED practice.

I did extensive research and found few uniform practices or standards on how to treat people with psychiatric disabilities in ED settings. The American Psychiatric Association Task Force on Psychiatric Emergency Services (2002) and the Consensus Guidelines on Treatment of Behavioral Emergencies (2001) contain recommendations that are helpful in the subject areas that are covered. However, neither addressed in depth the kinds of issues I was hearing from clients and ED staff. Nor were there any works summarizing the vast array of federal and state legal and regulatory standards that patients could invoke to seek relief or explaining the ways patients could advocate for themselves. Finally, there was little analysis of why these problems, which are so pervasive, are so generally ignored by policymakers. The analysis presented in this book suggests an explanation for the depth of the problems, their seeming intractability, and the vast silence from politicians and policymakers addressing health care and mental health issues.

Although I am a lawyer, the more I studied the issues, the less that I believed that litigation would provide the necessary solutions, except in the most egregious cases. Rather, working out new approaches for ED treatment of people with psychiatric disabilities requires an arduous process of dialogue and discussion between *all* the parties—the people who receive the services and ED professionals, of course, but also representatives of the public mental health system, managed care, accreditation bodies, the research community, Medicaid administrators, and those who have developed community crisis treatment alternatives.

I persuaded the Center for Public Representation, where I work, to focus on ED treatment of psychiatric patients as a major systemic initiative and to seek funding to work on developing these new approaches. The first step was to compile and analyze the research and case law on the standards governing the treatment of people with psychiatric disabilities in ED settings. Where there were no standards or significant disagreement, we assembled a group of experts representing the communities described above, and they assisted us in developing solutions and standards that were sensitive to the concerns and interests of all involved parties.

The Ittleson Foundation and the van Ameringen Foundation generously funded the project. This book and the recommendations appearing in its appendix represent these first two steps. But this book also reflects my conclusion that to focus solely on ED treatment of people with psychiatric disabilities is to miss an important larger picture. This picture includes more appropriate and less expensive crisis treatment alternatives, which are described in this book. It also includes a socio-legal analysis of the source of the problems and the larger solution to them. While some people with psychiatric disabilities blame EDs for the pain and damage they suffer, and some ED staff have little patience for the people they see repeatedly and can't seem to help, the policymakers whose problems are solved by this arrangement are not held accountable.

Emergency departments and their staff share some of the attributes of people with psychiatric disabilities they see—they go from crisis to crisis, with insufficient structural support and very little public understanding of the pressures they face. They inhabit a culture that few outsiders can comprehend. For many, the fact that they continue to function at all is heroic under the circumstances they face. Most of all, they are expected to shoulder the burdens of the unraveling public mental health care system, ever-diminishing Medicaid coverage and reimbursement, and inadequate or non-existent community crisis care services.

This book is about a major focal point of the health care crisis in this country. It offers solutions, from the concrete and mundane to more aspirational and systemic. If nothing else, it may serve as the springboard for a social policy conversation that should have started years ago.

Acknowledgments

This book was researched and written with the generous assistance of grants from the Ittelson Foundation and the van Ameringen Foundation. Anthony Wood of the Ittleson Foundation in particular was willing to fund the start-up costs of the Center for Public Representation's Emergency Department Project. Without him, this book would not exist.

The Center for Public Representation was also fortunate enough to attract an outstanding advisory council from across the nation for the Emergency Department Project. The members of the advisory council are Dr. Robert Factor, director of the Emergency Services Unit of the Mental Health Center of Dane County, who also provides emergency psychiatric services for the Veteran's Administration; Dr. Robert Glover, executive director of the National Association of State Mental Health Program Directors; Dr. Edward Knight, vice president for recovery, rehabilitation and mutual support of Value Options and Adjunct Professor, Rehabilitation Sciences, Boston University; J. Rock Johnson, J.D., of the National Association of Protection and Advocacy Systems; Dr. Charles Lidz, director of the Center for Mental Health Services Research, University of Massachusetts Medical School; Steven Miccio, executive director of PEOPLe, Inc., in Poughkeepsie, New York; and Dr. Robert Okin, chief of psychiatry at San Francisco General Hospital. The council was very much involved in developing the proposed standards and recommendations at the end of this book. They also read much of this book in draft and gave helpful comments. Opinions and conclusions expressed in the text of the book are my own.

I was also fortunate to receive outstanding research support from Kerry Kotar of Suffolk University Law School for two years, from Amy Cyphert of Harvard Law School for two years, and from Satyanand Satyanarayana of Harvard Law School for a semester. My colleagues at the Center for Public Representation, including Joy Bergman, Marcia Boundy, Bob Fleischner, Pam Long, and Steven Schwartz, devoted a great deal of time and energy to ensure the success of the Emergency Department Project, and I thank them for their continuing support. Amy Gunderson has been an extremely helpful and efficient secretary; this manuscript would never have made it out of the office without her assistance.

Scores of people have patiently given me the benefit of their first-hand experiences from working in and around emergency departments. There is insufficient space to thank them all here, but I would remiss not to particularly thank Nan Stromberg, Kathy Coughlin, and Michael Weeks of the Massachusetts Department of Mental Health Licensing Division; Dr. Anna Fitzgerald of Boston Medical Center; Dr. Robert Factor of the Mental Health Center of Dane County, Wisconsin; Amy Gremillion, R.N., of Austin, Texas; Deborah Provost and Ann Maynard, R.N., the director and nurse manager, respectively, of the Emergency Department at Baystate Medical Center in Springfield, Massachusetts; Beckie Child, of Choices for Change in Portland, Oregon; Maryann Spicer, Director of Corporate Compliance at Massachusetts General Hospital; Dr. Joel Dvoskin, Tucson, Arizona; and Russell Colling, Colling and Kramer Security Consultants, in Salida, Colorado.

Hundreds of people with psychiatric disabilities who received services in emergency departments were generous enough to fill out surveys, correspond with me, and speak to me regarding their experiences in emergency departments. Many of these people told me about experiences that have haunted and damaged them; their courage, humor, and resilience humbles me. For the most part, they have asked to remain anonymous, but some, like Cyndi McKnight and Louisa Smith, gave me permission to use their names, while others, like Linda Stalker, asked that their names be used, and I have gladly done so.

I also thank the dedicated attorneys and advocates with protection and advocacy agencies who shared with me insights from the work they have done to protect the rights of people with psychiatric disabilities in emergency department and crisis settings: Bill Brooks and Cliff Zucker in New York, Mark Joyce in Maine, Beth Mitchell in Texas, Kathy Wilde in Oregon, Patrick Washburn in Ohio, Laura Cain in Maryland, Emmett Dwyer in New Jersey, and Nancy Alisberg in Connecticut. I thank them for their assistance and for the work that they continue to do.

I have had a tremendously good experience with Oxford University Press. Heartfelt thanks to Dr. Ron Roesch for helpful edits and the benefit of his expertise, and to Joe Zito, Norman Hirschy, Cristina Wojdylo, and Keith Faivre for prompt, responsive, and professional assistance with my many questions.

Thanks to Laura Ziegler, Kermit Brown, Tom Behrendt, Ira Burnim, Adrienne Stefan, and Susan Mann for their love, support, wisdom, and their never-ending willingness to help me in moments of need.

Contents

Emergency Department Treatment
of the Psychiatric Patient

1

Introduction

I am feeling very traumatized because of a situation that happened at Baystate Emergency Room last Wednesday night. I was forced by police to go to the ER after I had gotten very flustered with PCS [crisis services] and hung up on them and they chose to call the police to do a check on me. The police came to my apartment and gave me the choice of going "voluntarily" or getting section 12ed [involuntarily detained]. Since I am terrified to end up in any hospital in this area I cooperated and went along peacefully. I was totally angry as I had already had a very bad day and at that point I just wanted to take my meds and go to bed.

When I arrived at the ER no one was paying attention so I spent about 15–20 minutes outside smoking figuring they would sooner or later catch up to me. I was eventually asked to come inside so I did and curled up on a stretcher as I was feeling totally overwhelmed and couldn't respond to anyone. That is when the trouble began. I was told to take my clothes off and get into a johnnie. When I didn't respond I was then wheeled into a small room and surrounded by several people both male and female and was forcibly undressed down to my underwear. I was pinned down and the orderly who had my arm held down was twisting so tight that I felt like he was going to break it. I begged him to release it but every time I moved he twisted it tighter. They put me into restraints and left me. To add insult to injury I was calling out a friend of mine's name to help calm me down and heard the hospital staff out in the hallway mocking me . . .

As a former trauma survivor this has had serious psychological effects on me. My sense of safety has been shattered . . . I am relating this to you because this is not an isolated case. So many consumers have horror stories of how they have been treated at emergency rooms yet the abuse is still continuing . . . Meanwhile I have no trust in ever getting help if I am in a crisis. The thought of ever ending up at the ER even for medical reasons absolutely terrifies me and no longer can I trust [crisis services] . . .

Linda Stalker
Northampton, Massachusetts (2001)[1]

This letter eloquently summarizes many common complaints that people with psychiatric disabilities have about their treatment when they are in crisis. They are unnecessarily and coercively taken to emergency departments (EDs) or hospitalized, often as a result of reaching out for help to crisis services or hotlines. Once at the ED, they may be ignored in the waiting area or left unattended on a gurney for hours. This may be because the ED is overcrowded and rushed. However, research discussed later in this book also confirms that emergency staff sometimes ignore psychiatric patients to "punish" them for coming in too often. People who present with psychiatric emergencies report being locked in small, bare rooms with no toilet and no knowledge of when the door might be unlocked—and these are people who were in emotional crisis in the first place. As was the case with Linda Stalker, sometimes people in psychiatric crisis are ordered to remove their clothing. If they resist, they may be forcibly stripped of their clothing by security guards. Many who bang on the locked doors or resist efforts to disrobe them are restrained with four-point leather restraints by security guards. People with psychiatric disabilities may be treated impatiently or roughly, without regard for how this treatment might affect an already fragile, vulnerable person. This is the experience of thousands and thousands of people with psychiatric disabilities, who view EDs with bitterness and distrust.

These experiences, of course, take place in a context. It is the context of EDs which are themselves in crisis, under pressure, and facing impossible demands with no end in sight. Many EDs are overcrowded, underfunded, and facing increasing staff shortages and a dwindling availability of hospital beds. Increasing ambulance diversions, as well as the ever-present threat of manmade or natural disasters, threaten to overwhelm an already teetering system. The shortage of nurses impacts EDs both in terms of staffing and in creating barriers to admitting patients to hospitals, which often have available beds but cannot accept patients because they do not have sufficient nurses available to provide safe care.

In this potent mix, the serious problems faced by people with psychiatric disabilities who seek treatment in EDs are often lost or obscured. Some of the problems that people with psychiatric disabilities encounter in EDs reflect common complaints: long delays, lack of inpatient beds or community follow up, and refusals by insurance or managed care to approve treatment. There is reason to suspect that people with psychiatric disabilities experience the worst of these common complaints: longer delays, fewer inpatient beds, sparser community resources and more denials of care by insurance companies.[2]

The good news is that some EDs rise to these challenges, genuinely seeking to improve the care they provide people with psychiatric disabilities. In fact, the ED staff at Baystate Medical Center, the hospital where Linda Stalker experienced the conditions described above, chose to embark on an ambitious program to improve ED care for people with psychiatric disabilities—a program whose successes have been published in *The Journal of Emergency Nursing* and presented around the country. They did this without additional funding or litigation. The story of the crafting of solutions by Baystate and other hospitals like it is as much a part of this book as the story of the people in great psychiatric distress who continue to be hurt unnecessarily by ED staff who are themselves stressed to the limits of their own endurance, and who do not understand (often because they have not been told) the harm that they are doing.

This book will analyze the treatment of people with psychiatric disabilities in ED settings through a number of lenses:

- federal and state legal and regulatory standards,
- case law,
- research literature (abundant in some areas and strikingly sparse in others),
- standards for treatment and practice proposed by a variety of professional groups, and
- people with psychiatric disabilities and the ED staff who serve them.

These voices have been gathered from survey responses by people with psychiatric disabilities and ED staff, as well as from a number of personal interviews. These interviews took place with authors of articles in the ED literature, following up information presented in the articles, or as follow ups to survey responses, when the respondents indicated that they did not mind further contact. The interview with Linda Stalker generated the interviews with the Baystate staff involved in responding to her situation.

The second chapter of this book presents the context of ED treatment of people with psychiatric disabilities, discussing the place of the ED in the hospital structure and in the mental health system. In addition, information about patterns of usage of EDs is presented, along with a description of the ways in which visits to the ED by people with known psychiatric disabilities are fundamentally different from visits by people who either do not have psychiatric disabilities or whose diagnoses are unknown to the ED staff. Myths about unnecessary use of EDs by uninsured people are debunked, as are assumptions about the frequency and subject matter of litigation against EDs on behalf of people with psychiatric disabilities.

Chapter 3 summarizes the principal complaints that people with psychiatric disabilities voice about their treatment in EDs. The majority of problems experienced in EDs by people with psychiatric disabilities are unique and are not shared by other ED patients. First, a level of force and coercion is directed at psychiatric patients in EDs that is not generally experienced by medical patients. The force and coercion arise in large part from the ED's duty to examine and detain patients who are believed to be dangerous to themselves or others as a result of mental illness. Emergency departments often involuntarily detain people who come voluntarily for help in a psychiatric crisis and who pose no danger until they can be assessed by a mental health professional, a practice whose questionable legality increases as the hours go by. In addition, to prevent psychiatric patients from leaving either prior to or after assessment EDs have adopted a host of policies, such as forced disrobing (even when the patient has a rape or trauma history), restraint to a gurney or bed for hours, and solitary hours and even days unattended in a locked room, all of which cause untold emotional and physical damage to the patient. Hospital EDs also have been known to use pepper spray and Taser guns on psychiatric patients.

In addition, patients with psychiatric histories who arrive at an ED seeking medical care often encounter a degree of skepticism that their medical concerns are imaginary or exaggerated not faced by people who do not have psychiatric histories. The use of force and the minimization of the medical complaints of people with psychiatric disabilities have led to injury and even death.

Other injuries are less visible but equally real. People who arrive seeking treatment for psychiatric emergencies are often treated by ED personnel with impatience, hostility, and contempt. Unlike most medical patients, psychiatric patients, especially so-called repeaters, can be perceived as manipulative, or not truly ill. Some ED personnel are so repelled by people they call "clutter"[3] that they engage in punitive responses. As one text notes: "The negative attitudes of emergency physicians, emergency nurses, and emergency medical technicians toward the person who requires treatment for attempted suicide are well documented. An attitude often expressed is that painful, punitive treatment will 'teach the patient a lesson' not to repeat the self-destructive behavior."[4]

Not surprisingly, ED staff have their own difficulties treating psychiatric patients. Some of these are mirror images of complaints expressed by people with psychiatric disabilities, and others are quite different. Chapter 4 canvasses the difficulties that administrators, physicians, nurses, psychiatrists, and other ED staff experience in the treatment of people with psychiatric disabilities. Because EDs have been historically ambivalent about whether psychiatric crises really belong in their domain, the development of standards of care for treating psychiatric emergencies has been slow, stalled, or non-existent. For example, as of today there is no agreement on what constitutes a psychiatric emergency that renders ED care "necessary."[5] There is no agreement on how a psychiatric assessment in an ED should be conducted.[6] An effort by the New York Office of Mental Health to develop a standard assessment tool failed. There is no agreement on the level of medical assessment required to constitute proper medical clearance, a serious problem since many illnesses present as psychiatric problems.[7] There is no agreement on whether medical clearance of psychiatric patients should, as a general rule, include toxicology tests for alcohol and drugs. There is no agreement on appropriate cognitive assessment in the psychiatric emergency service.[8] There are no standards, and little agreement, on when a psychiatric patient should be admitted rather than discharged to the community. There are no standards to guide the use of law enforcement/security personnel in EDs. Even a recent attempt to come up with guidelines for treatment of behavioral emergencies did not address these issues.[9]

Even where there are standards in emergency medicine's treatment of psychiatric patients, those standards often conflict with existing standards in the field of psychiatry. Nowhere is this more clear than in the area of seclusion and restraint. Other less publicized disagreements include the level of medical and laboratory tests that EDs should routinely administer to people presenting with psychiatric disabilities.

These issues, too, are inextricably intertwined with legal and regulatory issues relating to the right to evaluation and stabilization, civil commitment, rights to informed consent and to have advance directives honored, the right to be free from seclusion and restraint, the Americans with Disabilities Act, and other statutory and regulatory enactments. Although a plethora of complicated federal and state laws and regulations govern EDs, neither ED staff nor patients are familiar with their requirements. If the standards missing from ED treatment of people with psychiatric disabilities are to be developed, as a practical matter they must be developed or harmonized in the context of existing federal and state legal and licensing requirements. Chapter 5 delineates federal and state legal and regulatory requirements governing the treatment of people with psychiatric disabilities, covering questions such as to whom the laws apply, what standards they impose, and what questions arise uniquely in the context of ED treatment of people with psychiatric disabilities.

Most of the unique problems associated with the treatment of people with psychiatric emergencies are intertwined with the law and its requirements. Psychiatric patients, unlike other people at EDs, may be brought involuntarily and may not want treatment at all. Many of these patients are brought to EDs by police officers. Unlike other patients, individuals with psychiatric disabilities encounter ED doctors with the knowledge that those doctors have the legal authority to detain them against their will. Both the law and regulatory requirements are constantly changing. In the last few years, the Joint Commission on Accreditation of Health Care Organizations has added accreditation changes to attempt to address the issue of ED over-crowding.[10] The Bush administration amended the Emergency Medical Treatment and Active Labor Act (EMTALA) regulations on September 9, 2003, in response to urgent pressure from hospitals, ED administrators, and emergency services professionals. This book summarizes in one place federal and state licensing and accreditation requirements applicable to ED care of people with psychiatric disabilities for the benefit of ED patients and the people who serve them.

As the problems are unique, so the solutions must also be unique. Chapter 6 looks broadly at two different kinds of solutions to the problems discussed in this book: the development of alternatives to the use of EDs by people with psychiatric disabilities, and the improvement and modification of current standards and practices used by general hospital EDs and psychiatric emergency services. The first part of the chapter describes a number of alternatives currently in use around the country, from mobile crisis units to family foster homes and crisis hostels, with practical emphasis on how they are funded and research regarding their effectiveness. The second part of the chapter discusses proposed solutions to most of the problems discussed earlier in the book relating specifically to ED treatment of people with psychiatric disabilities. In addition, it delineates a number of very specific proposed standards and recommendations that, if adopted, would go a long way to improving the care received by people with psychiatric disabilities in ED settings. As the story of Baystate Medical Center shows, a staff that is highly motivated and well led can always improve the experience of people with psychiatric disabilities in EDs, through a commitment to see that experience "through the patient's eyes" and to tirelessly question assumptions and conclusions about the meaning of safety and protection to both hospital and patient.

Chapter 7 steps back and examines the factors that make the treatment of people with psychiatric disabilities different from medical patients in ED settings. In addition to the mandate to assess and involuntarily detain certain people with psychiatric disabilities—a mandate that does not extend to medical patients—another difference is the issue of the secondary utilizer of the ED. "Secondary utilizers" include the family members, police officer, or service provider who brings an individual to the ED—often against that individual's will—to solve a family problem or social conflict. Sometimes this happens at night, when regular treatment and service providers are not available. Sometimes the service providers seek a quick solution to a difficult problem by taking a client to the ED. In this way, the availability of EDs may contribute to inappropriate utilization individually and on a larger social level. Emergency departments provide cover for inadequate social service agencies suffering from budget cuts that make it difficult or impossible to provide the preventive and crisis stabilization services, medication, or sometimes just the reassurance and company that individuals in psychiatric crisis need. Thus, the larger solution to some ED problems must come from outside the hospital. At the same time, there is much that hospitals can do to improve their treatment of their patients with psychiatric disabilities without larger social change, and some hospitals are leading the way.

There are many issues that could have been covered in greater detail in this book: the role of police in detaining and bringing people to EDs, as happened to Linda Stalker; and a more exhaustive explanation of the complex reimbursement rules that govern ED care. Ultimately, this is a book about the people who visit EDs in psychiatric crisis, the staff who try to help them, the federal and state laws and regulations that govern them, and the policies that could improve the experience for everyone. No such book has ever been written, and my hope is that this will set the stage for discussions and, ultimately, for changes that benefit everyone, staff and patients alike.

2

Overview of Emergency Services for People with Psychiatric Disabilities

Emergency departments that serve people with psychiatric disabilities, whether they are general emergency departments (EDs) or psychiatric emergency services (PES), operate as part of two distinct worlds: the mental health service system, and the hospital in which they are physically located. Yet these EDs are in many important ways isolated from both worlds.

The problems facing EDs in their treatment of psychiatric patients are often a magnified version of the problems plaguing mental health services in general. Like mental health care systems, emergency services for people with psychiatric disabilities are underdiscussed, underfunded, fragmented, and isolated. Mental health and emergency service providers often bear the burden of social problems and tragedies—trauma, violence, poverty, and displacement—that preceded their involvement and that are out of their control.

Mental health services and EDs react to their isolation and increase that isolation by becoming their own small, insular worlds with distinctive rules and cultures, so much so that they have been the subjects of study by anthropologists and sociologists.[1] Despite the similar issues facing mental health services in general and psychiatric emergency services, however, the most striking fact about them is the degree to which they are isolated from each other, each conducting its operations in a vacuum from the other.

Public mental health services are generally overseen by a state mental health agency, which exercises considerable regulatory and funding control over treatment providers, such as state psychiatric hospitals and community residential providers. Generally, however, the state mental health agency has neither regulatory oversight nor funding control over EDs or psychiatric emergency services, which are tied to hospitals, regulated by public health agencies, and directly reimbursed by Medicaid, Medicare, or private insurance. Thus, the "continuum of services" overseen by state mental health agencies has a significant gap: emergency or crisis services. Some mental health agencies provide their own crisis services in the form of mobile crisis units, hot and warm lines, and respite settings. (These are described and discussed more fully in chapter 6.) But a substantial number of state mental health agency clients continue to use EDs, and state mental health agencies have little, if any, control or even influence over how their clients are treated within EDs.

In days gone by, private psychiatric providers often admitted their patients directly to private psychiatric hospitals, bypassing EDs altogether. Now, managed care has made that more difficult. The effort to control costs means that more private patients end up in the ED because inpatient stays and extended therapy have been limited. That does not mean, however, that private providers have increased their interactions with EDs.

The agencies that do regulate EDs, generally public health departments, often have very little expertise in the area of mental health, precisely because another state agency is responsible for that area. Thus, ED treatment of people with psychiatric disabilities remains generally unexamined, underregulated, and isolated from policy discussions on other mental health issues.

Emergency department services for people with psychiatric disabilities also share many of the problems of medical emergency services generally— they are underfunded, overstressed, and operate under a statutorily mandated "open door" policy exploited by policymakers and providers alike. Yet psychiatric patients and their problems are never quite considered a part of "real" emergency services. It is no secret that many emergency service personnel regard people in psychiatric crisis with distaste or fear, as "problems,"[2] "nuisances,"[3] or even "clutter."[4] Some staff who put in long and overwhelming hours saving lives have mixed feelings (at best) when a person comes in for self-injury or suicidality. Others, even those who want to provide good care for psychiatric patients, have competing demands on their time. As one director of nursing in an ED candidly acknowledged, "As an excellent, competent emergency nurse, I have someone in psychiatric crisis, someone who can't breathe from asthma attacks, and someone with cardiac arrest. Who do you think is going to get my attention?"[5]

This chapter will look at how emergency services in general, and psychiatric emergency services specifically, operate within hospitals and mental health systems without ever being fully integrated into either. It will examine the pressures exerted on EDs and the structural incentives under which they operate, many of which create unintentional barriers to optimal treatment of people in psychiatric crisis. As the American Psychiatric Association's Task Force on Psychiatric Emergency Services summarizes bluntly, "If any group of stakeholders were to design a system [to assist people in psychiatric crisis] *a priori*, the most common service currently available could not emerge from the deliberative process."[6]

Finally, this chapter will provide a statistical snapshot of EDs and psychiatric emergency services today and evaluate some of the most popular prevalent assumptions about the uses and abuses of EDs: that poor people use EDs for non-urgent medical needs, that most users of ED services are uninsured, and that EDs are a focal point of liability, especially in the case of suicidal patients. The research in the field, including the detailed statistical reports produced annually by the National Center for Health Statistics, shows that the first two assumptions are incorrect; surveys of case law show a more complex and ambiguous picture about ED liability issues. Finally, this chapter will examine the difference between medical and psychiatric emergency services, and set the stage for an analysis of problems facing psychiatric emergency services today and their solutions.

The History and Context of the Delivery of Emergency Services

Emergency Departments in the Context of Hospitals

Problems with Emergency Department Staffing

Emergency medicine is a latecomer to the field of medical specialties. Only in the last decade or two have "emergency rooms" graduated to department status at most hospitals.[7] Until quite recently, emergency rooms were staffed haphazardly—by rotating hospital physicians on a voluntary on-call basis, inexperienced residents, moonlighting physicians, or some combination of the three. Many EDs historically did not even operate on a round-the-clock basis. This was especially true in rural areas. The gap between rural and urban areas in medicine has always been wide, and it may be greatest in fields like emergency medicine, whose relatively low and unpredictable volume makes it impossible for many rural communities to sustain 24-hour preparedness in the variety of specialties that might be required.

Although the American College of Emergency Physicians was formed in 1968, emergency care as we know it today was still in its infancy at that time. In 1970, most of the private hospitals in New Orleans, for example, had no EDs and demanded substantial cash deposits from patients prior to admission.[8] The first hospital in Maine to have a full-time, around-the-clock ED was Central Maine Medical Center, which began to offer this new service in the summer of 1970.[9]

Governmental regulations, increased funding, and a series of court decisions establishing hospital liability for EDs' refusal to treat patients[10] began to change the landscape over the next decade. By 1979, when the American Medical Association recognized emergency medicine as America's 23rd medical specialty,[11] the situation had improved markedly in terms of staffing for most medical emergencies.

However, as late as 1990, the vast majority of psychiatric evaluations in two major New England EDs were provided by non-psychiatric physicians, a situation still prevalent in many rural, small town, and small city EDs.[12] Even in urban areas, EDs may still try to run operations on a shoestring. Until recently, at five major hospitals in Denver, Colorado (as in other locations), psychiatric evaluations were performed on an on-call basis through a contract with an outside agency. Sometimes the agency sent counselors, who often had no other mental health professional available with whom to consult when performing evaluations and assessments. In litigation arising from this situation, one counselor testified that her recommendations were routinely ordered by physicians who usually did not bother to read her notes.[13]

Ironically, emergency medicine claimed its status as a discrete professional specialty in a climate of crisis about the availability and staffing of emergency services. Perhaps the former was necessary as the first response to the latter. But it is important to remember today, amid declarations of an unprecedented crisis in emergency care, that this is not the first time that these alarms have been raised, especially in the field of psychiatric emergency services.

In 1988, a front page article in the *New York Times* noted that "On a Friday or Saturday night, it is not unusual to have 17 or 18 hospitals closed [in Los Angeles] . . . Many people mistakenly think this is a problem for the poor. But if there is no emergency room, it is not there for anyone. If the wealthiest person in the state is at a conference downtown and has chest pains, he will be taken to a county hospital."[14]

Between 1988 and 1990, the *average* length of stay in a major psychiatric emergency service in Los Angeles was running as high as 48 hours.[15] Many news accounts of the time have a timeless feel to them: the New York State Commission on the Quality of Care for the Mentally Disabled released a report on ED overcrowding for people with psychiatric disabilities in 1989.[16] This was a year after specialists in Florida refused to provide care in EDs in order to protest rising malpractice rates, resulting in a 13-hour treatment delay for a woman shot in the back. The seventh hospital contacted (Tampa General) agreed to treat her, and she was taken 150 miles for emergency surgery.[17]

Some aspects of staffing have certainly improved. Emergency departments do not report difficulty in attracting specialists in emergency medicine (although many are not satisfied with their employment, see below at pp. 16–17.[18] The nursing shortage does affect EDs,[19] and many are turning to staff with less training or experience to carry out tasks that nurses used to perform. Training for psychiatrists has begun to focus on psychiatric emergencies, although only quite recently. In the last 10 years, residents in general psychiatry programs have been required to receive training in emergency psychiatry.[20]

Communication Problems Between Hospitals and their Emergency Departments

Emergency departments in general are often ill connected to and ill treated by the hospitals in which they are located. Unlike most other departments in a hospital, the entire ED operation may be contracted out by hospitals to separate entities, usually physicians' groups, improving neither connection to nor communication with the hospital and its administration.[21] Historically, and to this day, the ED is not considered an integral part of the hospital.

The lack of communication with the hospital and the hospital's inattention to the needs of the ED may be a continuing legacy of the "emergency room," when emergency services were non-autonomous units in the hospital without the rights and responsibilities of hospital departments. The transformation of "emergency rooms" into hospital departments with all the appurtenant administrative benefits has taken place only in the last 10 to 15 years.[22] Being a department in a hospital carries important administrative advantages—having a director permits authority and responsibility to be centralized within the department, which promotes efficiency and organization. In addition, being a full fledged hospital department means that emergency services staff can have a voice in hospital governance and budget and policy decisions, and the opportunity to ensure that their concerns are heard at the hospital level.

Nevertheless, simply being a department in the hospital does not ensure adequate communication with other departments in the hospital. Lack of effective communication between the ED and the rest of the hospital can mean that patients are kept waiting for admission in the ED even when hospital beds are available. Differing fiscal priorities can mean that patients paying for expensive elective procedures are granted priority for beds over patients with greater medical needs but fewer financial resources.

The Joint Commission on Accreditation of Health Care Organizations recently concluded that the responsibility for overcrowding in EDs must be placed squarely at the hospital administrative level, and has added accreditation standards for hospitals under the leadership category to pressure hospitals to pay more attention to dispositional problems in their EDs.[23] Although hospitals are also increasingly turning to computerized models to streamline tests and admissions to inpatient units, recent research in the area of computerized prescriptions, designed to reduce mistakes associated with illegible handwriting, suggests that computerization may not reduce problems with incorrect dosages and may in fact create new problems associated with timely receipt of patient medication.[24]

Communication Problems within Emergency Departments

In addition to communication problems between the ED and hospital wards, communications problems often exist within the ED. The ED generally does not employ the physicians, psychiatrists, or mental health professionals who assess patients or supervise their assessments. Nor does the ED have much control over these physicians and specialists. This issue was raised in almost every interview I conducted with ED staff.

Although coverage and professionalism have improved, tensions between ED staff, especially nurses who often run the ED, consulting physicians in the ED, and psychiatrists for the hospital's inpatient units continue to be a major factor in the life of an ED. The department administrator and nursing staff of the ED may have different concerns and priorities than the physicians who see (or, according to some ED staff, contrive to avoid seeing) psychiatric patients in the EDs. In addition, each of these groups have different incentive structures than the medical residents rotating through, who are often assigned to assess difficult psychiatric patients late at night with little available supervision.[25]

Residents and ED physicians and psychiatrists also have different incentives and pressures than the physicians who work on the hospital's inpatient units. For example, an ED's incentives to free beds for new patients, speed patient disposition, and lower its statistics of "boarding" patients may conflict with an assessing psychiatrist's desire to perform a number of medical screening tests and await their outcome prior to making dispositional decisions, or to keep a patient in the ED pending the availability of an inpatient bed rather than risk legal liability associated with discharge. Some psychiatrists acknowledge seeking to avoid working late nights or wishing to duck a well-known and difficult patient altogether.

Meanwhile, all emergency staff are growing more dissatisfied with their working conditions. A survey of 1050 emergency physicians reflected that "75% felt they had been financially exploited by the ED contract holder" and almost half "considered leaving their employer because of unfair business practices."[26] Disturbingly, "a majority of the physicians reported encountering instances of substandard emergency medical care, most commonly in settings with multi-hospital contract company coverage."[27]

Emergency nurses are equally unhappy. The American Nurses Association conducted a survey of 76,000 nurses throughout the country in 2005 and reported that "[l]evels of job satisfaction . . . varied," with ED nurses (along with medical-surgical and step-down units) reporting the "lowest" satisfaction.[28] Emergency department nurses were also among the three groups of nurses reporting the highest increase in working extra hours.[29] In another survey of nurse "burnout," ED nurses were significantly more likely to suffer burnout than other nurses, especially in areas such as emotional exhaustion.[30]

One emergency nurse interviewed for this book said that when she worked at a Level 1 trauma center ED,[31] she longed to return to her former job as an air traffic controller at a busy airport, where the stress was much lower and the job environment much calmer.[32] She eventually changed jobs to another ED that was not a trauma center, and is now much more satisfied. However, she still doesn't feel she has enough time to devote to the psychiatric clients that come through.

Space Problems

Space has always been a major consideration in emergency services provided in a hospital setting for people with psychiatric disabilities. This is true whether emergency services are provided to psychiatric patients in a separate location or within the general ED. In 1984, the physical plant at Harbor-UCLA for psychiatric emergency services, that saw 6000 patients a year, was a 500 square foot space with two seclusion rooms and a small holding cell.[33] As emergency rooms progressed to EDs, more space was added. Bellevue Hospital's ED occupies 65,000 square feet.

Space remains, however, a pressing problem in many EDs that serve people in psychiatric crisis. As the American Psychiatric Association (APA) Task Force on Psychiatric Emergency Services notes, "[s]pace is often the most vexing issue confronting emergency services."[34] If there is not adequate space, issues of safety and privacy arise. Perhaps most importantly, cramped, crowded, and noisy spaces may exacerbate the psychiatric crisis that brought an individual to the ED in the first place. Lack of space makes patient management difficult and increases the probability that force will be used and mistakes will be made in both paperwork and human interactions.

Financial Pressures

As noted above, the relationship between hospitals and their EDs is not only plagued by difficulties in communication and in integrating the ED into the rest of the hospital. In addition, EDs are increasingly perceived by hospital administration as financial drains, whose federally mandated open doors threaten the hospital's fiscal integrity. EDs are also seen as sources of legal liability. As the business model encroaches on health care, this matters more and more.

The large-scale addition or improvement of emergency rooms to hospitals began because of fiscal incentives. An Internal Revenue Service ruling in 1969 provided that hospitals claiming tax-exempt status as charities were required to have EDs.[35] Although the Hill-Burton Act, passed in 1946, required hospitals receiving federal financial assistance to provide medical care to some people unable to afford it, this requirement was ignored until the mid-1970s, when both congressional and executive branch regulatory action forced hospitals to begin to comply with the requirements. In 1986, after years of complaints about hospitals turning pregnant women and dangerously sick people from their doors because they were not insured, Congress passed the Emergency Medical Treatment and Active Labor Act (EMTALA), requiring EDs to provide screening for all presenting patients and stabilization of those found to be in emergency condition, regardless of ability to pay. At first, the statute had virtually no impact because the Department of Health and Human Services failed to issue regulations until 1988. Beginning in 1988, however, cases against hospitals for patient dumping—turning away or transferring patients because of their inability to pay—began to increase. EMTALA and its implications for people with psychiatric disabilities are discussed at length in chapter 5.

At the same time, managed care was beginning to emerge as a force in medicine. Managed care companies began to refuse to reimburse EDs when, in the judgment of the managed care company reviewing the claim, the patient's condition did not warrant emergency status. As states contracted with managed care companies to provide Medicaid services, managed care's refusal to pay for emergency services became a national problem. Between 1996 and 1998, the percentage of total ED charges actually paid dropped from 60.3% to 53%.[36] Interestingly, the percentage of charges paid by Medicaid, Medicare, and the uninsured remained constant, but the percentage of charges paid by private insurance fell from 75.1% to 63.4%.[37] Although Congress passed legislation in 1997 requiring Medicare and Medicaid to cover all ED visits that a prudent layperson would deem necessary, the issue was finally resolved only in 2001 with the adoption of regulations requiring that managed care companies that provided services under contract with state governments also abide by the prudent layperson standard. Some state legislatures have also imposed additional requirements on managed care companies. These initiatives are discussed further in chapter 5.

The average cost of an ED visit in 1998 was $798, with average charges varying depending on whether the patient was privately insured ($813) or uninsured ($740), although both groups experienced statistically significant increases in charges over the two-year period between 1996 and 1998.

Emergency Departments as Part of the Mental Health System: Crisis Services as a Critical Component of Public Mental Health Care

Although emergency rooms have existed for at least 100 years, the concept of publicly funded psychiatric emergency services was introduced on a national level in 1963 with the Community Mental Health Act, which mandated emergency services as part of a comprehensive system of community mental health care.[38] Ten years later, the Emergency Medical Systems Act provided that the ability to provide services for psychiatric emergencies was a critical component of emergency room care.[39] The mid-1970s saw the beginning of the impact of deinstitutionalization, with EDs bearing the brunt of insufficient community services.[40] The plan was that the funding for the clients would follow them into the community, but state hospitals often stayed open, consuming capital costs, and state funds remained institutionalized, locked in the hospital long after the patients had left the wards.

In 1978, the APA formed the Task Force on Psychiatric Emergency Services, chaired by Dr. Gail Barton.[41] The Task Force report was issued in 1983, but the APA refused to publish it, for reasons that remain unclear to this day.[42]

The beginning of the modern era in psychiatric emergency services began in 1980, around the time that "the psychiatric emergency service had become a chief entry point and sole source of treatment for many of the chronically mentally ill."[43] That year saw the publication of Samuel Gerson and Ellen Bassuk's influential article examining the role of the ED in providing services to psychiatric clients.[44] This article, which has been cited in hundreds of subsequent articles and books about ED treatment of psychiatric patients, was the first to look at the function of the ED as part of the mental health service system. It raised a number of issues that are still being grappled with today, including ED staff's dislike of and discomfort with psychiatric patients:

> A more subtle situational factor affecting the treatment of psychiatric patients is the generally negative attitude toward such patients of the [emergency room] medical staff, the senior psychiatric staff, and, often, the therapists themselves . . . Psychiatric staff and patients are often seen as intrusions into the essential business and are at best tolerated. This view often results in neglect of and at times even hostile reactions to psychiatric staff and patients by the rest of the [emergency room] personnel . . . These maladaptive coping mechanisms are often reflected in strong negative attitudes and feelings about specific patients or types of patients.[45]

The early 1980s also saw the beginnings of the movement toward bringing crisis caregivers to the client in the community to perform assessments and ward off hospitalization if possible. Dr. Len Stein and others established the first PACT or psychiatric assertive community treatment team in the country in Dane County, Wisconsin. The so-called Madison model of handling crises in the community to avoid unnecessary hospitalization drew mental health policy makers from across the country and around the world.[46] Dr. Bassuk continued to publish articles on psychiatric emergency services, and the first treatises and textbooks began to emerge on the subject of psychiatric emergency services.[47]

By the mid-1980s, with deinstitutionalization well under way, the ED had assumed the role it retains to this day: the gatekeeper into the public mental health system, the arbiter of inpatient services, and (all too often) the final drop-off point for the problem client or family member.

Problems with Emergency Department Delivery
of Psychiatric Emergency Services

Emergency rooms and EDs had never imagined themselves as serving a crucial role in the public mental health system, and they were both reluctant and ill-prepared to fulfill this function. In 1988, New York City's Health and Hospital Corporation was sued by a class of plaintiffs who were stuck for days in crowded city psychiatric emergency rooms. They challenged the lack of care and treatment, physical restraint (including being handcuffed to wheelchairs and tied to gurneys), and lack of opportunities for personal hygiene.[48]

The chaos was not limited to New York City. The atmosphere at California's Harbor-UCLA in 1984 was summarized in a graphic description by an emergency psychiatrist who worked there: "one of the freely roaming psychotic patients in the holding cell proceeded to put a cigarette out in [a] restrained patient's ear."[49] Although Harbor-UCLA got a new PES department and a great deal more space, it isn't clear that conditions for clients in Southern California have improved. An editorial several years ago depicted conditions at Los Angeles County-University of Southern California Medical Center's psychiatric ED, where a patient trying to escape crashed through the ceiling into a trauma room, a patient leaped off a gurney onto a doctor, and a young woman who had just been raped cowered in a corner in a room crowded with "older male mental patients" also awaiting psychiatric evaluation.[50] More recently, King-Drew Hospital, also in Los Angeles, was threatened with loss of federal funding because hospital staff called in police to use Taser guns on psychiatric patients.[51]

These dramatic stories are picked up by the media, but mundane problems are more widespread and more pressing: system fragmentation, with little or no communication between mental health providers and EDs, let alone integration of services; inappropriate admissions decisions (both decisions to admit and failures to admit), and the use of EDs to solve myriad individual and systemic problems.

Inappropriate Utilization of the Emergency Department

Inappropriate utilization of the ED is usually associated with the patient who is known as a "repeater" or (more derogatorily) a "frequent flyer." This issue will be discussed in chapter 4. However, less well recognized is the inappropriate utilization of EDs by people other than the ostensible patient. These secondary utilizers of EDs include family members, police, and a variety of mental health service providers, including group home operators, case managers, and day treatment programs. There is some indication that EDs are used by these groups to solve interpersonal conflicts and other problems presented by people with psychiatric disabilities. The literature suggests that up to one-half of admissions to psychiatric inpatient programs may be the result of interpersonal conflicts between a person with a psychiatric diagnosis and his or her family, provider, or others in the community.[52] The individual's known psychiatric disability leads others to label his or her behavior as symptomatic of illness rather than an artifact of interpersonal conflict, and an ED assessment may be requested, with inpatient hospitalization solving the conflict from the point of view of the family member or service provider. Police can similarly resolve complaints in the community arising from erratic behavior that may not constitute criminal conduct by taking the individual to the ED.

Emergency department researchers have found that when individuals are brought to the ED by these secondary utilizers of ED services, the individual is more likely to be hospitalized.[53] This is true regardless of the clinical appropriateness of inpatient admission: "the familial and social service staff who escort patients to emergency rooms . . . are likely to be strong advocates for inpatient hospitalization. . . . these patients are more likely to be admitted regardless of their true symptomatology."[54] Skilled ED practitioners deal with these secondary utilizers as a fact of life:

> Often family, friends, housemates, emergency department staff, landlords, employers, and police have their own views of the problem and their own needs that must be met . . . A decision to support a patient in the community may be an appropriate way to deal with the patient's crisis, but it may do little to help the family with their sense of responsibility, the landlord with his or her disturbing tenant, or the police who must wait in the emergency room as follow-up arrangements are made. If the clinician understands the needs of all the people connected with the crisis, it will be easier to come up with a solution that all parties can accept.[55]

The scenarios in this excerpt mirror other articles, treatises, and books about secondary utilizers who bring their children or clients to the ED because of their own concerns (however valid), needs, and imperatives, rather than because the person being brought has asked for help or expressed distress. As Dr. Factor and Dr. Diamond advise the ED clinician: "Ask yourself, 'For whom is this a crisis?'"[56]

For example, people with histories of childhood sexual and physical abuse often are given diagnoses of borderline personality disorder. Known hallmarks of this diagnosis are difficult interpersonal relationships and conflict with service providers.[57] Thus, looking for interpersonal conflict or resolution of a program problem as a potential source of ED utilization is especially salient for this population, who are likely to be frequent users of ED services.

Some inappropriate use of the ED is tied to social phenomena. "There has been a tremendous proliferation of children and adolescents presenting nationally in the emergency department," said Glenn Currier, M.D., president of the American Association for Emergency Psychiatry. "In part this has been fueled by [the 1999 school shooting at] Columbine, because teachers now have a policy of zero tolerance and often bypass parents in deciding to send kids to the ED, often when sub-acute emergency mental health services would have been sufficient if available."[58] This also relates to one of the key reasons that EDs are inappropriately utilized: in order for appropriate sub-acute mental health services to be used in these circumstances, they would have to be (1) available, (2) known to the teacher, and (3) obliged to see the student immediately. These factors explain many inappropriate uses of EDs by secondary utilizers, who may not have the time or knowledge to access more appropriate sources of mental health assessment or treatment.

An illustration of these and other inappropriate uses of EDs can be found on the Web site of the PES department of the University of New Mexico Psychiatric Center, which warns that among "services not included" are "termination of care of a difficult patient (fired patient). The patient will be referred back to the primary therapist until an orderly transfer of care takes place."[59] Other "services not included" are competency evaluations for criminal courts. Finally, the Web site cautions, "nor does the psychiatric emergency services provide evaluations for the clients of lawyers who have Social Security disability practices."[60]

Medicaid "Reform," Managed Care, and the Role of the Emergency Department

Mental health service providers and lawyers with social security disability practices are not the only secondary utilizers of EDs. State legislatures and departments of medical assistance enact Medicaid "reforms" that reduce state financial burdens by cutting needed medical and psychiatric services, knowing that hospital EDs will be forced to take up the slack as individuals deprived of Medicaid coverage turn to EDs for needed but increasingly uncompensated care.

Financing explains why the history of psychiatric emergency services for the private patient is more limited and did not truly begin until the advent of managed care. In the private psychiatric sector, there was very little emergency psychiatry. Patients could afford long-term therapy with the same therapist and extended hospital stays, and this generally obviated much of the need for crisis services. This is changing with managed care's emphasis on capitation and cost containment, which reduces outpatient treatment and inpatient days. Trends in the private psychiatric sector include the emergence of 24-hour observation beds, private psychiatric mobile response teams, and psychiatric interventionists under contract.

Managed care's concern with saving money on expensive services connected to ED utilization has also pioneered innovations in crisis care that have improved the lives of people with psychiatric disabilities. Some of these models are discussed in chapter 6. Although these models have been successful, they have not been widely replicated. And though the problems that EDs have with fragmentation, isolation, and inappropriate utilization are expensive and frustrating, there are structural reasons why they continue to flourish.

Structural Disincentives for Appropriate Psychiatric Assessment and Treatment in the Emergency Department

The current system is supported by a number of incentives. For example, fragmentation of services and isolation from the mental health community are attractive to overburdened emergency services because they are perceived as keeping the caseload manageable. Many EDs—whether general EDs or PES—prefer to have virtually no ongoing connection with the mental health systems for which they serve as crucial gatekeepers. As one ED psychiatrist candidly admitted, "the culture of the PES has resulted in survival strategies that are protectionist and isolating in nature. When you have an over-abundance of patients you don't exactly want to collaborate with outside agencies. The inherent fear in the old paradigm is that collaborative linkages will result in even more patients presenting for emergency care."[61]

In addition, the structure of the mental health and emergency services system discourages integration. Licensing and oversight of institutional and community mental health services are generally provided by a state's de-partment of mental health. By contrast, an ED, even a PES, is most often licensed and regulated as part of the state's department of public health, which may have little expertise or interest in mental health issues that are considered to be the jurisdiction of a sister agency.

Emergency departments also have a variety of structural incentives re-lating to disposition that are not related to a patient's needs. Length of stay is a key measure of ED performance, and quick dispositions may be favored over appropriate ones. Emergency department staff receive absolutely no rewards for ensuring that a patient is transferred to the best or most appro-priate setting. As Dr. Mendoza ironically characterized the attitude of a par-ticular era in California, "If a patient had Medi-Cal insurance, we wouldn't even think about whether the patient might clear in a few hours, a common practice just a year before. Life was grand—a dispo is a dispo, right?"[62] If the patient returned to the ED shortly thereafter, it would count statistically as a new episode of care, with the clock starting at zero for disposition. On the other hand, if the ED kept the patient a few extra hours to make a better disposition, especially if those hours pushed the stay over into the "board-ing" category, the hours would count against the ED.

Fear of liability also motivates some ED dispositional decisions. Over and over again, ED staff interviewed for this book told of admitting patients when their clinical judgment would have favored discharge because of con-cerns about liability. Books recounting ED experience simply assume this behavior,[63] describing a ritual understood by all: patients recognize that they must claim to be suicidal in order to get a bed, and the doctor writes an admission order against his or her clinical judgment because "the patient is telling a story scary enough to make a doctor think that his or her medical license may die along with the patient's suicide."[64] This practice is so prevalent that it has a name: contingent suicidality. Contingent suicidality has been studied, with findings that patients who threaten suicide if they don't get admitted do not, in fact, end up attempting or committing suicide.[65]

Ironically, much clinically inappropriate practice springs from inadequate to nonexistent knowledge of the law. Research shows that the less a physician is acquainted with the law, the more likely he or she is to order unnecessary tests.[66] But even ED staff who do not operate out of fear of liability and who have ample dispositional alternatives condense their concept of their duty to psychiatric patients into one recurring phrase: "we have to keep them and us safe." Misunderstandings of which practices actually contribute to safety, and inability to see the damage that total focus on physical safety creates, is a crucial problem with EDs consistently reported by people with psychiatric disabilities.

The mid- to late 1990s saw a resurgence of academic and policy interest in psychiatric emergency treatment. In 1998, the APA formed its second task force on psychiatric emergency treatment. The task force released its report in 2002; this time the APA did publish the report.[67] The report identified the variety of settings in which psychiatric emergency services were offered and acknowledged the lack of standards governing psychiatric emergency care. The report went on to suggest a series of minimum staffing, space, and evaluation standards across various sites offering emergency psychiatric treatment. Finally, the report identified financing as one of the most pressing problems facing EDs in the 21st century.

In 2003, the Center for Public Representation, a public interest law firm advocating on behalf of people with psychiatric disabilities, began a collaborative ED project, intended to identify problems and propose solutions relating to the treatment of people with psychiatric disabilities in ED settings. A group of cross-disciplinary experts assembled and made findings and proposed new standards and recommendations for the treatment of people with psychiatric disabilities in ED settings. These standards, discussed more fully in chapter 6, are found at appendix A of this book.

Snapshot of Emergency Services Today

Use of Emergency Departments in General

Every year, more than 100 million people visit EDs for care.[68] Of these, 31 million are children and adolescents.[69] About 82% of patients are seen in metropolitan areas.[70] The ED at New York City's Bellevue Hospital alone sees 100,000 people a year. The people seen at Bellevue's Comprehensive Psychiatric Emergency Program constitute about 6% of this total.[71]

For many years, there has been an upward trend in visits to EDs. During

2002, about 110.2 million visits were made to EDs, or about 38.9 visits for every 100 people in the population.[72] This figure has risen relative to 2001, when there were 107.5 million visits to the ED.[73] There had been some hope that use of EDs had peaked, since the 2001 figures were slightly lower than the figures for 2000, which counted more than 108 million visits.[74] However, the 2002 figures appear to continue the trend of increasing visits to the ED.

The increase in ED utilization over the decade prior to 2001 is popularly thought to be attributable to the number of uninsured people seeking treatment at EDs for non-urgent medical problems. In fact, these assumptions are incorrect. The increase was mostly due to an increase in visits by people with insurance, and very few visits were classified as "non-urgent" (see below). In 2002, as before, private insurance continued to be "the dominant expected source of payment," with about 40% of people seeking care at EDs in 2001 and 2002 covered by private insurance.[75] Of the remaining visits, roughly 18–20% were covered by either Medicaid or State Children's Health Insurance Program, and 15% were covered by Medicare.[76] For both years, injury, poisoning, and adverse effects of medical care, such as allergic reactions to medications or complications from surgery, accounted for more than one-third of all visits.[77]

Almost 2% of people who went to the ED in 2002 left without being seen by a physician, up from 1.5% in 2001.[78] The average length of an ED visit is about three hours, or five hours if the person is admitted to the hospital.[79] The number of patients who "board" in EDs—whose stay exceeds 24 hours—is increasing.[80] According to recent surveys and research, psychiatric patients (particularly adolescents and children) are especially at risk of boarding in EDs.[81]

Race and Use of Emergency Departments

The African-American population used the ED at a rate 76% higher than the white population in 2000.[82] By 2002, the rate was still vastly disproportionate, but the disproportion had reduced significantly: African Americans used the ED just under twice as much as whites.[83] Use of the ED by individuals classified as "Asian" is extremely low: just over half the rate of white users and more than three times less than African American usage.[84] Almost one third of Native Americans visited an ED once in the year 2000, compared to 19.4% of the white population.[85] Interestingly, several studies have found higher rates of ED usage by Hispanics with language discordant primary care physicians, compared with primary care physicians who spoke Spanish.[86] There is conflicting data on whether minority children are higher or lower users of emergency services than white children.[87]

Poverty and Use of Emergency Departments

It is commonly known that poor people, and people without primary physicians, make far greater use of EDs than people who have higher incomes and/or family physicians or primary physicians. In the year 2000, 30.2% of adults with one ED visit were poor, compared with 18.6% of non-poor people. In the same year, the source of payment for medical services, if any, was a powerful predictor of how often individuals used EDs. Fully 41.8% of adults aged 18–64 on Medicaid visited an ED once in 2000; 20.7% of individuals on Medicaid visited an ED more than twice in 2000. Only 17.5% of individuals with private insurance visited an ED once in 2000; 5.1% of individuals with private insurance visited an ED more than twice.[88]

Some studies suggest that homeless people also have a higher rate of ED use, stay longer, and cost more to treat. Housing, even marginal housing, cuts down on ED use to such an extent that in San Francisco, the Department of Public Health has started to provide housing as a way of saving hospital and ED expenses. A study of homeless people who were high users of the ED showed that they tended to be "younger, female, homeless versus marginally housed, and Medicaid or Medicare insured (as opposed to uninsured). In addition to mental illness and substance abuse, other factors associated with high ED use included: poorer health status and involvement in crime (either as perpetrator or victim)."[89]

Unnecessary Use of Emergency Departments

Although it is commonly believed that overcrowding in EDs is due to people seeking routine or non-emergency care, only 9.1% of visits in 2001 and 10.2% of visits in 2002 were characterized as "non-urgent."[90] (In coming to this figure, EDs failed to provide triage data for 23.6% of visits in 2001 and 14.8% in 2002, figures that might make a substantial difference.)[91] The categories into which visits are triaged are: "emergent," where the patient must be seen in less than 15 minutes, the category describing 22.3% of all visits in 2002; "urgent," where the triage nurse judges the patient must be seen in 15–60 minutes, which constituted 34.2% of visits; and "semi-urgent," in which the patient must be seen in 1–2 hours, which accounted for 18.5% of visits.[92]

Public opinion erroneously conflates the high use of EDs by poor people, homeless people, or people with other psychosocial difficulties with unnecessary use. In fact, use of EDs by poor people tends to be for more serious medical and psychiatric problems. A research study examined the use of EDs to see whether non-emergent complaints would be higher among individuals with high levels of psycho-social problems, such as illiteracy, drug dependency, homelessness, and similar problems.[93] The study concluded that the groups with psychosocial difficulties had similar rates of emergent visits compared to groups without those difficulties (58% for those with difficulties; 50% for those who did not fall into that category).[94] If anything, the numbers show that individuals with psychosocial problems presented more often with truly emergent conditions.

Litigation Related to the Use of Emergency Departments

Much attention was generated by the publication of the Institute of Medicine's (IOM) 2000 report on deaths and injuries caused by preventable medical errors.[95] According to the IOM report, ED errors account for about 70–80% of preventable medical errors causing mortality, serious injury, or disability.[96] Nevertheless, separate figures indicate that only about 20% of inhospital medical malpractice suits involve ED care.[97] Very few lawsuits are filed on behalf of people with psychiatric disabilities against ED personnel or hospitals. Although ED personnel appear to be primarily attuned to and concerned about litigation involving people who commit suicide or hurt others after discharge from the ED, a survey of actual litigation reveals a greater variety of litigation related to decision making in the ED setting.

For example, substantial litigation has been filed on behalf of people who were assaulted by hospital security guards. Thomas Jefferson Hospital in Philadelphia lost two cases involving violence by its security guards in two consecutive months in 1992: the total damage award exceeded $300,000 (not including attorney's fees and other costs of litigation).[98] Other cases involve patients with psychiatric histories whose medical conditions were ignored, not diagnosed, or mistaken for psychiatric symptoms. Still other successful damage actions have been brought on behalf of people who were restrained, secluded, or drugged against their will and people who were subjected to forced disrobing or sexual assault. An increasing number of successful cases, with jury verdicts over $1 million dollars, have been litigated challenging improper involuntary detention in EDs following cursory evaluations, evaluations that did not reflect dangerousness on the part of the patient, or evaluations that reflected bad faith or improper influence in the decision to commit. These cases and the underlying legal claims are discussed in chapter 5.

The Use of Emergency Departments by People with Psychiatric Disabilities

Of 110.2 million visits to the ED in 2002, just over two million visits (or 1.9%) involved patients who gave "symptoms related to psychological/mental disorder" as the principal reason for the visit.[99] Interestingly, "mental disorders" was the primary diagnosis given to almost 3.5 million (or 3.2%) of the patients.[100] It is not clear whether the contrast in the two figures reflects the experience of people with psychiatric disabilities who report that they go for treatment of medical problems and are inappropriately treated for psychiatric disabilities, or the experience of people whose somatic presenting symptoms (headaches, sleeplessness, etc.) are correctly identified by ED staff as caused by psychiatric problems.

Some hospitals see psychiatric patients along with all their other patients in an ED; other, usually larger, hospitals operate specialized separate psychiatric EDs, called psychiatric emergency services. The PES is a self-enclosed space dedicated solely to seeing people with psychiatric emergencies. There are 142 facilities in the United States that provide psychiatric emergency services.[101] Some of these facilities see as many as 900 patients a month.[102] A number of larger hospitals have added acute care units, where individuals can be held for up to 72 hours, in the hope that this will prevent longer-term admissions.

Although the number of people seeking help in EDs for psychiatric problems in general has risen, the proportion of ED visits arising from psychiatric problems has stayed relatively stable. However, if sub-populations of people with psychiatric difficulties are examined, use of EDs by some sub-populations has increased substantially. Between 1992 and 2002, visits to EDs for depression among those 18–44 years of age increased by 106%.[103] A study by the Department of Public Health in Massachusetts demonstrated that the proportion of people seeking ED assistance for psychiatric problems varies dramatically depending on the source of funding.[104] The proportion of people with Medicaid coverage who seek ED assistance for psychiatric crises is far higher than the proportion of people with private insurance or with Medicare.

People who were brought to the ED from institutions (including nursing homes, group homes, prisons, or psychiatric hospitals) accounted for 2,608,000 million visits, or 2.4% of all ED visits.[105] Many of these visits, of course, were from nursing homes.

Reasons for Presentation at Emergency Departments

About 38% of the two million people who visit the ED in psychiatric crisis are suicidal or have attempted suicide.[106] It is possible to extrapolate the number of people who have actually attempted suicide by comparing this figure, 760,000 people, to the number of nonfatal self-inflicted injuries seen in EDs that are possibly or probably suicide attempts, around 185,000 people, predominantly white adolescents.[107]

About 26–28% of persons who visit EDs with psychiatric complaints demonstrate psychotic symptoms.[108] Statistics relating to ED usage by people with psychiatric disabilities focus on usage for psychiatric problems. However, many of the problems reported by people with psychiatric disabilities in EDs relate to their attempts to receive care for medical problems. Although there is a great deal of research on latent medical problems of people who present at EDs for psychiatric reasons, there is relatively little research on course and outcomes for people with known psychiatric problems presenting at the ED for medical reasons.

A substantial number of people, 32% in one study, who present to a PES are acutely intoxicated with drugs or alcohol (the corresponding figure for general EDs is 17%).[109] It is unclear whether this is simply because professionals in a PES expect and look for intoxication. Research indicates that ED physicians tend to underdiagnose substance abuse in persons seeking psychiatric help in ED settings.

Unnecessary Use of Emergency Departments by People with Psychiatric Disabilities

The question of when an ED visit is "necessary" for a person in psychiatric crisis is more complicated than in the case of bullet wounds or heart attacks. There is little or no consensus on what makes an ED visit "necessary,"[110] and the research on the actual experience of ED professionals is contradictory. In one study, professionals deemed the vast majority of visits to be necessary; another reflected the belief that most people who visit EDs in psychiatric crisis are malingering.[111]

Race and Use of Emergency Departments for Psychiatric Needs

Research shows inconclusive results on the issue of whether race affects decisions to involuntarily detain individuals in ED settings. A study of visits to the ED, which looked at a number of factors including diagnosis, demographics, and substance use, found that three variables were significantly associated with a larger number of visits to a PES: a past history of visits, moderate alcohol use, and black race.[112]

Early research also showed a disproportionately high rate of involuntary detention among black patients brought to an ED.[113] Later studies replicated the correlation but found that it could be almost wholly accounted for by the greater likelihood that individuals brought in by the police are more likely to be involuntarily detained, and blacks are more likely than whites to be brought to the ED by police.[114] A later study showed blacks somewhat less likely to be involuntarily detained than whites, but showed a strikingly disproportionate number of Hispanics detained.[115] The few surveys that have been done regarding the experiences of people with psychiatric disabilities in EDs, including by the Center for Public Representation, tend to drastically underrepresent the experience of members of ethnic minorities.[116]

Overcrowding in Psychiatric Emergency Services

Although overcrowding of EDs is a national phenomenon, it is even more of a problem with psychiatric patients. This is an issue of both physical space and patient flow.

Patient flow contributes to overcrowding. This is because a great deal of overcrowding is attributable not so much to an increase in volume entering the ED as to a drastic decrease in disposition options.[117] This decrease is at its greatest when it comes to psychiatric beds. Within psychiatric populations, the problem is worst with children and adolescents. In one study of "boarding" patients, i.e. psychiatric patients held inappropriately in medical wards, one third of children who required psychiatric admission were boarded. Interestingly, predictors of boarding versus placement included not only race (black children were more likely to be boarders) but also severity of homicidality or suicidality (those with more severe ideations were more likely to be boarders).[118]

Overcrowding in EDs because of lack of dispositional alternatives is not new. On September 24, 1985, the New York City Health and Hospitals Corporation was sued by the American Civil Liberties Union because New York City psychiatric EDs were so crowded that patients were being handcuffed to wheelchairs or tied to gurneys for days at a time.[119] Although cases continue to be brought against EDs, for the most part they now revolve around inadequate assessments leading to unnecessary detention, involuntary medications or restraints, and injuries caused by security guards.

Distinctions Between ED Experiences of Psychiatric and Medical Clients

Voluntary Versus Involuntary Visits

Visits to the ED for psychiatric emergencies are different in a variety of ways from visits for medical problems. Although some people arrive voluntarily, many others are brought involuntarily by the police. In New York City alone, police escorted at least 24,788 people considered "EDPs" (emotionally disturbed persons) to hospital EDs in 1999.[120] About one third of people with psychiatric disabilities are brought into EDs involuntarily.[121] Often visits to the ED fall into a gray area: legally voluntary, but coerced by ambulance technicians, police, family, or friends.[122] One survey respondent, asked whether a visit to the ED was voluntary, involuntary, or other, checked "other" and wrote "the police explained it was in my best interests to go."[123] Surveys show a range of rates of accompaniment: between 22–71% of psychiatric ED patients are accompanied by others.[124]

Disposition

Although about 12% of all ED visits result in hospital admission, most studies report that between 25–50% of people who come to the ED for psychiatric emergencies are hospitalized.[125] In one study that appears to be an outlier, 90% of people who came to the ED for psychiatric reasons were hospitalized.[126] The large range between 25–50% is explained by different factors associated with presentation: the proportion of people who are hospitalized is usually higher for people who are accompanied to the ED, and higher for people who are brought in by the police[127] (although, in one recent study of police specially trained in crisis intervention, hospitalization rates were no higher than for self-referred subjects).[128] Finally, hospitalization rates are higher for people who are brought in pursuant to a petition for evaluation.[129] Of those who are hospitalized, about half are involuntarily hospitalized and half are voluntarily hospitalized.[130]

Evaluations of Successful Treatment

It is much more difficult to evaluate the quality of ED care for people with psychiatric disabilities than for people with medical problems.[131] Many of the standard measurements—mortality, recidivism, and leaving without being seen—are confounded by the particular nature of the ED visit for people with psychiatric disabilities. People with psychiatric disabilities are often not permitted to make the choice of leaving without being seen, and relatively few people die.[132] The issue of how to appropriately evaluate the quality of treatment that EDs provide for people with psychiatric disabilities who present to them is an important one, and is discussed at length in chapter 6.

Social Control and Gatekeeper Function

Far more than for medical conditions, EDs function as the gatekeeper that determines the level of care the individual will receive: inpatient hospitalization or discharge to an uncertain community mental health system. And far more than for medical conditions, the use of force is common in relation to psychiatric patients: force to keep them in the ED, and force to calm or control them in the ED, especially if they are upset about not being allowed to leave. As noted above, a medical patient may almost always leave the ED, regardless of his or her condition, but often psychiatric patients are not or cannot be permitted to leave, and this makes a world of difference in their treatment and the conditions they experience. Few medical patients will experience being Tasered by police in an ED[133] but few medical patients are brought to the ED by police. As discussed at length throughout this book, the social function served by EDs in assessment and treatment of psychiatric patients is utterly different from the function served by EDs in treating medical patients, and is central to the difficulties that people with psychiatric disabilities and ED staff have in their interactions with each other.

Thus, the modern ED is a complex culture, little known or understood by outsiders, which is required to perform multiple functions far beyond the average citizen's notions of the scope of ED practice. Cultures vary widely from ED to ED, even within the same city, and these cultures dictate a wide variety of practices toward people with psychiatric disabilities. These practices are discussed in the next chapter.

3

Patients' Problems with Emergency
Department Care

Patients with psychiatric disabilities who seek (or are brought unwillingly to) emergency departments (EDs) have a different perspective on problems with ED treatment than professionals who work in emergency room settings and researchers and policymakers. Yet the problems are clearly related: patient complaints about not being allowed to leave the ED are related to professional fears of legal liability for permitting such departures. The use of force dreaded by clients with psychiatric disabilities is related to professional fears of violence in emergency room settings. This, in turn, implicates policy and regulatory decisions about permissible searches of patients, use of seclusion and restraint, and the presence of security guards, including the arms they will be permitted to carry and use and who will supervise them.

The Center for Public Representation researched the experience of people with psychiatric disabilities in emergency rooms through a variety of sources: books, articles, and testimony by people with psychiatric disabilities in congressional and state legislative hearings. In addition, three surveys were consulted: a survey in 1999 conducted by the Office of Protection and Advocacy for Connecticut, a state agency responsible for protecting the rights of people with psychiatric disabilities;[1] a survey in 2002 designed and funded by Comprehensive NeuroScience, Inc., as part of its Emergency Services Project;[2] and another ongoing survey created and distributed by the Center for Public Representation.[3] Survey respondents in all cases were self-selected, and none of the distributors of these surveys make any claims to rigorous design or random selection. But I could not write a book about the treatment of people with psychiatric disabilities in EDs without seeking as much information as possible through as many means as possible from people with psychiatric disabilities themselves.

Nevertheless, even with the above disclaimer, the three surveys of patients conducted at different times, in different places, and with different questions, reflect strikingly similar complaints. Some experiences reported in patient surveys were positive (20% in the Connecticut survey), although more were negative (perhaps to be expected when respondents were self-selected). Interestingly, the vast majority of positive responses did not refer to the effectiveness of treatment, but rather to caring and respectful treatment by staff at the ED. The importance of being treated with respect and dignity appears to outweigh many considerations that might be considered more substantive.

By contrast, patients who reported negative experiences had a variety of complaints. Some referred to being treated with disrespect and even hostility; others to having their medical complaints ignored because they were psychiatric patients, still others to the fear and discomfort of isolation and seclusion, or to the terror they experienced in restraints. The individuals surveyed also complained about the use of force or threat of force in a variety of different contexts: force by security guards, forcible removal of clothing, and forced catheterization or blood draws. They also wrote of long delays, far longer than the national average, and of the refusal to permit relatives and friends to accompany them when they were frightened and vulnerable. Some also raised issues relating to reimbursement, the physical surroundings of the ED, and the inability to smoke, eat, or drink while waiting.

Use of Force

Psychiatric patients experience force in the emergency room from two distinct sources. There is force or threat of force by hospital security guards, especially those armed with pepper spray, mace, Taser guns, batons, and guns. Security guards are often involved in restraints of patients. A number of cases examined by the Center for Public Representation concerned psychiatric patients who were injured—and some who died—in emergency room settings resulted from the use of force by security guards.[4] Emergency room professionals, including doctors and nurses, also order restraints and other forms of force, including forced disrobing, seclusion, and medications. These are experienced as being conducive to safety by ED staff, but are experienced as frightening uses of force by patients.

Use of Force by Security Personnel

Patient deaths and injuries at the hands of hospital security guards often take place, as in the case of psychiatric hospitals, during a restraint procedure. Some of these deaths result in court cases,[5] and others are investigated by police or a grand jury. For instance, Gregory Cooper died after being sedated and restrained face down on a gurney with a towel over his mouth and a backboard and blanket on top of him. The restraint was accomplished by four police officers, three hospital security guards, and two ambulance workers. The Lake County Coroner ruled that Mr. Cooper's death by suffocation was a "homicide caused by the restraints" although the county prosecutor decided not to bring criminal charges.[6] The Ohio Legal Rights Service issued a report about general problems relating to force by security guards in emergency rooms.[7] Inspection by the federal government led to the hospital's banning the use of handcuffs as restraints.[8] Since then, the federal government has issued regulations banning the use of handcuffs as restraint devices in hospital and ED settings.[9]

People are also injured by security guards in emergency room settings. A survey of Connecticut emergency rooms revealed that many emergency room security guards were armed with pepper spray, although Bridgeport Hospital, an emergency room in a high-volume, urban, high-crime area, refuses to use pepper spray. In Ohio, the protection and advocacy agency succeeded in prohibiting the use of pepper spray in inpatient units. Some cases involve the use of force by security guards against patients who are trying to leave. In some cases, family members are injured by security guards.[10]

Charles Lidz and his colleagues, reporting on coercion in the emergency room, alluded in passing to the use of force in 69 of 405 (17%) cases they observed in the emergency room of a large psychiatric hospital. Force was defined broadly, including security officers blocking the departure of a patient who tried to leave, but also included incidents such as holding a patient down on the floor. Interestingly, "in 35% of the cases in which force was used against a patient, the patient was either admitted voluntarily or not admitted at all."[11]

Policy Issues Concerning Proper Function of Security Personnel

Hospitals are required by licensing standards to provide adequate security,[12] and have responded in a variety of ways. As the American Psychiatric Association Task Force on Emergency Psychiatry noted perceptively, "[t]he numbers and training of the mental health staff [in EDs] will determine the role of security officers. Smaller services tend to rely more heavily on armed security."[13] Some employ off-duty police, some contract with security guard companies, and others employ their own security staff. The degree to which hospitals train these individuals in the use of force in the hospital or emergency room setting also varies. Some hospitals rely entirely on police training when they employ off-duty police officers.[14] Others have training and policies of their own. Russell Colling, a leading expert in health care security, recommends that hospitals steer clear of hiring off-duty police officers for a variety of reasons, including "high costs, virtually no organized system, little or no security training, and lack of continuity."[15]

While the presence of security guards may make some medical patients feel safer, many patients with a history of psychiatric disability have had unpleasant encounters with the police, and are uncomfortable and frightened by the presence of uniformed, armed security guards. A number of surveys completed by individuals with psychiatric disabilities about their experiences in EDs complained about the presence of and treatment by security guards. Other comments were brief, leaving the reader to guess at the stories behind them: "Get the security guards away"[16] or, in response to a question soliciting suggestions on how to improve ED treatment of people with psychiatric disabilities, "Minimize presence of security guards."[17] It appears that while some individual security guards have been sensitive and kind to psychiatric patients, armed and uniformed guards in an emergency department can be upsetting to psychiatric patients and are perceived as contributing to both the atmosphere and actuality of force in the ED.[18] Russell Colling notes that he has consulted in a number of cases where a moderately agitated psychiatric patient escalated severely when uniformed security guards were brought in to handle the situation.[19]

There is very little research and very few standards to guide the use of police or security guards in the ED. As one of the few articles in this area notes, there are certain inevitable functions in an emergency room that can be assigned to clinicians, police, or be a shared responsibility, including "control of violent behavior, pursuit and securing of dangerous patients, enforcement of hospital regulations, consultation on possible law enforcement responses to unusual behavior, and performance of liaison functions with community police departments and courts."[20]

It is incumbent on hospitals to decide how these functions will be divided, and to make the decision clear to all staff who will be expected to perform such functions. Security guards should operate only under the direction of the nursing or professional staff of the hospital. Their performance evaluations should be completed by those individuals, and it should be made clear to them that the expectations of the health care milieu are different from expectations ordinarily placed on security guards.

Weapons

GUNS. Approximately 15–20% of the health care security forces carry guns, down from approximately 30% in 1992.[21] Health care security expert Russell Colling notes that "[p]erhaps as many as half of the security officers presently carrying weapons should be disarmed,"[22] because they are simply incompetent to use the weapons. Arming security guards is sometimes justified by reference to patients who might become violent and/or patients who enter the ED carrying weapons themselves. At least among patients in psychiatric emergency rooms, this seems to be a relatively small number (between 4–8%).[23] News reports of security officers discharging weapons in emergency room settings are sparse, suggesting little misuse in this area.[24]

CHEMICAL GAS, MACE, AND PEPPER SPRAY. Approximately 20–30% of security guards in hospital settings carry pepper spray. Arming security guards with pepper spray is less a function of the level of crime in the area of the hospital, and more a function of the degree to which hospitals maintain active involvement and oversight of their security guards. Some hospitals located in high-crime areas do not arm their security guards, while other hospitals in low-crime areas do permit their guards to carry pepper spray. Pepper spray and mace are used far more frequently than guns in hospital emergency rooms. This is true even though the use of mace and pepper spray is risky for people who have medical conditions such as asthma or emphysema, and although there is a major danger associated with contamination in indoor settings. Pepper spray has been associated with deaths in custody when used on agitated individuals who are being restrained. Some hospitals have lowered the risk of contamination by using pepper foam, but pepper foam also carries health risks.[25] This is especially true if an individual or area has not been properly decontaminated.

The Center for Medicare and Medicaid Services (CMS) and state licensing authorities have investigated the use of pepper spray on patients, including psychiatric patients, and have punished hospitals for such use. For example, in 1999, the federal government threatened to revoke the accreditation of Backus Hospital in Norwich, Connecticut, after finding that the hospital had improperly used pepper spray to subdue psychiatric patients.[26]

The Center for Medicare and Medicaid Services has underscored in interpretive guidance to its regulations regarding patient rights that "pepper spray, mace, nightsticks, [T]asers, cattle prods, stun guns, pistols and other such devices" are considered weapons, and that "CMS does not consider the use of weapons in the application of restraint as safe appropriate health care interventions . . . CMS does not approve the use of weapons by an hospital staff as a means of subduing a patient to place that patient in patient restraint/seclusion."[27]

Litigation has been filed in federal district court seeking to limit or ban the use of pepper spray in emergency rooms.[28] The case, which is under seal to protect the patient's privacy,[29] charges that security guards use pepper spray to prevent psychiatric patients from leaving the hospital, even when patients have a legal right to leave. The case raises claims under the Americans with Disabilities Act (ADA) and Section 504 of the Rehabilitation Act because it is alleged that psychiatric patients constitute virtually all of the patients subjected to pepper spray. The case also raises state claims under the state Patients' Right Act and tort claims of false imprisonment, battery, and negligence.

TASER GUNS, NIGHT STICKS, AND BATONS. Some health care security personnel carry collapsible or non-collapsible batons. Still others are armed with Taser guns, which are essentially stun guns. In other EDs, health care security personnel carry night sticks and batons. In Madison, Wisconsin, the police consider Taser guns superior to pepper spray because Taser guns can be directed at only one person, while pepper spray may contaminate an entire room and affect a number of people, including the officer. The effect of Tasers can be controlled by the officer; and, unlike pepper spray, the effect ends at the moment that the Taser gun is turned off.[30] In one well-publicized incident, a young man was pepper sprayed and then Tasered, and the electric current from the Taser gun ignited the pepper spray. Recently, the use of Taser guns has been associated with deaths in the case of juveniles and people with health conditions.

The use of batons emerges less frequently in litigation, perhaps because baton manufacturers do not claim that someone can be safely hit with their product, or because (for similar reasons) baton use may be more clearly perceived by a lay jury as undue force. At least one case against a hospital involved a claim that a security guard beat the plaintiff with a baton, even after the plaintiff was handcuffed.[31]

HANDCUFFS. Although Russell Colling believes that handcuffs are "an important piece of equipment carried by the majority of healthcare security officers," he advises that "[b]ecause handcuffs reinforce the police image, they should be completely enclosed within a leather case rather than exposed."[32] In addition, he states handcuffs should be used only when a security officer is alone and trying to handle a difficult and potentially violent patient. In most hospital situations, there is no call for the use of handcuffs because security officers have backup by nurses, aides, and other trained officials.

The Center for Medicare and Medicaid Services may have a more strict approach. Although CMS does not regulate the use of handcuffs by police officers,[33] it restricts its exception to law enforcement officers not employed by or under contract with the health care facility. If medical or other personnel were to use handcuffs, they would be regulated as "law enforcement restraint devices" and CMS makes clear that it is inappropriate to use them for purposes of any restraint related to health care.[34]

Litigation regarding the use of handcuffs on people with psychiatric disabilities has generally failed. However, such litigation has usually been brought against police officers transporting individuals who have already behaved in dangerous ways or who have been adjudicated as dangerous, rather than hospital security guards handcuffing patients.[35]

Searching Patients

The question of when and how to search patients coming to the ED has been raised for over 25 years. Many treatises recommend asking individuals whether they are armed and asking them to voluntarily turn over any weapons for safekeeping. In a list of 13 possible security measures an ED may consider, the Joint Commission on Accreditation of Health Care Organizations (JCAHO) does not include searching patients for weapons. The commission does suggest that "ED staff or security who observe that a violent patient has a weapon, or has an object that can be used as one, can request that it be turned over before he or she is treated."[36]

Various means of searching potential patients for weapons, such as patting them down, requiring them to take off their clothes, or strip searching them, can be extremely traumatizing for psychiatric patients and can be a primary reason for avoiding the emergency room altogether. Some large urban hospitals use metal detectors. However, most hospitals regard metal detectors as unaffordable (the machines cost about $100,000 and require a staff person to operate them) and impractical for a variety of reasons.

Chapter 6 and appendix A contain recommendations and standards relating to disrobement of patients. The requirement of mandatory disrobing has resulted in more complaints registered in the surveys than pat downs. Pat downs may also be problematic, and should be conducted only when necessary and with attention to a patient's trauma history.

Use of Force by Emergency Room Personnel

Restraint in Emergency Room Settings

People who arrive at the emergency room seeking help for severe emotional distress are often secluded or restrained, sometimes for no better reason than to keep them from leaving the hospital. For many psychiatric patients, being restrained in emergency rooms overshadows all other complaints. One 18-year-old man with mental retardation was kept in restraints in an emergency room cubicle at Prince George's County Hospital for 11 days.[37] The hospital's executive vice-president, Thomas Crowley, was quoted as saying that patient rights rules in this case "could be waived because of the man's mental disability."[38] The hospital has been cited for rights violations by the State of Maryland and the federal government.

The use of restraint and seclusion is now regarded by many government and licensing agencies as a sign of treatment failure on the part of the provider who employs them. The President's New Freedom Commission on Mental Health, the Department of Health and Human Services Substance Abuse and Mental Health Services Administration, the National Association of State Mental Health Program Directors, JCAHO, and many state governments have taken strong positions against the use of restraint and seclusion.

This applies to emergency room settings, as well as inpatient settings. The federal government and the National Association of State Mental Health Program Directors have urged the mental health field to work toward the elimination of seclusion and restraint. They cite the example of the Commonwealth of Pennsylvania, which reduced its use of restraint by more than 80%. A number of state hospitals in Pennsylvania have not used restraints in several years.

Emergency department restraint rates vary so much that the variance cannot be explained by differences in setting—rural versus urban—or type of patient seen. "[A]s with studies in other settings, restraint rates were not correlated with staff assault rates or with volume of patients treated."[39] It is the general consensus in the field that the most important variable in minimizing or eliminating the use of restraint is the commitment of hospital leadership to do so, including providing the appropriate training and staffing.

The National Association of State Mental Health Program Directors has also supported the proposition, which is part of the language of state policies such as those of the Department of Public Welfare in Pennsylvania, that the use of restraint reflects a failure of treatment. Licensing and accrediting organizations, such as JCAHO and the Center for Medicaid and Medicare Services, as well as major professional organizations such as the National Association of State Mental Health Program Directors, have expressed particular concern about the use of restraints in recent years. Both CMS and JCAHO have enacted new, more stringent regulations on the use of restraints to manage behavioral emergencies.

Restraining a patient places his or her health at risk, especially when emergency room personnel are unaware of the person's recent ingestion of intoxicants or other health factors that increase the risk in use of restraints. In addition, if harm comes to a restrained patient in the emergency room, or if a patient in restraints escapes the hospital, legal liability is highly likely.[40]

Seclusion in Emergency Room Settings

Often, when clients present in emergency rooms with psychiatric disabilities, they are placed in rooms alone and are not permitted to leave. Sometimes the rooms are locked; sometimes patients are told they cannot leave (and physically prevented from doing so if they try). The ED may not make a distinction between patients who voluntarily self-present and who are legally free to leave and patients who are brought in by police on certificates of detention. Detaining individuals without completing the necessary paperwork is a practice that is beginning to be challenged in litigation by patients' advocates.[41] Often, seclusion is so disturbing or frightening to the individual (who was already experiencing some form of psychiatric crisis) that he or she bangs on the door or starts yelling, which usually results in the application of restraints, both physical and chemical.[42]

The use of seclusion is regulated by the federal government, implicates accreditation requirements, and may constitute false imprisonment under state tort statutes. Seclusion, defined as "the involuntary confinement of a person in a room or an area where the person is physically prevented from leaving," implicates both seclusion rooms and locked waiting areas in psychiatric EDs.[43] Seclusion cannot be used for the convenience of ED staff, or to coerce a patient, and can only be used if needed to ensure the patient's *physical* safety and less restrictive interventions have been determined to be ineffective."[44] Thus, emergency department policies and practices which provide for automatic seclusion of patients presenting in psychiatric crisis, and possibly locked waiting areas in psychiatric emergency rooms, may be illegal under the regulations of the Center for Medicare and Medicaid Services.

Forced Disrobing in Emergency Room Settings

One way that hospitals ensure that patients will not leave prior to assessment is to force them to remove their clothing. While some hospitals require this of all ED patients, many restrict the requirement to patients presenting with psychiatric disabilities. Others have policies requiring patients who are subject to emergency detention orders to disrobe.

A survey by the Office of Protection and Advocacy in Connecticut in 1999 found that 56% of patients presenting with psychiatric complaints to emergency departments were asked to remove their clothes, compared with 40% of psychiatric patients presenting with medical complaints.[45] One hospital in Maryland requires that all patients disrobe who are brought in subject to an order of detention for psychiatric reasons, although this requirement is not imposed on patients subject to criminal detention.[46] This practice is particularly difficult for people with trauma histories, who feel vulnerable and unsafe, and at least one court has held that a hospital's policy of requiring psychiatric clients to disrobe, by force if necessary, stated a claim under the ADA.[47]

Forced Medication in Emergency Room Settings

A common complaint by people presenting for treatment in emergency room settings, especially people brought in involuntarily by police, is that they are medicated without consent. Both case law and licensing requirements make clear that emergency room personnel are subject to the same legal requirements to obtain informed consent as other physicians before medicating individuals, unless the situation meets state law definitions of an emergency.[48] The definitions of "emergency" are more stringent than simply seeking care in an emergency setting, and will be discussed in chapter 5. Forced medication is particularly problematic when ordered over the telephone by a physician or psychiatrist who has not seen the patient[49] or when ordered prior to receipt of results from medical examinations and laboratory tests.

Other Issues

Ignoring or Minimizing Medical Complaints of People with Psychiatric Disabilities

When it was considering passage of the ADA, Congress heard testimony that emergency departments discriminated against people with psychiatric disabilities by ignoring or minimizing their medical complaints. Dr. Patricia Deegan of Massachusetts told a Congressional committee about a woman known to have a psychiatric disability who went to Cape Cod Hospital's ED reporting that she was pregnant. The woman "was thought to be delusional and was ignored, and later that evening, while wandering the streets, she miscarried with serious hemorrhaging."[50]

Respondents in all surveys reviewed for this book confirm that disbelieving medical complaints of people with psychiatric histories continues to be a major problem.[51] As one survey respondent wrote, in response to a question about how EDs could improve their treatment: "Treat people on psychotropic meds with a medical complaint with care and in a dignified, serious manner. Just because one is on psych meds doesn't mean that they're not credible."[52] A respondent to the Connecticut Protection and Advocacy survey noted, "for stomach pains they kept saying it was all in my mind . . . it was a bleeding ulcer."[53] Another wrote, "I swear once they see psych drugs you're treated different. They told me nothing was wrong . . . The following morning they called and said I had pneumonia . . . I felt very isolated in that little room."[54] Simply taking a patient's medical complaints seriously earns gratitude. One patient praised Lexington County Hospital in Lexington, South Carolina:

> Vital signs were taken and when I said I thought I had a urinary
> tract infection, the nurse immediately ordered a urine sample—
> turned out to be a kidney infection. I received very appropriate
> medical treatment, was not treated as a nutcase or talked down to—
> everyone was pleasant and helpful and treated me like a fully
> functioning human being who had a medical problem.[55]

This survey response was typical of respondents who were pleased with the care they had received in EDs for medical problems.

The degree to which people with psychiatric disabilities complain that their medical problems are minimized or ignored is interesting because it conflicts somewhat with equally strong complaints by ED professionals that they are forced to do unnecessarily thorough medical "clearances" of people who present with psychiatric disabilities before they can be seen by psychiatrists or admitted to psychiatric units or facilities.[56]

The interrelationship of medical and psychiatric conditions has long been standard knowledge in the research literature. However, it is clear that although people with psychiatric disabilities often have comorbid medical conditions, ED staff still tend to interpret reported medical symptoms of people with psychiatric histories with skepticism.

Medical Conditions That Cause, Mimic, or Exacerbate Psychiatric Conditions

A person seeking help in the emergency room may not know whether the condition he or she is experiencing is medical or psychiatric. Often, the symptoms a person is experiencing represent a combination of medical and psychiatric conditions, with the medical condition causing or exacerbating psychiatric symptomatology. As one treatise notes, "[i]t is particularly important to recognize underlying medical illness that presents primarily with psychiatric symptoms; this scenario has accounted for more than one-third of patients hospitalized on psychiatric wards in some studies. Delayed diagnosis of subdural hematoma, toxic encephalopathy, or metabolic disturbance may result in permanent disability or death."[57] Numerous metabolic, endocrine and other disorders mimic psychiatric disabilities. In addition, some medications, notably steroids such as prednisone, can result in "steroid-induced psychoses."[58] Yet if a person has a history of psychiatric disabilities, all too often triage nurses or examining physicians reach the conclusion that a presenting condition is psychiatric.

For more than 40 years, research has shown that people who present at emergency rooms with psychiatric complaints often have serious medical conditions. "These unrecognized physical illnesses may have the symptoms of depression, anxiety states, apathy, aggressive outbursts, personality changes, sexual dysfunctions, delusions, hallucinations, or schizophreniform or manic-like psychotic states."[59] One of a number of early studies to document this phenomenon examined 100 consecutively admitted patients to a psychiatric ward; 46% had an unrecognized medical illness that either caused or exacerbated their psychiatric symptoms.[60] As the study noted, these patients "in all probability would have been committed to the state hospital."[61] Given medical treatment for the underlying condition, half of these patients displayed rapid and significant improvement of their psychiatric symptomatology.[62] Since then, studies have shown that 63% of "new" psychiatric patients in an ED had organic etiology to explain their presentations.[63] This is an example of a fact, like the trauma histories of women with severe psychiatric disabilities, that has been known to researchers for decades and yet has not changed the practice in the field to any substantial extent.

A number of lawsuits have been brought by the relatives of people who died because emergency room personnel diagnosed serious physical conditions as psychiatric complaints. These are discussed further in chapter 5.

Medical Conditions Caused by Psychiatric Treatments

Although recently pharmaceutical companies have alerted physicians to the relationship between Zyprexa and diabetes,[64] and risperidone and stroke,[65] some conditions caused by psychiatric treatments, such as neuroleptic malignant syndrome or dystonia, have long been known and yet are often not considered by emergency room physicians or psychiatrists. Currier, Allen, and colleagues make the point that psychiatrists rather than physicians are in a better position to recognize that "many of the serious medical co-morbidities encountered in people with psychiatric illness may actually be caused by psychiatric treatment (e.g., dystonia)."[66] At least one case against a hospital involved a patient who was medically cleared but died due to a toxic level of psychotropic medication in his blood.[67] High levels of anti-psychotic medications can cause psychotic delirium, which in turn leads to cardiac arrhythmia and death, especially in cases involving restraints.

Medical Conditions Whose Treatment Is Complicated by Psychiatric Problems

> I generally wind up going to the ER with her because of how challenging she is and the ER's difficulty in working with people who aren't compliant and nice. She also frequently has hygiene issues as well. But when she's had to have MRIs or CT scans, the techs frequently get frustrated with her and if I wasn't there talking to her and telling them how to work with her, they wouldn't do the tests because she's not compliant, and she screams and yells a lot—to the point it feels like verbal abuse.[68]

Emergency departments are busy places and do not have time to facilitate the kinds of accommodations often needed by people with psychiatric disabilities in the treatment of their medical problems. Especially when medical treatments involve intrusive or frightening procedures, the individual with psychiatric disabilities may present objections or demands that are difficult to meet in a crowded, rushed ED environment. This may lead either to forcible treatment, with long-lasting traumatic consequences for the individual, or no treatment, with potentially serious medical consequences. Various solutions are possible: EDs can permit accompaniment by a trusted family member, friend, or advocate who can help to calm the individual's apprehensions. Many EDs are reluctant to permit accompaniment, especially by an unrelated person, but if desired by the individual with a psychiatric disability, accompaniment could solve a number of problems. Sometimes the hospital employs a patient advocate who can assist. Many mental health treatment providers who advise their patients to seek assistance in an ED could assist enormously by asking their patient's permission to call the ED prior to that patient's arrival with information about the patient's specific accommodation needs and how they could be met. If the patient is a frequent visitor to the ED, creating a plan that gives treatment providers assistance on necessary accommodations may save time and preclude escalation.

Treating Psychiatric Emergencies with Contempt or Derision

The most universal complaint of people with psychiatric disabilities about their treatment in the emergency room, as reflected from survey responses, concerned the lack of respect and even hostility they faced when they sought emergency care. One survey respondent wrote, "Some of the psych techs made fun of some of the patients . . . saying that we thought the hospital was a 'Holiday Inn' where we come when we need a break or just to take a shower and get a hot meal . . ."[69] The same respondent wrote of listening to nurses "making jokes" about a patient who was suicidal, saying he "was stupid because he only shot himself in the shoulder."[70]

This feeling is confirmed by books and treatises on emergency room treatment and practitioners' journals, which acknowledge that "[p]sychiatric patients tend to be regarded as a nuisance or sometimes even a hindrance to the work of the ED because they frequently have accompanying behavioral disturbance."[71] Other articles and books state that psychiatric patients in emergency rooms "are often seen as a burden,"[72] "are often seen as intrusions,"[73] and note that "to a degree the emergency psychiatric patient represents the unwanted patient."[74]

Repeatedly, survey respondents who were pleased with their care in emergency settings cited respectful and responsive treatment as the primary reason for their satisfaction. Even the tiniest gestures of concern and empathy were remembered by people who might have appeared to be in a state where they would have remembered very little of how they were treated.

Lack of Privacy

Although privacy and confidentiality issues may overlap, we use them separately here to make an important distinction. "Privacy" refers to the experience of the patient him or herself: being able to make private phone calls, being interviewed by doctors or nurses in private, having a private space if necessary to be in crisis. "Confidentiality" refers to information about the patient. The lack of privacy is part of what makes an emergency room experience difficult for a patient undergoing a psychiatric crisis, and he or she will generally be fully aware of privacy violations. The patient may not personally experience a breach of confidentiality; he or she may never learn that confidentiality has been violated.

The JCAHO standards make clear that "Patients who must make private phone calls should have access to space and phones appropriate to their clinical condition. Physically challenged individuals have similar access."[75] In addition, the conditions of participation for hospitals receiving Medicaid and Medicare funds from the federal government require that those hospitals ensure that "the patient has the right to personal privacy," which is interpreted as meaning "that patients have privacy during personal hygiene activities (e.g., toileting, bathing, dressing), during medical/nursing treatments, and when requested as appropriate."[76] This means that "people not involved in the care of the patient should not be present without his/her consent while he/she is being examined or treated, nor should video or other electronic monitoring/recording methods be used while he/she is being examined without his/her consent."[77]

Confidentiality

Confidentiality concerns are especially important for patients with psychiatric disabilities, as people with diagnoses of mental illness can face discrimination and adverse treatment if their condition is known. Requirements of confidentiality apply to the public through both the Health Insurance Portability and Accountability Act (HIPAA) regulations (discussed in chapter 5) and JCAHO standards, which unequivocally state: "[u]nder no circumstances is it advisable to post a patient's name, diagnosis, and treatment protocol on a white board for public viewing."[78] The JCAHO standards advise that the health care organization has an obligation to inform the community it serves that filming or videotaping may be occurring when emergency services are provided. "Patients can be informed . . . by the posting of advance notice signs in the public areas of the hospital and emergency department."[79] It is not clear what recourse is available to patients who object to such videotaping.

Media and Confidentiality

It is obviously very important to protect the identity of patients who have not consented to be filmed or taped when the media enters the ED. Again, JCAHO cautions that it "supports videotaping or filming of television programs in the ED only when patients, their family members, or surrogate decision makers give fully informed consent . . . EDs may film or videotape patient care activities in the emergency room, but they must obtain informed consent from the patient, his or her family members, or surrogate [decision makers]."[80] The ability of family members or surrogate decision makers to consent to taping or filming of their relative is not clear as a legal matter. Certainly, courts might not agree with the JCAHO standard that taping can occur without informed consent if the patient is not competent and no alternate decision maker is available. In any event, consent must be obtained before using the tape in any way.

HIPAA provides that patients have a right to see their own records, subject to very few exceptions. In addition, HIPAA permits patients to request that their records be amended. These standards are discussed in detail in chapter 5.

Delays in Emergency Room Treatment

Overcrowded emergency rooms are a national crisis. The Joint Commission on Accreditation of Health Care Organizations has held several conferences on the issue, plans to issue a white paper on ED overcrowding,[81] and has issued new accreditation standards under "Hospital Leadership" to include measurement of emergency room overcrowding as an accreditation issue. The surveys conducted by the Center for Public Representation anecdotally confirm the gravity of the problem: "This particular emergency room [in South Carolina] according to the guy in charge of it who I heard talk in a meeting recently . . . now keeps psychotic mental patients in the ER for as long as [five] days without a psychiatrist seeing them, without any meds, etc."[82]

Another complaint concerned an emergency room stay in Portland, Oregon, that lasted for four days before a person from the court investigating team visited to determine that no petition for involuntary civil commitment would be filed. Delayed treatment in emergency rooms is often linked inextricably to demand that cannot be met by existing resources. Patients may wait for treatment on gurneys in hallways; this has become so standard that gurneys are now assigned permanent stations by some EDs. Psychiatric patients complain, as do other patients in emergency rooms, of inordinate delays in receiving treatment in emergency rooms. Psychiatric patients, unlike other patients, may be tied to gurneys or handcuffed to wheelchairs to prevent them from leaving. Again, the involuntary nature of the detention can implicate constitutional and statutory rights.

According to the Centers for Disease Control, the average waiting time in an ED for a non-emergency condition increased from 51 minutes to 67.6 minutes between 1997 and 2000.[83] By 2004, the National Center for Health Statistics was reporting that duration in the ED (as measured by the time between arrival and discharge) was an average of 3.2 hours.[84] The Joint Commission on Accreditation of Health Care Organizations agrees: "many patients can wait three, four, five, or many more hours."[85] Newspaper reports of actual conditions across the country highlight far higher figures at EDs that are particularly pressed.[86] Studies of emergency room delays have found that psychiatric patients wait longer than the average patient, and it is psychiatric patients who raise the average waiting time when delays are measured.[87]

However, because other patients are free to leave if they become impatient, and psychiatric patients are often prevented from leaving, delays may implicate constitutional rights. A case filed in 1985 and settled in 1992 challenged New York City Health and Hospital Corporation's practice of keeping psychiatric patients for "days at a time" in the emergency room while they waited transfer to scarce beds.[88] Another case filed more recently in the State of Washington established for the first time that patients have a due process interest under the federal and state constitution in not being unreasonably detained in emergency rooms, and put the burden of proof on the hospital to show that the delay was reasonable.[89] These cases are discussed more fully in chapter 5.

Many states have statutes that limit the amount of time that an emergency room can hold an individual. These statutes are also discussed in chapter 5.

Access Issues for Specific Populations

Although the emergency room is considered to be accessible on a 24-hour basis, just because an individual can enter an emergency room does not mean that he or she will receive adequate care once inside. Access to care for psychiatric clients who are deaf, have trauma histories, speak languages other than English, are not citizens, or use service animals is often fraught with difficulty. Ironically, many of these individuals may end up in emergency room settings because of inability to obtain adequate health and psychiatric care from their primary care providers.[90]

Deaf Clients

People with psychiatric disabilities who are deaf present particularly significant issues in hospitals and EDs. If a person who is deaf is restrained, he or she cannot communicate except by vocalizations that may be frightening and incomprehensible to staff who have no experience with deaf people. Many behaviors common to deaf culture—stamping the floor or hitting the table to indicate a desire to communicate—may be misunderstood by staff, and this is especially likely if staff know that the deaf person has a psychiatric disability.

Hospitals and emergency rooms are notoriously inaccessible to deaf patients, despite clear federal requirements under both Medicaid law and the ADA that deaf people are entitled to effective communication and equal access to services. In addition, accreditation requirements by JCAHO specifically require that hospitals respect patients' right to and need for effective communication.

The ADA applies to private hospitals through Title III, which requires "public accommodations"—accommodations open to and doing business with the public—to provide effective communication and equal access to hospital services to people who are deaf.[91] The ADA applies to state and county hospitals through Title II of the ADA, which applies to "public entities" such as state and local governments, and has similar requirements regarding effective communications and equal access to services.

The Department of Justice's regulations implementing Title III specifically provide that a public accommodation such as a hospital "shall furnish appropriate auxiliary aids and services where necessary to ensure effective communication with individuals with disabilities."[92] "Auxiliary aids and services," in turn, are defined to include

> qualified interpreters, computer-aided transcriptions services, written materials, telephone handset amplifiers, assistive listening devices, assisted listening systems, telephones compatible with hearing aids, closed caption decoders, open and closed captioning, telecommunications devices for deaf persons (TDDs), videotext displays, or other effective methods of making aurally delivered materials available to individuals with hearing impairments.[93]

The Department of Justice has brought a series of lawsuits under the ADA against hospitals on behalf of deaf people who could not access the hospital's services.[94] There have been a number of private lawsuits against hospitals and EDs for failing to provide interpreter services for deaf individuals under the ADA as well.[95] Because Title III only allows cases for injunctive relief to be brought by private individuals (the Department of Justice is empowered to seek damages), the private cases have sometimes lost because plaintiffs cannot show that they are likely to visit the hospital and suffer the same injury again.

Hospitals are subject to conditions of participation under Medicare and Medicaid that require communications with people who are deaf to be effective. First, all provider agreements contain an agreement to comply with civil rights laws, such as Section 504 of the Rehabilitation Act of 1973, which ensure that hospitals will use alternative communication techniques or aids or take other steps as needed to effectively communicate with patients.[96] Information about patients' rights is subject to this requirement.[97] In its "Guidance to Surveyors," the Center for Medicare and Medicaid Services emphasizes, "The hospital's obligation to inform [patients of their rights] requires that the hospital presents information in a manner and form that can be understood, e.g., . . . specialized programs to inform individuals who are deaf or blind, use of interpreters."[98]

The Joint Commission on the Accreditation of Health Care Organizations also includes a requirement that hospitals, including EDs, meet the needs of deaf patients for effective communications. It includes a standard in its patients' rights section that provides: "The hospital respects the patient's right to and need for effective communication."[99] In meeting the standard, surveyors look to "Elements of Performance" including that "the hospital facilitates provision of interpretation, including translation services as necessary[100] and "the hospital addresses the needs of those with vision, speech, hearing, language and cognitive impairments."[101]

New technology is being developed that allows live video conferencing to be used for emergency interpreting needs before a local interpreter arrives. It is not intended to take the place of such interpreters, but to allow for some communication in the crucial time before an interpreter reaches the hospital. The hospital pays a monthly fee and a per-minute rate, and in return is guaranteed access on a 24-hour-a-day basis to interpreters. Among the hospitals using this service are Baystate Medical Center in Springfield, Massachusetts; St. Elizabeth's Hospital in Cambridge, Massachusetts; and Montefiore Hospital in the Bronx, New York.

People with Trauma Histories

Most women with complex psychiatric histories who are frequent utilizers of psychiatric emergency services are survivors of childhood physical and sexual abuse. There is a clear relationship between an individual's experience of severe trauma, such as childhood abuse, and later psychiatric and emotional difficulties, including self-injury. This is even more true of adolescents and children.[102] People with trauma histories are frequently the highest users of costly mental health crisis and emergency services.[103] These women are often diagnosed with borderline personality disorder or post-traumatic stress disorder (PTSD). As Rosenberg and Sulkowicz note, the PTSD may go un-identified in the ED:

> Not surprisingly, the PTSD patient can present to the [psychiatric emergency service] long after occurrence of the trauma, often as a consequence of the disruptive effect of avoidance, impaired sleep, or use of drugs and alcohol as a way of coping. PTSD is often unrecognized at the time of a [psychiatric emergency service] presentation unless there is specific inquiry made about traumatic experiences.[104]

Trauma survivors also come to the emergency room seeking care for self-inflicted burns, cuts, or other wounds. This creates deep emotional conflicts for ED personnel, who feel overloaded caring for persons whose wounds and injuries were inflicted by others. ED personnel often respond with deep hostility to people with self-inflicted wounds.

One activist, Deb Martinson, has created a Web site for people who self-injure and those who treat them in the emergency room. This helpful site includes guidance for ED personnel, citations from the research literature, and forms that the individual can fill out to expedite care and minimize confusion.[105]

Trauma survivors often have particularly strong reactions to being locked in rooms, restrained, or having their clothes taken from them in EDs. These experiences can feel more damaging than the crisis that brought them to the ED in the first place.

People Who Speak Different Languages

In urban areas in the United States, one of the major problems in hospital emergency rooms is responding to the communication needs of a diverse population. Close to 20% of all patients at Beth Israel Deaconess Medical Center in Boston require interpreters.[106] This is obviously a crucial problem for psychiatric patients. Patients cannot give informed consent if they do not understand their diagnosis, the possible outcome of the procedure or course of treatment, and the reasons the treatment is necessary. Federal law, many state laws, and licensing and accreditation requirements all clearly require hospitals to provide interpreter services for clients who cannot speak English.

The Joint Commission on Accreditation of Health Care Organizations emphasizes that "if EDs are not fortunate enough to have staffers from the ethnic backgrounds in question to translate for them" they must "see to it that they have ready access to translators, either through a hot line or from community referrals."[107] The commission makes clear that

> it is critical that patients be able to understand medical staff who speak to them, which can be a challenge if they do not under-stand English. The ED can overcome this barrier by conducting a survey of the predominant languages in the neighborhood and hiring staff who can speak those languages. For patients who speak a less common language, emergency department staff might consult with a medical translating service. It is important that the service is properly credentialed or certified.[108]

In addition to JCAHO accreditation standards, the United States Department of Health and Human Services Office of Minority Health has promulgated Standards for Culturally and Linguistically Appropriate Services in Health. These standards provide that "[h]ealth care organizations must offer and provide language assistance services, including bilingual staff and interpreter services, at no cost to each patient with limited English proficiency at all points of contact in a timely manner during all hours of operation";[109] that "[h]ealth care organizations must provide to patients in their preferred language both verbal orders and written notices informing them of their right to receive language assistance services,"[110] and that "[f]amilies and friends should not be used to provide interpretation services (except on request of the patient)."[111]

Non-Citizens

As of this writing, the Emergency Medical Treatment and Active Labor Act (EMTALA) applies to non-citizens. In addition, undocumented immigrants and aliens are entitled to "emergency" Medicaid, if they would otherwise meet Medicaid requirements, even though they are not eligible for the Medicaid program in general.[112]

Although federal Medicaid regulations and the state Medicaid manual state that an emergency condition must result from the "sudden onset" of an illness or injury, this requirement is not in the Medicaid statute. Courts have struggled to interpret the scope of the "emergency" medical care to which undocumented aliens are entitled and have come up with conflicting formulas. Some courts, such as the Second Circuit, look to "sudden, severe and short-lived physical injuries or illnesses that require immediate treatment in order to prevent future harm,"[113] and emphasize "severity, temporality and urgency." In *Greenery*, the Second Circuit rejected the proposition that because such emergencies had caused the plaintiffs' initial conditions, ongoing treatment for those conditions was covered by Medicaid. Thus, although both plaintiffs in *Greenery* had suffered severe brain injuries, and one was tube-fed and had to be monitored constantly for infection and malnutrition, while the other could not get his own food and was taking multiple medications that required constant monitoring, the court held that neither of these conditions was an "emergency" within the intention of the drafters of the emergency exception.

The Arizona Supreme Court disagreed with the Second Circuit's interpretation as too narrow, holding that the appropriate question was whether the patient's "current medical condition is a non-chronic condition presently manifesting itself by acute symptoms of sufficient severity that the absence of immediate medical treatment could result in one of the three adverse conditions . . ."[114]

Different states can adopt their own policy interpretations of when an emergency ends for purposes of the emergency exception to the Medicaid statute, as long as those interpretations fall within the language of the federal statute and regulations. State coverage varies considerably. For example, in Louisiana, state policy (Louisiana Medicaid Eligibility Manual, H-1721.6 [June 1, 1996]) provides that the certification period for emergency Medicaid "is limited to the length of time the recipient is receiving emergency hospital services, including labor and delivery." Nothing in federal law or policy suggests that such restriction is warranted.

Even if an undocumented alien is eligible for emergency Medicaid, obtaining care and coverage for psychiatric conditions can be problematic. First, in most communities, there may be little public awareness of the availability of emergency Medicaid for non-qualified aliens. Immigrants and providers need to be educated about the availability of emergency medical coverage. Second, while imminent suicidality appears to clearly qualify as an emergency condition under the language of the regulations, the language of court decisions has, without analysis, appeared to limit emergency situations to physical injuries, even though EMTALA and Medicaid explicitly apply to both medical and psychiatric conditions. For example, in *Greenery*, the court referred to "sudden, severe and short-lived *physical* injuries or illnesses that require immediate treatment to prevent future harm."[115]

No court decision has been found applying the emergency Medicaid provision to undocumented immigrants with psychiatric problems. This is probably because such individuals, if their psychiatric situation is truly emergent, are transferred to state mental health facilities.[116] From there, it is virtually impossible to discharge them, because Medicaid will not cover their care in the community. The emergency provisions of the Medicaid Act apply only to treatment in hospitals and EDs and cannot be used to fund community care for undocumented immigrants. There is currently a case in Massachusetts involving the interpretation of emergency Medicaid requirements as they apply to people with psychiatric disabilities that is attempting to expand state coverage to community crisis facilities and teams.

If, however, state Medicaid agencies officially interpret the emergency Medicaid provision to exclude all people with psychiatric disabilities who were receiving short-term emergency care in hospital facilities, no matter how urgent their conditions, such an exclusion might violate Title II of the ADA, as discussed later in chapter 5.

Service Animals

Although it is not commonly realized, people with psychiatric disabilities sometimes use service animals. The Department of Justice's regulations to the ADA generally require public accommodations to admit service animals.[117] However, hospital emergency rooms typically do not allow service animals, although hospitals have different practices, and some hospitals permit them in some areas and not in others.[118] The Department of Justice has ruled that in order to exclude service animals, the hospital must show that permitting service animals would create a fundamental alteration in the provision of services or constitute a direct threat to others.

Although cases involving service animals in hospitals are few, patients with service animals have generally lost, with courts giving deference to the testimony of hospital professionals.[119]

Accompaniment While Waiting

One issue frequently mentioned in surveys was the loneliness and frightening nature of waiting alone in an assessment room, uncertain when ED personnel would arrive and what would happen next. Many survey respondents expressed a desire that family, friends, or advocates be permitted to stay with them while they waited. Since research indicates that between

22–43% of psychiatric emergency room patients are accompanied by others, in many cases a potential source of comfort is available, but waiting in the waiting room.[120] It should simultaneously be underscored that this only applies to people whose presence is desired by the individual. In many cases, family members accompany unwilling patients and may be requesting hospitalization that the individual does not want.[121] The survey responses confirmed this; some respondents expressed the desire for a comforting presence, while others expressed the strong position that they did not want to be assessed in the presence of family members without a professional seeking their permission. In some cases, respondents noted, their abusers brought them to EDs.[122] Therefore, an individual's preference both for accompaniment and to choose who would provide accompaniment is a crucial part of this issue.

Many hospital EDs permit such accompaniment, but others do not. Some have a blanket policy prohibiting accompaniment in the case of psychiatric patients, although a family member or friend might be permitted to accompany a medical patient. Some EDs permit family members to be present during resuscitation or treatment.[123] However, having a family member or friend simply wait with a psychiatric patient is not permitted in many hospitals. For example, Civista Hospital in Maryland's policy states that, as to patients subject to a petition for involuntary commitment, "No visitors will be allowed until after patient is evaluated by [emergency personnel staff] and then only at the discretion of the ED [s]taff."[124]

Hospital EDs give a number of reasons for these policies: concerns for the safety of the person accompanying the patient; concern that the patient's condition might clinically deteriorate; discomfort with having an advocate in the ED, and (more rarely) concern for the safety of the patient. One ED professional acknowledged (on condition of anonymity) that EDs that lock psychiatric patients in assessment rooms do not permit accompaniment because they do not want to lock non-patients in the room.

The Joint Commission on Accreditation of Health Care Organizations and the Center for Medicare and Medicaid Services have no regulations directly addressing this issue, but they do have a number of regulations that support the proposition that patients should be allowed to ask for a friend or relative to accompany them while they wait. For example, both bodies underscore the importance of respecting the individual's requests, involving the individual in decisions regarding care, as well as involving family members when appropriate, and of ensuring that the patient can obtain a personal advocate when appropriate.

Lack of Effective Grievance Mechanisms or Advocacy

One of the most frequent complaints of psychiatric patients in emergency room settings is being left alone, unable to ask questions, gain information, or complain without fear of retaliation. One of the most popular recommendations in surveys of psychiatric patients is to establish an advocate/ombudsman/grievance function in the emergency room to help answer questions or resolve complaints. Such a system might help keep frustrations in check, avoid misunderstandings, and sometimes even avert tragedies.

Hospitals are supposed to have such a mechanism in place already. Hospitals receiving Medicare or Medicaid funds "must establish a process for prompt resolution of patients grievances and must inform each patient whom to contact to file a grievance" [42 C.F.R. 482.13]. The Joint Commission on Accreditation of Health Care Organizations has a similar requirement, RI.2.3, requiring facilities to have a system to "address the resolution of complaints from patients and their families."

However, when the Center for Public Representation surveyed Boston-area acute care hospitals to assess their grievance mechanisms in 2004, the findings were discouraging. Although all hospitals had some process for resolving patient grievances, there were significant differences in notice to patients about the procedures, ease of access to the procedures, and understandability of the hospital's description of the process. Very few hospitals had a grievance process that could reliably provide a real-time response to patients' complaints or questions. The few notable exceptions demonstrated that it is possible to have effective patient grievance systems in place.

Sixteen Boston-area hospitals were assessed. The following criteria were evaluated: access to information regarding patient ombudsman or advocate services through the hospital's Web site, by telephone, or in person; the information provided regarding those services; and the staffing of the grievance office, site of the office, ease of access to individuals to report grievances, and likelihood of real-time solution to problems. Thus, the assessment was not based on visits to the hospital. However, the information gathered through this process suggested that in many cases, hospital visits would not have yielded significant additional information regarding the availability of assistance.

First, the hospital's Web site was checked for patient advocate or grievance information. Then, the individual or office listed (if any) was called with basic questions about the operations of the office and how a specific hypothetical situation would be handled.

Just over half of the hospitals (9 out of 16) had any apparent reference to a grievance process on their Web pages. These were accessed typically through a "visitor information" or "patient guide" link. The best Web sites had multiple references and two or three different ways to obtain grievance process information. For example, the Massachusetts General Hospital Web site prominently calls attention to and explains their patient advocate process at the bottom of the "patient information" page, or through the "patient advocate" or "patient rights" links. Notably, few of the other hospitals had a direct reference to a grievance process even when they had a "patients' rights" page or link. A few hospitals indicated that complaints could be filed under the "patient responsibilities" heading, but did not include any contact information or other information as to how to file a complaint.

The nine hospitals with references to a grievance process, patient advocacy, or patient relations Web page links generally provided sufficient information (telephone numbers, business hours, etc.) to enable a patient to directly contact the responsible person to file a complaint or grievance. Many hospitals have electronic contact features built into their Web pages, but it is unclear where the messages are routed. An exception is the Beth Israel Deaconess Medical Center's Web page, which routes electronic messages directly to patient relations through a feature that pops up a form that permits patients to email the office directly.

Staffing and Access

Obtaining timely, direct access to a hospital's grievance process can be difficult, even during business hours, for all but the larger hospitals. Staffing arrangements for hospital grievance processes included a range from full-time paid staff to part-time to volunteer advocates. After hours calls were likely to be referred to the nursing supervisor or administrator on call. No hospital offered patient advocate services on Sunday. Only Brigham and Women's Hospital offers such services on Saturday, and only three others have between four and 12 staff persons available full-time during normal weekday business hours. In these hospitals, it was always possible to reach a live person during business hours to discuss a complaint. Eleven hospitals had one or two full or part-time staff members handling complaints. In these hospitals, reaching a staff member to personally discuss an issue was virtually impossible. One hospital used only an answering service to receive all patient complaints. The answering service advised that if deemed necessary (presumably by the answering service) the patient advocate would be paged.

For all hospitals, telephone calls after normal business hours are answered by voice messaging systems. Only one or two of the messaging systems explained that urgent after hours matters could be addressed by having the switchboard operator contact the nursing supervisor or administrator on call.

Few hospitals had any special training or mechanism for handling complaints from psychiatric patients. Although hospitals that treat psychiatric patients are required to have a human rights officer, only some of the grievance personnel knew to refer patients with complaints related explicitly to their psychiatric treatment to the human rights officer.

Cambridge Hospital, which receives a significant number of psychiatric emergencies, has a best practice worth noting. The hospital's patient relations office is located in close proximity to the ED, so that both ED patients and staff have ready access to the responsible grievance person. In certain situations, the ED medical staff will call patient relations to assist with a difficult or uncooperative patient. Alternatively, a disgruntled patient may be actively encouraged by the ED staff to seek the services of the patient relations office. In either event, potential patient grievances are avoided or handled in real time.

Obviously, people with psychiatric disabilities have a number of concerns about how they are treated in ED settings. In the end, almost all fit into one of two categories: force, including seclusion, restraint, forced medication, and mandatory disrobing; and discrimination and differential treatment, including minimization of medical complaints and even hostility based on the person's status as someone with a psychiatric history or who was taking psychiatric medications. When survey respondents described differential treatment, it was often (although not always) to the disadvantage of the person with psychiatric disabilities. Most of the difficulties could have been averted if staff had more time to listen and to treat the person with consideration, empathy, and respect.

Many ED staff interviewed for this book concurred substantially in these assessments. They tended to justify the complaints about force in terms of the need for safety, and translated the complaints about respect, consideration and empathy into the need to spend more time with clients with psychiatric histories (and the need for additional staff that this implies). In this way, professional perspectives dovetailed (if not perfectly) with patient perspectives. However, ED professionals also have unique concerns of their own. These are described in the next chapter.

4

Professional Issues in Emergency Department Care

Not surprisingly, the problems expressed by emergency department (ED) professionals when interviewed for this book differed significantly from the problems described by the people with psychiatric disabilities who used ED services. Nevertheless, it does not take very much insight to understand how the difficulties described by professionals result in the problems described by the patients.

Accreditation and Evaluation Systems Create Incentives That Undermine Appropriate Psychiatric Evaluation and Treatment

Emergency departments are measured on how swiftly they conduct competent triage, assessment, and disposition of patients who present for care. An anthropologist who studied a psychiatric emergency service titled her book *Emptying Beds: The Work of an Emergency Psychiatric Unit.*[1] She noted that one of the reasons that she chose to study the unit was "the contradictory nature of the task: the staff described themselves as having the 'impossible mandate' that required that they discharge patients quickly yet treat them adequately."[2]

Although people in psychiatric crisis need a calm person who can take the time to listen and be reassuring, EDs do not have the staffing to provide the attention that individuals in emotional crisis need. Nor is the culture of the ED one that supports quiet reassurance. There are multiple pressures on ED physicians and staff to do something, to act quickly—their own professional culture of being decisive and in control, the demands of the ED, the knowledge that their performance will be measured on how many assessments and dispositions can be accomplished, and, often, the pressures of secondary utilizers, such as police who have to get back on the job or providers who have to get back to their residence. The patient may feel desperate and urgent. Yet experts in emergency psychiatry and crisis resolution advise that the best thing to do is to slow down, listen, and *not* make quick decisions.[3] Sometimes, an individual in crisis simply needs a safe place to be for a while, or to be monitored after a medication change. However, for EDs that are measured on "input-throughput-output"—speedy evaluations and dispositions—keeping a patient over 24 hours is known as "boarding" the patient, and the failure of an ED is measured by the number of boarders who occupy beds needed for new emergency patients. Some hospitals have developed adjunct crisis units that can take patients from EDs and keep them for one to three days, which is considered superior to boarding in the ED. However, the crisis units often simply become repositories for patients who need admission, but for whom no hospital bed is available.

Sometimes, listening to a patient or that patient's friends or family for another half hour will provide solutions or answers that can prevent expensive inpatient hospitalization. But there is no formal system that rewards this kind of cost savings; rather, the incentives are to keep the interview short and make the disposition decision speedily. Keeping patients too long leads to overcrowding, another area that is currently receiving a great deal of attention.

There are few incentives to conduct a thorough and detailed assessment of a person presenting in psychiatric crisis, and many incentives to evaluate as quickly as possible. Hasty and inadequate emergency room assessments of people with psychiatric disabilities are rarely reviewed, monitored, or challenged. On the other hand, the length of time that people wait to be seen and the overcrowding of EDs are scrutinized by licensing authorities and the media. Thus, the evaluation of a person presenting with a psychiatric emergency may take very little time, as little as five to 15 minutes, before decisions are made regarding admission, detention, or discharge.[4]

Nor are there many incentives to inform a patient of alternatives, negotiate with reluctant or hostile patients, or work to achieve an optimal rather than the most conveniently available disposition. It is no surprise that agitated patients find themselves in restraints or required to remove clothing to prevent their departure as they wait for extensive periods. These kinds of requirements sometimes result in confrontations with increasingly well-armed security guards. Some of these confrontations escalate into force and violence, and an individual who might have come for comfort and solace finds himself or herself in greater crisis than before.

Cursory assessments lead to hasty decisions to involuntarily detain the individual. In some cases, plaintiffs charge that admission was a foregone conclusion prior to the assessment.[5] The inadequacy of emergency room assessments of people with psychiatric disabilities has become so marked that a number of assessments have recently been successfully challenged in damage actions in court. At least three verdicts of over $1 million dollars each were reached in the year 2003–2004 alone.[6]

Many emergency room professionals are compassionate, thorough, and take the time to listen to the patient and provide individualized care and attention. However, there are currently few structural mechanisms that provide any incentive for them to behave this way, other than their own personal integrity. By contrast, the current emergency room culture creates many incentives to conduct speedy examinations and make quick dispositions. New Joint Commission on Accreditation of Health Care Organizations (JCAHO) standards intended to reduce overcrowding may contribute to this pressure.

The only systemic counter pressure favoring thorough examinations is the increase in litigation by patients, accompanied by high verdicts and adverse publicity. It would be preferable to conduct a more focused and organized discussion of this issue, rather than permitting the current system of pressure and counter pressure to result in unthinking reactions that benefit neither the hospital organization nor the patients it serves.

The Lack of Standards in Emergency Room Practice

Emergency departments lack standards in the most basic elements of evaluation and treatment with regard to people with psychiatric disabilities. Emergency department professionals readily admit that no clear, comprehensive standards exist as to what constitutes an adequate assessment of a client presenting with psychiatric problems in an emergency room.[7]

Some very basic standards regarding assessment of clients presenting with psychiatric problems have emerged from treatises, recently produced expert consensus guidelines, and case law.[8] It is clear that some form of medical evaluation should be done to ensure that the presenting problem is neither medical nor primarily related to substance abuse. It is not clear, however, what kind of tests, if any, are necessary beyond taking core vital signs and a history from the patient. Nor is it clear who should be responsible for determining the necessary tests: the ED or the facility receiving the patient. Many conflicts are generated by the refusal of psychiatric wards to accept patients without tests that ED staff consider unnecessary.

It is also clear that a mental status examination should be done to screen for organic brain injury, dementia, and other conditions. Again, experts disagree as to the utility or validity of clinical interviews as compared to the use of instruments developed and marketed to perform these evaluations. Among those who favor the instruments there is disagreement as to which instrument to use.

The professional consensus (and statutory requirement) to evaluate suicidality and danger to others founders on an inability to make accurate predictions, especially in the brief time period ordinarily allotted to ED assessments. The difficulty of these predictions is compounded by the inexperience of the residents, medical students, and mental health counselors assigned to do the assessments. Patient profiling (i.e., simply looking at the patient's demographic and historical facts, such as past acts of violence or self-harm) can be more accurate at predicting dangerousness, but instruments developed for this purpose (typically to analyze the likelihood of future dangerousness of a criminal proposed for parole) generally take much longer to perform—at least an hour—than most physicians can spend with a given patient in an ED. Recently, an instrument has been developed for more abbreviated risk assessment, which would be more appropriate for use in ED settings, the Classification of Violence Risk Instrument.[9] This is discussed at greater length below.

Nor is there consensus on what kind of treatment an ED should provide in psychiatric emergencies. As one recent report that attempted to establish consensus noted, key constructs such as agitation have not been adequately operationalized so that the criteria defining a behavioral emergency are vague. Second, there are few data on which to base clinical policies, given the relative lack of research in this area. A consensus about key elements in the management of behavioral emergencies has not yet been articulated by the provider community.[10]

In summary, the primary task of the ED evaluation of an individual in psychiatric distress is to determine appropriate diagnosis, treatment, and disposition, but there are no standard methods to accomplish this. Decisions are often influenced by the availability of beds in the hospital and the community, as well as reimbursement and health care coverage.

Standards for Medical Assessment of People in Psychiatric Crisis

All texts and treatises, as well as Policy Statements by the American College of Emergency Physicians[11] and the Expert Consensus Guidelines, agree that a patient presenting for psychiatric reasons should receive some form of medical examination. The importance of this cannot be overstated, since apparent psychiatric symptoms may be caused by or exacerbated by underlying medical or substance abuse problems.[12] Because of the number of medical conditions that cause psychiatric-seeming symptoms, the standard of care requires a medical screening even when both the patient and the emergency room perceive the patient's primary complaint as psychiatric.

As noted above, the scope of this medical screening or clearance is the subject of considerable controversy and dispute. Researchers agree that "no consensus has been reached regarding a clinical pathway outlining the scope and extent of the PMSE [psychiatric medical screening examination]."[13] In addition, a patient presenting for psychiatric reasons may have serious medical problems that are unrelated to the psychiatric problems but that can and should be diagnosed with relative ease, such as hypertension or diabetes. These conditions are especially important to consider in light of recent findings associating some common psychiatric drugs, such as Zyprexa, with increased vulnerability to diabetes.[14]

There appears to be uniform agreement that all persons presenting for psychiatric evaluation should have their vital signs taken, be asked for basic medical history, and have a physical examination performed as a matter of course. However, there is controversy on whether taking a history from the patient suffices to spot possible medical reasons for the psychiatric complaints, or whether certain medical tests should be routinely conducted.[15] These tests include toxicology screenings, serum electrolytes, blood counts, enzyme measurements, or pregnancy tests. Whether these tests should be done routinely is a matter of debate. Some argue that medical and substance abuse problems are so prevalent in psychiatric patients that toxicology screenings must be done as a matter of course.[16] Others consider them necessary only if specific history or clinical findings point to substance abuse, overdose, or medical problems.[17]

One early study suggested that if emergency room patients presenting with psychiatric symptoms were given "a battery consisting of careful physical, psychiatric and neurological examination, SMA-34 blood chemistry, including CBC [complete blood count], routine urinalysis, ECG [electrocardiogram], EEG [electroencephalogram] after sleep deprivation, their medical illness would be defined in more than 90% of cases."[18] More recently, the authors of a study that revealed that 63 of 100 consecutively presenting patients who came to the emergency room with new psychiatric symptoms had organic etiologies, suggested that medical histories, physical examinations, alcohol and drug screens, computed tomography scans, lumbar puncture, SMA-7 tests, and calcium tests be administered routinely, and that a creatine phosphokinase test be performed if there is possible myoglobinuria.[19]

On the other hand, tests can be expensive and time-consuming, and other authors point to studies indicating that routine laboratory testing or screening detects only 0.05%–20% of medical illnesses.[20] Emergency room physicians responding to a survey indicated that they believed few, if any, laboratory tests were useful; only about a third endorsed tests to detect alcohol or drugs in a presenting patient.[21] Yet many psychiatrists and outpatient providers rely on the emergency room physician for medical screenings and tests that most emergency room physicians believe are unnecessary and resent being expected to perform.[22]

In part, as an exchange in *Academic Emergency Medicine* between a psychiatrist and an emergency room physician underscored, psychiatrists and emergency room physicians have different goals in performing the tests. The emergency room physician who wrote the initial article looks at disposition of patients, and notes that laboratory tests of psychiatric patients rarely influence disposition, and most of the useful information can be extracted from interviewing the patient or clinical examination. The psychiatrist who responded focuses on treatment; identification of substance abuse, or of medical conditions that contraindicate certain psychiatric medications, is of primary importance in shaping treatment.[23] She points out that many clients dislike repeated blood draws, and prefer that all necessary tests be accomplished with one blood draw. The psychiatrist notes a final benefit to doing lab tests: "[r]outine health maintenance screening is also important when psychiatric patients are seen in acute settings, since such individuals have increased rates of medical morbidity and mortality yet often receive inadequate medical attention in the community."[24]

This last comment illustrates the crux of the conflict between psychiatry and emergency medicine: in response, the original author writes, "Dr. Fochtmann's final suggestion that the ED should be responsible for routine health maintenance screening of psychiatric patients should be a wake-up call to all EPs [emergency physicians] working in the overcrowded front lines of the health care system, that abuse of the ED can originate from other medical specialties. Further, why should EPs shoulder the responsibility for the added cost and time, especially when prolonging the psychiatric patient's time in the ED will prolong his or her exposure to a relatively unsafe environment? In this age of ED overcrowding, it would seem counterintuitive to keep psychiatric patients in the ED to perform tests that are not necessary for their immediate stabilization."[25] This raises the policy issue, also the subject of great debate, as to whether EDs should reject or embrace the greatly broadened role in community health care that they are playing by default.

One point of consensus, which is crucial in light of the frequency with which it is violated in practice, is that "before intervening with medication, the experts considered it most important to determine if there is a causal medical etiology that should be managed first, to review the patient's records if available, and to determine if substance abuse may be complicating the presentation."[26]

The thoroughness of medical assessment may depend on a variety of factors, including the patient's age, physical condition, whether he or she is already known to ED staff, and whether he or she has an ongoing relationship with medical providers in the community. In cases where the patient's symptoms suggest a medical origin—including but not limited to sudden onset of confusion, disorientation, difficulty concentrating, nausea, or headaches—ruling out possible physical causes is important. Whether the responsibility to do so rests with the patient's primary health care providers or the EDs depends on the gravity of the situation. In one case, a patient began treatment at a mental health clinic for confusion, poor memory, expressive difficulties and non-responsiveness, and presented the same month at an ED with these symptoms. The ED physician performed a neurological examination, but no neurological testing. Her doctor at the mental health clinic attributed her symptoms to mental illness and the side effects of medication. The doctor told the patient that if she was concerned, she could obtain a neurological evaluation, but he did not order one himself. As it happened, the plaintiff had a slow-growing brain tumor, which was diagnosed and removed two years later; the removal alleviated her symptoms. In subsequent litigation, the community mental health clinic and its doctor were found to be liable for more than $200,000 for failing to order neurological tests, while the ED doctor and the ED doctor were found to have no liability for the same omission.[27]

Standards for Mental Status Assessment of People in Psychiatric Crisis

The most common instrument used to assess mental status is the Mini-Mental State Exam (MMSE). First developed in 1975, this is a short test designed to measure "orientation, immediate and short-term recall, language, and the ability to follow simple verbal and written commands."[28] Texts and treatises disagree as to its utility. Although the Expert Consensus Guidelines recommend "a cognitive examination (e.g., a Mini-Mental State Examination),"[29] one text on ED evaluations states that "The Mini-Mental Status [sic] Exam (MMSE) is a brief and useful screening cognitive examination but does not substitute for a full mental status examination."[30] Another text, noting that the MMSE was developed for geriatric populations, concludes "the MMSE is not sensitive to detection of cognitive deficits in many groups of psychiatric and dementia patients" and unequivocally recommends that other screening devices be used.[31] In cognitive and mental status testing, as in predictions of dangerousness, clinical evaluations have been shown to be unreliable compared to evaluations using standard testing instruments.[32]

Standards for Psychiatric Assessment of People in Psychiatric Crisis

Although most articles and treatises agree on the need to develop instruments to enhance the reliability of assessments, efforts to do so have failed when tested in the field. This is due to the fact that accurate psychiatric assessments take more time than EDs actually allot to conducting those assessments. The Office of Mental Health in New York received a substantial grant to create such an instrument, and assembled a consensus panel of experts. The instrument that emerged would probably have been an excellent means of making judgments regarding admission and detention, but, tellingly, physicians who worked in EDs rejected it as taking too long to administer and being too complicated.[33] The instrument contained 73 questions, of which 44 were designated as "must ask." As one implementation site responded, in order to be utilized to make triage or admission decisions, "it must be doable in minutes."[34] When the developers of the Expert Consensus Guidelines considered the extent of assessment necessary to create a plan of care in an ED setting, they noted, "to create a plan of care, the experts considered a brief assessment leading to the determination of a general category of presentation (e.g. intoxication, psychosis) adequate. A more comprehensive assessment leading to a specific diagnosis was also supported, but may be impractical for various reasons."[35]

The tension between the need to do a thorough and comprehensive assessment of an individual presenting at an emergency room with psychiatric disabilities, whose liberty may hang in the balance, and the rushed and understaffed reality of many emergency rooms, has led some jurisdictions to allocate the function of assessment for purposes of involuntary detention and inpatient admission to other entities.[36] This has the advantage of theoretically increasing reliability of the assessment, but the disadvantage of creating delay as individuals wait for two assessments: the assessment of the ED professionals that the outside team should be called, and the assessment of the mobile team itself.

These delays led to litigation in at least one case. The Washington State Supreme Court held that involuntary detention of an individual between the time of his or her arrival at the ED and the time that the outside team was called implicated due process interests, although the standard it created to address those rights—the hospital must show that the delay is justified—is relatively easy to meet.[37]

Assessment of Dangerousness

There are no agreed-upon clinical standards on how to appropriately assess psychiatric patients in the ED and when they should be admitted to inpatient care. Yet every state has a statute that creates standards on when a patient should be involuntarily detained for assessment of his or her dangerousness. Assessing a patient to determine whether he or she needs inpatient care is obviously related to determining whether to involuntarily detain the patient, but these are distinct inquiries. An individual can be voluntarily admitted based solely on the severity of his or her psychiatric condition. Involuntary detention may only be considered if the individual's psychiatric condition, however severe, will likely cause him or her to be dangerous to himself or herself or others.

A finding of dangerousness involves a number of assessments: the likelihood of the danger, the seriousness of the likely danger, the imminence of the likely danger, the degree of confidence that a predictor has in the above judgments, and the existence of alternatives to ameliorate or mitigate the risk of danger. Some state statutes essentially leave the issue of how to balance these judgments to the physician; others provide guidance in consideration of these factors: the danger must be "serious" or "substantial," the danger must be "imminent" or "present," and the physician must make a specific finding that no willing family members or friends are available to help avoid the danger.

Although the requirement of finding dangerousness is statutory, the Second and Ninth Circuits, as well as the Washington Supreme Court, have held that the act of detention in EDs implicates constitutional rights.[38] However, courts have generally been content to leave protection of constitutional rights in the hands of medical experts. Thus, the Second Circuit held that the question of "which indicia of dangerousness satisfies the statute is guided by the medical principles generally accepted in the community."[39]

Unlike the problem with ED assessments in general, which is that workable standards do not exist, the difficulty with predicting dangerousness—either to self in the form of suicidality or to others in the form of physical aggression—is that the statutorily established standards cannot be met with any degree of accuracy.

There are three distinct problems with assessments of dangerousness for purposes of involuntary detention that have been reported consistently in the research literature for several decades. First, some assessors who are charged with assessing dangerousness actually base involuntary detention decisions on other grounds, from the availability of inpatient beds to the weather outside.[40] Second, even when assessing dangerousness, individuals are involuntarily detained on the basis of behavior that may not rise to the level of dangerousness contemplated by involuntary commitment statutes. Third, in the best of all worlds, where mental health professionals perform careful assessments that track the language of the involuntary commitment statutes, they are largely unable to accurately predict dangerousness based on unstructured clinical interviews, and most ED assessments rely solely on unstructured clinical interviews. Even structured clinical interviews or actuarial assessments, discussed below, are not extremely accurate.

Despite these difficulties, physicians and other assessors in EDs must at least *try* to assess dangerousness. It is probably a departure from the standard of care not to inquire or elicit of the individual information about whether he or she intends to or is likely to harm himself or others.[41] In addition, some cases have held and some authors have cautiously suggested that in a given situation, the failure to attempt to obtain collateral information—information from sources other than the individual—may be malpractice, particularly when the collateral sources were readily available, and had information that, if known to the assessor, might have averted an adverse outcome.[42] Of course, this may conflict with new requirements imposed by the Health Insurance Portability and Accountability Act (discussed in chapter 5). The appropriate course is to attempt to obtain consent from the patient to interview collateral sources and carefully document a patient's consent or refusal.

Although research is conflicting on whether decisions to involuntarily detain individuals are based primarily on an assessment of dangerousness or on severity of symptomatology,[43] there is strong support for the proposition that other factors come into play in a decision to involuntarily detain an individual. As noted below, less experienced residents tend to make admissions decisions based on inappropriate factors. In addition, admission decisions can be governed or at least influenced by external factors, such as the preferences or attitude of the managed care organization or other reimbursing entity, which often must be consulted prior to inpatient admission and to authorize inpatient care.[44] One study showed a strong correlation between the availability of collateral information from police or family members and decisions in favor of involuntary detention.[45] Although these factors are more difficult to prove in a case challenging individual involuntary detention, at least one attorney is currently litigating a class action lawsuit that asserts that clinicians improperly base decisions to involuntarily detain an individual on the basis of their perceptions of the individual's need for treatment rather than an assessment of dangerousness.[46]

Evaluations That a Patient Is Dangerous Are Based on Behavior That Is Itself Only Tenuously Connected with Dangerousness

Both case law and research confirm that individuals in ED settings are judged to be dangerous on the basis of behavior that is defined far more broadly than permitted under commitment statutes.[47] Recent studies reflect that behavior considered dangerous in earlier studies included verbal aggressiveness or behavior that made others afraid, e.g., a prediction of dangerousness was scored as "accurate" if the individual was verbally aggressive.[48] Other studies considered an individual violent if he or she was arrested.[49] In one study, a prediction of dangerousness was scored as accurate if the patient ended up in seclusion. These are not the kinds of dangerousness that are intended to be predicted by those who drafted involuntary detention statutes. Yet, as Dr. Charles Lidz has demonstrated, clinicians' predictions of violence, which are "relatively inaccurate" in the first place, do not increase in accuracy for patients that clinicians believe to be the most dangerous.[50] Case law supports this research. In one case, a psychiatrist testified that his conclusion that the individual was dangerous was based on the patient's "body language," a conclusion the judge found to be legally insufficient to support involuntary detention.[51] In another case, a mental health professional acknowledged that she petitioned for her patient's commitment because she was afraid that the patient's spouse might harm her.[52]

Clinical Interviews Cannot Predict Dangerous Behavior

However, even if a psychiatrist or physician focuses on dangerousness, and attempts to predict the likelihood of injury or physical harm to the patient or others, the research literature confirms that clinical interviews simply cannot accomplish this objective. The inability to predict dangerousness to others is well documented.[53] The American Psychiatric Association (APA) has never receded from its position that the unreliability of clinical predictions of dangerousness "is an established fact."[54] There are a number of reasons for this. First, suicide and seriously aggressive behavior toward others occur so rarely that it is extremely difficult to predict them accurately. Even using a sample of people who were already more violent than the norm, clinicians' predictions of violence show a 60% sensitivity rate (compared with an expected chance accuracy rate of 50%), and there is no increase in accuracy for patients judged by clinicians to be especially dangerous.[55] Interestingly, the ability to predict dangerousness in men was better than chance, but the ability to predict violence in women was no better than chance.[56] Finally, when individuals who were predicted to be violent actually were violent, only 14.4% of the violence was serious violence, involving any injury to another person. Second, physicians and psychiatrists are subject to the same flawed heuristics that undermine the accuracy of lay decision makers: they overlook the significance of rare base rates, tend to be swayed by stereotypes and prejudices, and tend to neither keep track of their own errors nor modify their decision making in response to discovered errors.[57] Furthermore, one research study showed that when asked, mental health professionals overstate the number of police referrals of people with psychiatric disabilities or people who jeopardized staff safety, because the drama of a few cases caused their retelling, while the more mundane cases faded from memory.[58]

Psychiatric Assessments Are Not Reliable

The reliability of a standard means that different people, applying the same standard, will reach the same results. Even when supplied with very specific instructions and specific characteristics to measure, including psychopathology, impulse control problems, danger to self, and disposition, and when viewing identical tapes of emergency room patients, one study found that there was no better than chance agreement among experienced emergency room professionals in identifying individuals who were believed to display those characteristics or symptoms.[59] In another study, researchers looking at the same emergency room charts had a low level of agreement about whether the behavior described could be categorized as "bizarre."[60]

Evaluators Are Often Inexperienced

Adding to the difficulty of valid psychiatric assessments in the emergency room is that in the one place in which people are in greatest crisis, they are most likely to be assessed by extremely inexperienced people—residents and interns barely emerged from student status.[61] Not only do these individuals have a limited range of professional experience with individuals who are mentally ill, but they are unlikely to have any specific training or education in risk assessment. Residents and interns are obviously supervised by more senior staff, but the intensity of the supervision may vary from facility to facility. Increasingly, plaintiffs are asserting failure to train and failure to supervise claims against EDs in connection with assessments made by residents and even medical students that were given inappropriate weight by physicians whose duty and responsibility was to provide supervision.

The role of residents in psychiatric assessments is particularly important given the fact that residents tend to over hospitalize and inappropriately hospitalize. One study of the decision to hospitalize among first-year residents found that over a year of residency, admission rates declined from 34–19%, and that the initial admissions had been associated with diagnosis and symptomatology rather than dangerousness.[62] By the end of the first year, only dangerousness and overall symptomatology were factors in admission. Given the stress, pace, and time pressure of EDs, it is likely that many involuntary detention decisions are effectively made by individuals unqualified to make them who have a demonstrated tendency to involuntarily hospitalize without following the statutory requirements.

Alternatives to Standard Psychiatric Assessments of Dangerousness

The field of risk assessment has progressed far beyond unstructured clinical interviews, everywhere except the ED. Although "virtually no one in the field would support basing judgments of future risk, either immediate or long-term, on the basis of unstructured clinical interviews,"[63] almost all assessments of dangerousness in ED settings are conducted through unstructured clinical interviews.

There are three general approaches that a clinician could use to attempt to determine whether the individual before him will cause injury to others in the near future if he or she is permitted to remain at liberty.[64] As previously noted, because violence toward others, especially any serious violence, is extremely rare, it is very difficult to predict accurately.

CLINICAL JUDGMENT. This approach, which gives total discretion to the clinician to seek whatever information he or she deems appropriate through an unstructured interview, and draw conclusions about this information according to his or her professional judgment, has been subject to severe criticism and has generally been invalidated by the research literature. Basing a prediction of dangerousness solely on clinical judgment results in "unsystematic and widely different approaches to data gathering and synthesis,"[65] and the resulting predictions of dangerousness have little reliability or validity. Even Professor Thomas R. Litwack, who defends clinical assessments against claims that pure actuarial assessments are superior, concedes that "good clinical practice may well entail, or even require, considering the results of an appropriate actuarial assessment, relevant base rate data, or both."[66]

Basing involuntary detentions in EDs on unstructured clinical assessments may soon be subject to legal challenge under the Supreme Court cases of *Daubert v. Merrell-Dow,*[67] *Kumho Tire v. Carmicheal,*[68] and *General Electric v. Joiner,*[69] which require that expert testimony be reliable and that the methodology used have a valid scientific basis. Although lower courts have granted psychological and psychiatric testimony some leeway in these requirements, there is considerable doubt as to whether a 15-minute un-structured clinical interview meets the standard of *Daubert* and *Kumho.*[70] The Fourth Circuit recently declined to rule whether a Daubert analysis was applicable to psychiatric testimony, but found that the combination of a clinical interview and an actuarial test was sufficient to meet a reliability standard for prediction of dangerousness.[71] It is not clear how the court would have decided if the actuarial test had not been used.

STRUCTURED CLINICAL JUDGMENT. This approach requires a structured inter-view, with required questions or factors to be considered, but allows for clinical judgment in interpretation of the results of the interview, including the weight to ascribe to the numbers generated by an actuarial test, or to any particular factor in the test. Psychological instruments can be used as part of the assessment. The Historical, Clinical, and Risk Management 20 (HCR-20) is an example of an instrument that can be used in a structured clinical judgment assessment.

ACTUARIAL ASSESSMENT. This approach is specifically geared to limiting clin-ical judgment and replacing it with research-based predictions of risk. The Classification of Violent Risk (COVR), for example, gives the clinician one of five numbers: a 1%, 8%, 26%, 56%, or 76% chance that a person will be violent to others in the next five months.[72] Actuarial assessments are gen-erally based on historical facts: the number of arrests, age of first offense, etc. Examples of actuarial instruments developed for assessing general vio-lence include the Violence Risk Appraisal Guide (VRAG), as well as violence risk assessments for specific populations such as minors or sex offenders, the Three Ratings of Involuntary Admissibility (TRIAD), and the COVR, introduced in August 2005.

It has increasingly been demonstrated that the best way to assess a patient (at least for the purposes of predicting dangerousness) is by way of the patient's demographic and other background and current characteristics, whether by using an actuarial instrument or simply by asking a series of questions regarding, for example, past history of criminality or violence or current substance abuse. Research shows that simply predicting violence based on a history of past violence, which any layperson can do, is just as accurate, or more accurate, than unstructured clinical assessments based on interviews.[73] A lay person with access to historical data about an individual has been shown to be able to predict dangerousness more accurately than a psychiatrist conducting an unstructured interview without reference to such information.[74] No risk factor for future violence and criminality has been more thoroughly validated than past violence and criminality.[75] However, even those predictions, which are better than clinical predictions based on unstructured interviews, are not very accurate,[76] and are even less accurate if asked to predict immediate or imminent dangerousness.

Although all tests confirm the correlation of past violence with future violence, other factors have also been identified as being positively correlated to future violence, including current alcohol or substance abuse, abuse and neglect as a child, male gender, young age, and prior failure on programs, such as conditional release. It is important to note that none of these factors, standing alone, has high predictive power: it is their combination that creates the quantifiable risk. Some standardized instruments have been developed that could assist in predicting dangerousness in the ED, such as the HCR-20 and the COVR, because they can be adapted to the short time available in ED settings more readily than the TRIAD or VRAG.[77] While the VRAG may take days to administer, the COVR can be completed in 10 minutes.

The criticism of actuarial tests is that they do not sufficiently take into consideration individual factors unique to each person's presentation, rely too much on static rather than dynamic factors, and do not give enough weight to the experience and judgment of the professional (assuming the professional has experience, see above).

In addition, few if any of these tests claim to predict imminent violence or even violence within a day, a week, or a month. While imminence requirements in emergency detention statutes and civil commitment statutes have been weakened tremendously in the past decade,[78] none have been so diluted that a prediction of dangerousness within one year, or eventually, would suffice to support involuntary detention or commitment. The COVR predicts violence within the next five months. While some researchers claim that mental health professionals are *better* at predicting violence against others in the short term than in the long term through clinical evaluation,[79] the methodology used in these studies has been strongly criticized for including too broad, contingent, and subjective a description of "violence," e.g., ending up in seclusion has been equated with violence.[80]

The HCR-20 and others like it are tests for violence against others, developed primarily for sentencing and parole purposes. But the vast majority of people who are detained in EDs involuntarily for psychiatric reasons are dangerous to themselves—either judged to be suicidal, self-injuring, or gravely disabled enough to raise doubts about their ability to care for themselves. As in violence toward others, one of the best predictors of eventual suicide is previous suicidal attempts, especially serious ones. Even more than in the case of violence toward others, however, "[a]lthough statistical methods can identify subgroups of patients with unusually high rates of subsequent suicide, the base rate of suicide is so low that even a predictive test with high specificity and sensitivity will still include far too many false-positives for practical use."[81] As in the case of prediction of violence toward others, while actuarial factors may be somewhat useful in predicting suicide over the long term, they do not (and do not claim to) have any predictive value when it comes to imminent suicidality.

Given the demonstrated tendency of physicians and psychiatrists (especially less experienced ones) to over-assess dangerousness, and with the demonstrated unreliability of assessments based on clinical impression alone, EDs need to adopt a brief, usable, objective risk assessment instrument to be used as a check *against* decisions to admit (rather than a decision to discharge).

Financing Emergency Room Care

One of the most bitter and frequently voiced complaints by emergency room professionals is the sense of being caught between the Emergency Medical Treatment and Active Labor Act's (EMTALA) requirement of screening and treatment, and the refusal of managed care companies and other insurance entities to reimburse appropriately, or at all, for the treatment provided. In addition, of course, many patients who come to the emergency room are uninsured.

Managed Care and the Emergency Room Setting

The relationship between managed care and emergency room treatment is a complex one, mediated by federal and state statutes and the different practices of different managed care companies. Experience ranges from the managed care company that redefined medical patients' emergency needs as psychiatric emergencies to avoid paying for their care,[82] managed care companies that redefined children's psychiatric problems as criminal or juvenile detention problems to avoid paying for care,[83] or the managed care company that had no provision for outpatient psychiatric consultation, which resulted in the most seriously ill clients being sent to the emergency room for care. Some managed care companies have been forces for positive change, such as the companies that have "become a strong stimulus for the development of extended-evaluation beds and mobile outreach to deal with acute situations while avoiding the use of more expensive systems of care such as inpatient hospitalization."[84] Value Options received an award for development of its crisis hostel program in La Junta, Colorado, which enhanced opportunities for empowerment and recovery and avoided unnecessary ED expenses.

Medicaid regulations require that Medicaid reimburse emergency room care and treatment provided under the "prudent layperson standard." This standard requires reimbursement if the reasonable layperson is experiencing the sudden onset of symptoms, including pain, so severe that he or she could reasonably believe that his or her health would be in serious jeopardy without medical treatment.[85] In addition, Medicaid requires managed care organizations to cover and pay for post-stabilization care services related to the emergency medical condition.[86]

Medicare regulations cover emergency services under the Medicare+ Choice program, which provides a managed care option to both Medicare A and B programs. The regulations parallel the Medicaid regulations outlined above.[87]

State Legal Standards

More than 30 states have laws requiring managed care companies to reimburse for emergency room care provided under the prudent layperson or reasonable layperson standard.[88] Many of these statutes also ban managed care companies from requiring prior authorization in order to reimburse for a trip to the emergency room.[89] Some require them to pay for emergency ambulance services.[90] In some states, the prohibition on requiring prior authorization extends to specialty consultations,[91] if the managed care company is notified and "fails to identify an appropriate specialist who is available and willing to assume the care of the enrollee."[92]

The Arizona statute also requires managed care services that require prior authorization to maintain 24-hour access by telephone or fax, to have a physician available to assist in making determinations as to prior authorization,[93] and provides that prior authorization will be deemed granted if the hospital does not receive a denial or direction of care instructions within a reasonable time.[94] Furthermore, the statute prohibits managed care companies from rescinding or modifying prior authorization after the care has been provided.

The Problem of Lack of Continuity Between Emergency Rooms and Community Care

One of the key reasons for problems that people with psychiatric disabilities experience in emergency rooms is the lack of communications, coordination, and shared responsibility/accountability between the mental health service system and the ED. Licensing, accreditation, and reimbursement of the ED are almost always handled by a state agency that has little or no experience with or responsibility for the care of people with psychiatric disabilities. Usually the state's mental health agency has little or no formal or informal relationship with EDs. As a result, EDs are not held accountable for their treatment of people with psychiatric disabilities, and have no outlet for their resentments at being used as a "dumping ground" by group homes, at being refused placements for psychiatric clients, or having placements conditioned on medical examinations that are expensive and perceived as unnecessary.

One significant policy question is whether the appropriate approach to resolving these problems is through diversion to mobile crisis units or crisis hostels or whether the ED's functions should be expanded to include three-day acute beds or even temporary housing associated with the hospital to which people could be discharged.

Those advocating the former approach span a wide spectrum. A team of emergency medical experts in Las Vegas, Nevada, released a report for reforming emergency room practices, including "keeping drunks and the mentally ill out of EDs when there is not a medical crisis."[95] Others are current and former psychiatric patients who have worked hard to create and fund peer-run alternatives, such as drop-in centers, peer hostels, and hot and warm lines. Mental health agencies have funded family foster care, crisis houses, and other ways to divert people with psychiatric disabilities from the emergency room.

Those advocating the latter approach argue that people are already coming to the ED for their primary health care needs, and EDs need to reconfigure themselves to address the needs of this population by expanding the care provided. This would permit emergency rooms to initiate crisis hospitalization, provide "outpatient" appointments, and deliver non-emergent care at a newly configured ED.

Medications in Emergency Care

For many years, the vast majority of agitated or distressed psychiatric patients in the ED have been given Haldol and/or Ativan to calm them. Although these medications were recommended virtually universally in texts and treatises, there was relatively little research supporting their use.

Recently, there has been increased discussion in the research literature as to whether these medications remain the medication of choice, given the advent of the new atypical antipsychotics. Arguments against the use of Haldol note that it produces sedation, as well as tranquilization, and sedation may lead to misdiagnosis of the patient's underlying problem because the emergency room physician confuses side effects of Haldol with psychiatric symptomatology.[96] Haldol and Ativan are, of course, considerably less expensive than the newer atypicals, several of which are now available in injectable form. One problem with the newer medications that is of particular concern to ED staff is that some of them may be dangerous for people with medical conditions, such as diabetes or heart arrhythmia, that patients may not know they have, and ED staff may not be able to discover in time.

"Repeaters"

> I felt bad enough that I was bothering the people in the ER because I've been there frequently, so when the nurses are rude to me, I feel like I deserve it in a way. It hurts when I can hear the nurses at the station laughing and joking about why I came this time. They think I can't hear, but they are so loud it's hard not

to hear. I would rather not hear. The last time I was at UConn's ER, the APRN who I saw in the morning was very helpful. She listened and was courteous and caring. I told her I was hurt by the attitude of some of the nurses who were on the night shift. She said I was right, that I was not imagining that they talked badly and joked about me. She said it is a common problem for people who frequent the ER for psych reasons. I am glad she was honest with me and didn't try to make me feel more crazy by pretending there was no such problem.[97]

From the point of view of professionals who provide services in emergency room settings, one of the major problems associated with providing care to people with psychiatric disabilities are the individuals known (in the most charitable term of many used in the emergency room setting) as "repeaters." Every treatise, book, or interview with ED professionals regarding use of emergency rooms by people with psychiatric disabilities identifies people who are frequent users of emergency room services as a major problem.[98]

It does appear that a very few people account for a great deal of emergency room use: in one study, 7.9% of homeless patients who used the ED accounted for 54.5% of the visits.[99] In this study, "frequent use" was defined as four or more visits per year. One individual had 50 visits in one year.

Despite the universal acknowledgement by professionals of the frustration and expense associated with frequent users of the ED, especially those with mental health problems, very few systematic efforts have been made to design programs to specifically identify the individuals and understand what systemic failures are responsible for their repeated use of the ED. Staff tend to blame the individuals themselves, and sometimes take frankly punitive actions against them, including deliberately ignoring them, sometimes for hours at a time.[100] Often, "repeaters" come because of a lack of appropriate services in the community; sometimes, it is simply the familiarity and availability of the ED. A chapter in the *Manual of Emergency Psychiatry* describing "Emergency Room Repeaters" contains a section entitled "Patients Who Make Psychiatric Emergency Services Part of Their Social Network."[101] Dr. Barker advises that "It is helpful to develop a plan that allows patients some access to staff while affirming their now-improved status. Allowing them contact with the triage nurse on an as-needed basis without registering, scheduled contacts with an identified staff member, or informal brief entries into the service to say hello may all be legitimate options."[102]

This would not meet the needs of every frequent patient. One survey respondent told me frankly that she often had to go to the ED at the end of the month when her scant supplemental security income allotment would no longer pay for food and she was hungry.

A more time-consuming but ultimately more fruitful plan may be to take a proactive approach with frequent patients, assessing why they come so often, and (with the patient's permission) working with community providers and the patient to create joint plans to assist ED staff in behaving with consistency and understanding when the patients return. Crisis plans such as wellness recovery action plans may be of assistance for patients in this situation, and ED staff can help patients by familiarizing themselves with and introducing frequent visitors to the ED to the possibility that such plans might assist them (see chapter 6). In addition, many frequent visitors to the ED may have trauma histories, and ED staff should take this into consideration when attempting to understand the nature and frequency of the visits (see chapter 6).

Facilities That Use On-Call Systems Face a Variety of Problems

Emergency rooms that do not specialize in psychiatric evaluations may rely on on-call psychiatrists to perform evaluations, which often create delays. Although new EMTALA regulations have eased the requirement that hospitals maintain specialists on staff, the use of on-call psychiatrists creates problems of its own. Many of these psychiatrists give orders over the telephone before meeting with the patient, including orders of involuntary detention and medication based on information received from nurses. Both of these practices are of questionable legality and certainly implicate the physician's ethical duties. They also create problems if litigation should ensue. In one recent case involving an involuntarily detained and medicated woman, the doctor who gave the orders met her for the first time at trial, a fact that was noted by the court.[103] The woman won a judgment of $50,000 in compensatory damages, $100,000 in punitive damages, and her attorneys won $49,797 in fees. All of these awards were affirmed on appeal.[104]

An even riskier practice is to rely on less qualified on-call personnel. Recently, at five major hospitals in the Denver area, evaluations of psychiatric patients were performed by on-call evaluators, including mental health counselors. One such counselor testified in subsequent litigation that although she had no other mental health professional available with whom to consult, her recommendations were routinely ordered by physicians who did not read her notes.[105]

Florida passed legislation in 2004 that permits mental health counselors to evaluate people in psychiatric crisis and apply for involuntary commitment. This may well create further litigation if people are inappropriately detained at psychiatric facilities based on the evaluations of insufficiently trained individuals.

The problems and difficulties expressed by both patients and providers in EDs are almost all subject to laws and regulations. Neither patients nor providers are familiar with these regulations and laws, and they are not necessarily easy to find. Even when found, the language of many regulations is quite cryptic, and has been decoded in different ways by different courts, whose decisions are also difficult to access. The next chapter attempts to gather as much of this information in one place as possible.

5

Legal Rights and Standards in Emergency Department Treatment of People with Psychiatric Disabilities

Federal Laws and Regulations

The legal rights of people in emergency departments (EDs) arise from a variety of sources. Federal law creates some rights, which apply equally to all citizens (and sometimes to non-citizens). Federal rights take the form of constitutional rights, which generally only apply in the case of action by state or local government officials, and an array of statutory rights, such as the Americans with Disabilities Act (ADA) or the Emergency Medical Treatment and Active Labor Act (EMTALA), which apply to both private entities and government actors. Each of these statutes has interpretive regulations.

Under some circumstances, these constitutional, statutory, and regulatory rights can be asserted and enforced by individuals themselves.[1] In addition, the Protection and Advocacy for Individuals with Mental Illness Act (PAIMI)[2] creates an agency in each state charged with protecting the rights of and advocating for individuals with mental illness and gives each agency statutory access to facilities which provide treatment to people with mental illness, including EDs. Congress gave protection and advocacy agencies the right of access to facilities, records, and patients when the agency receives a complaint or has probable cause to believe that a person with a psychiatric disability is subject to abuse or neglect under the statute.[3] The agencies also have standing to bring lawsuits to protect the rights of their constituents with psychiatric disabilities. While protection and advocacy agencies have not historically focused on emergency services, this may be changing, and is discussed below.

This section will begin by looking at federal constitutional rights, then federal statutory rights, and finally rights created by federal regulations. The section will seek to answer a few basic questions about each federal law or constitutional provision: Who is liable? What rights are created, and how can they be enforced? What are special issues facing psychiatric patients in EDs under these laws and regulations?

Constitutional Requirements

Liability

The U.S. Constitution provides protection against the violation of rights by federal, state, and local governments. The Constitution applies in the ED when people are detained or injured under state authority; that is, by agents of the state or "state actors." The term "state actors" is not limited to state or local government employees; in certain limited circumstances, private individuals can be state actors for purposes of liability under 42 U.S.C. 1983, a statute that permits individuals to sue state actors for violations of their federal statutory and constitutional rights.

For the most part, courts have held that private psychiatrists are not state actors when they act under their state authority to detain individuals for examination,[4] although they may be considered state actors if they act pursuant to special arrangements with a state agency, or take the word of state agents for an individual's mental illness and dangerousness.[5] Sometimes when private hospital employees act in concert with police officers or other agents of the state, it is argued that they were state actors for the purposes of constitutional claims.[6] In the few cases involving mobile crisis teams that are not state employees, courts have held that members of the mobile crisis team are not state actors.[7] However, when EDs hire off-duty police officers, the officers have been considered state actors for purposes of constitutional challenges to their actions.[8]

Requirements

The constitutional guarantee of substantive due process ensures that people cannot be arbitrarily deprived of their liberty by the state. The right to liberty includes freedom from unreasonable restraint. This freedom applies to involuntary transportation to the ED and restraint from leaving the ED in all its forms: locked doors, being told that leaving will not be permitted, being restrained by security guards. In addition, freedom from restraint means freedom from unreasonable seclusion and restraint. Finally, the substantive due process right to liberty gives an individual certain rights to refuse unwanted treatment.

The guarantee of procedural due process protects people from deprivations of liberty without procedural protections such as notice, hearing, or the right to confront witnesses. Courts typically use a balancing test to decide what kinds of procedural protections are due before liberty or property may be taken from an individual, weighing the deprivation to the individual against the state's interests in each case.

The Fourth Amendment protects individuals against unreasonable searches or seizures. It is well settled that Fourth Amendment protections apply to the initial detention of a person for involuntary psychiatric assessment.[9] This means that a person cannot be detained for psychiatric assessment absent probable cause to believe that he or she meets the statutory standard for detention, which usually involves mental illness and dangerousness. This is a highly fact-specific inquiry. A detention amounts to a seizure if the individual reasonably believes that he or she is not free to leave.[10]

Fourth Amendment protections also apply to a number of other specific situations: a person prevented from leaving the emergency room is subject to seizure for Fourth Amendment purposes. Blood and urine testing constitute searches for Fourth Amendment purposes. Involuntary medication also implicates Fourth Amendment rights. The Fourth Amendment is more often invoked against police who bring individuals to emergency rooms than against the emergency rooms themselves, but a few cases have arisen in which emergency rooms were involved. These are discussed below.

A person also has a right to equal protection of the law, that is, not to be subject to discriminatory treatment based on membership in a particular group. Claims that this right was violated are subject to particularly strict scrutiny by courts if a person claims that he or she was treated differently because of race and to a higher level of scrutiny if a person alleges gender discrimination. Although differential treatment on the basis of disability may violate a person's constitutional rights, if the defendant had a rational reason for the differential treatment, the plaintiff will lose the case.

Finally, a person involuntarily detained by the state has the right to have professional judgment exercised on his or her behalf in decisions relating to treatment, restraint, seclusion, and protection from harm. When actions by agents of the state constitute a substantial departure from professional judgment, standards, or practice, the individual's rights under the Constitution have been violated. The deviation from professional standards required to prevail in a case asserting a deprivation of constitutional rights is harder to meet than a malpractice standard.

In emergency room settings, this has translated to cases raising questions about the right of emergency rooms to detain individuals, the length of time for which they can be detained, restraint in emergency room settings, involuntary treatment in ED settings, and the degree to which people can be searched in emergency room settings.

Special Issues

Non-Consensual Blood Draws, Urinalyses, and Other Searches

A number of U.S. Supreme Court cases are relevant to the treatment of people with psychiatric disabilities in emergency room settings by agents of the state. In 2001, the U.S. Supreme Court held that individuals' Fourth Amendment rights were violated by the policy of an emergency room to test pregnant patients for illegal drugs and reveal positive test results to law enforcement officers.[11] Although blood and urine tests, and tests for the presence of drugs, do implicate the Fourth Amendment, these tests are likely to be upheld in the context of psychiatric evaluations. This is because of the "special needs" doctrine, which allows some searches by the state if they fulfill special state needs and will not be used for law enforcement purposes.[12] In *Anthony v. City of New York*[13] various actions by police and emergency room professionals in detaining a woman with Down syndrome for involuntary examination were challenged as violating the woman's constitutional rights. Although the court acknowledged that the blood and urine tests performed on her constituted searches under the fourth amendment, it upheld them under the "special needs" doctrine.[14]

Although challenges to involuntary blood draws and urine testing may not prevail on constitutional grounds, they may well succeed as claims of assault and battery under state tort law (see below).

Competence, Voluntariness, and Informed Consent to Treatment

> Getting her to consent to the surgery nearly required an act of God. She told the surgeon how much she didn't like the scar from the last hernia surgery 3 years ago and he told her he would cut the scar tissue out. She interpreted what he said very literally and thought he would cut a chunk of her stomach out . . . So after three trips to the ER, three trips to the surgeon to have him explain and re-explain what he is going to do (this surgeon is an absolute gem of a surgeon)—she said she would have the surgery if I could get the one psychiatrist she trusts to observe the surgery . . . I knew that she hadn't really consented and we had several conversations about this . . . I also explained to her that if she continued to show up at the ER for the hernia pain and the docs kept recommending surgery to fix the hernia but she kept refusing that at some point she was going to have a doctor say that she didn't have capacity . . . She did consent to have the surgery. And that was an ordeal all by itself . . . When we were in the pre-op area, she was refusing to let them put the IV in, she wouldn't get into the hospital gown, she wouldn't lay on the gurney. Once they gave her the Versed and it took effect . . . we were able to get

her to put the gown on, get on the gurney and let them put the
IV in ... She told someone after the surgery about how glad she
was that she'd had the surgery ... [15]

Modern law acknowledges that competence is a spectrum rather than
an either/or proposition,[16] and some difficult legal quandaries arise with the
voluntariness of decision making by arguably incompetent people in ED
settings.

Zinermon v. Burch considers the right of individuals to liberty and to
informed consent in the context of the incompetent assenter to hospitalization and treatment. The Supreme Court held that a man who had been
hospitalized as a voluntary patient in an inpatient facility for months while
clearly incompetent to consent to hospitalization or treatment could sue for
violation of his due process rights. This case is probably largely limited to
inpatient settings, but it may require an emergency room physician or psychiatrist to at least informally assess and document the individual's competence in his or her charts.

There are a variety of reasons that *Zinermon* is unlikely to apply in the
emergency room setting.[17] First, the harm to Burch—months of hospitalization and medication—does not arise in the emergency room context. Second, the state interest in providing care to an individual in crisis prior to
invoking formal or informal legal processes is likely to be considered greater
by a court than the interest of a state mental health center.[18]

The question of how to treat people who are obviously not competent
to give informed consent is obviously a situation frequently faced by EDs.
Since most of these departments are private entities rather than state entities,
the issue of competence to accept or refuse treatment will probably arise
under the requirement of informed consent and is discussed at length in
the "state law" section of this chapter.

Involuntary Detention Prior to Psychiatric Assessment

The other side of the *Zinermon* coin—depriving an individual who wishes
to leave an emergency room of his or her liberty to leave—also implicates
due process concerns. While all states have statutes permitting the detention
of an individual after a professional assessment concludes that the person is
mentally ill and a danger to himself or herself or others, these statutes do
not answer the question of the basis for authority to involuntarily detain an
individual *prior* to a professional evaluation.

The few courts to have considered such challenges have concluded that
hospitals are entitled to involuntarily detain a person for a small window of
time to enable them to conduct the evaluation. All courts have underscored
that this time must be brief in order to meet constitutional standards. For
example, the Third Circuit has held that the Constitution did not require a
hearing to justify short-term involuntary detention, such as that required

for assessment by an ED, but cautioned that this finding was premised on the fact that detention was "for a maximum of several hours to permit an examination" which "continues for only a short period of time,"[19] and that while being held, the individual "was constantly evaluated by [defendant] physicians."[20] In a case involving a delay of less than an hour, an appellate court in California noted: "The prior temporary restraint of [the plaintiff] until professional evaluation could be obtained is inherent in the process contemplated by the provisions of the [Lanterman-Petris-Short] LPS Act authorizing detentions. If the homicidal or suicidal must go free unless an 'authorized person' is always immediately available, the LPS Act is futile."[21]

This is not to say that constitutional due process protections do not apply at all to these brief involuntary detentions. Thus, in *C.W. v. State of Washington*,[22] in the context of interpreting a state statutory requirement that limited the amount of time an individual can be held in an emergency room to six hours,[23] the court found that constitutional due process protections applied to limit the amount of time that an emergency room could detain a person pending evaluation by its staff. The court found that "it is necessary to impose due process safeguards on the time between a person's arrival at a hospital or agency and the professional staffs' determination that referral to the CDMHP [county designated mental health professional] is necessary to protect against the potential deprivation that may occur because of the lack of statutory time restraints on the time it takes professional staff to evaluate a person."[24] The court placed on the hospital the burden to prove, by a preponderance of the evidence, that any delay between a person's arrival at the ED and detention, and the professional staffs' determination to refer the person to the county designated mental health professional is justified. The court underscored that the state could meet its burden in most cases "by reference to hospital records and statements by hospital personnel." In the case before it, which involved six petitioners, the court affirmed the finding below that the hospital had not met its burden in two cases. However, it refused petitioner's request to dismiss the commitments of those individuals, finding that dismissal would only be appropriate if the hospital staff or the county designated mental health professionals had "totally disregarded the requirements of the statute."[25] The court stated that it did not necessarily agree with petitioner's contention that they lacked a civil remedy for the two patients who had been held in violation of the statute, and did not discuss the remedy for constitutional violations at all.

Emergency Department Conditions

In addition to the constitutional issues raised by detaining people and preventing them from leaving the emergency room before any evaluation has been completed, other emergency room conditions have been subject to constitutional challenge. In *Lizotte v. New York City Health and Hospital*

Corporations et al.,[26] plaintiffs in crowded city psychiatric emergency rooms challenged the lack of care and treatment, physical restraint, and lengthy stays.[27] The case eventually settled, with the City of New York promising not to keep patients in psychiatric EDs for over 24 hours (with some exceptions); not to use handcuffs except in emergencies (with some exceptions); and to provide clean linens, a change of clothes or pajamas, and reasonable accommodations for sleeping, including dimmed lights, for those detained overnight. All patients were guaranteed access to showers, clean towels, and toothbrushes. The court maintained jurisdiction over the case for seven years.[28]

Federal Statutory and Regulatory Standards

The Americans with Disabilities Act

The ADA was passed in 1990 as a landmark piece of legislation intended to end discrimination on the basis of disability in the public and private sectors. It does not cover specific disabilities, such as diabetes or schizophrenia, but rather protects anyone who has a physical or mental impairment that substantially limits one or more major life activities (such as working, sleeping, or caring for one's self), or who has a history of such an impairment, or who is perceived by others to have such an impairment.

Who Is Liable?

The ADA is divided into a number of different titles, each dealing with different kinds of discrimination and different defendants. Title I of the ADA covers discrimination in employment on the basis of disability, and any employer with a payroll of 15 or more persons can be liable.

Under Title II, any "public entity" including any state, county, or municipal hospital or agency can be sued for discriminating against a qualified individual with a disability. Federal hospitals are not subject to the ADA. Generally, individuals are not liable for damages (i.e., monetary relief). The question of whether state agencies or state hospitals are liable for damages has been left open by the Supreme Court; in all likelihood, they would not be subject to damages under the ADA. County, city, or municipal hospitals or agencies remain liable for damages under the ADA.

In addition, state and local agencies and hospitals can be sued for injunctive relief. This means that they can be sued if their policies, practices, or conduct are alleged to discriminate on the basis of disability, and a court can order them to change such policies or practices. If a case under Title II for injunctive relief is successful, while the hospital or agency does not have to pay monetary damages to the plaintiff, it may have to pay attorneys' fees.

Under Title III[29] of the ADA, any private hospital or medical practice can be sued.[30] Individuals may be liable if they effectively control the actions of the practice.[31] No monetary damages can be awarded in an action brought under Title III by a private individual.[32] However, the Department of Justice can bring an action for damages if it finds that the defendant has engaged in a pattern or practice of discrimination that raises an issue of general public importance.[33] The Department of Justice has a record of numerous cases against hospitals and emergency rooms under Title III of the ADA, especially cases involving failure to provide interpreters to deaf people.[34]

Requirements

The statute requires that people with disabilities not be subject to discrimination on the basis of their disabilities. "Discrimination" is defined to include unequal treatment, unequal access to benefits provided by a program, screening on the basis of disability, adverse treatment, exclusion or refusal of care, and segregation of people with disabilities. It is also discriminatory to refuse to provide reasonable accommodations to people with disabilities, including refusal to modify policies with an adverse impact on people with disabilities, unless providing the accommodation would require a fundamental alteration of the program provided by the agency or hospital. It is illegal to use administrative methods that result in discrimination against people with disabilities.

Special Issues

A number of cases have been brought against emergency rooms under the ADA, challenging refusal of care on the basis of disability[35] or the provision of delayed or inferior care on the basis of disability.[36] In addition, cases confirm the obligation of emergency rooms to provide interpreters to deaf clients[37] and permit emergency rooms to exclude service dogs if they can show that the presence of these animals would either fundamentally alter the services provided or present a direct threat to the safety of patients in the emergency room.[38]

The ADA prohibits unequal and adverse treatment on the basis of disability, including psychiatric disability. Emergency departments that have blanket policies or practices singling out people with psychiatric disabilities for differential or adverse treatment without requiring individualized determinations may be subject to liability. For example, the practice of requiring psychiatric patients to disrobe when other patients are able to remain in street clothing or a policy requiring psychiatric patients to wait in locked rooms may violate the ADA. In two cases, hospitals have been sued under the ADA for discrimination against psychiatric patients: one case involved a hospital policy that required psychiatric patients to disrobe.[39] The other case challenged a hospital's practice of pepper spraying psychiatric patients to control their behavior or prevent them from leaving the hospital.

REQUIREMENTS OF TREATMENT IN INTEGRATED SETTINGS. The ADA includes a requirement that services be provided in the most integrated setting possible, and prohibits unjustified segregation of persons with psychiatric disabilities. The increasing practice of segregating psychiatric emergency rooms from emergency rooms providing general medical care may be subject to the ADA. The ADA does permit provision of "a separate benefit" if it is "necessary to provide the individual or class of individuals with a good, service, facility, privilege, advantage or accommodation, or other opportunity, that is as effective as that provided to others."[40] However, the ADA also prohibits a public accommodation from requiring a person with a disability to use this separate facility or benefit if he or she prefers to use the one that is used by non-disabled people.[41] As a practical matter, this means that hospitals may create psychiatric EDs, but they may not exclude a person with a psychiatric disability from the regular hospital ED. Additionally, the practice of locking emergency room patients in seclusion rooms to keep them from leaving may possibly constitute unjustified segregation under the ADA.

People with psychiatric disabilities have mixed feelings about such separate services. Some call for increased availability of professionals with expertise in psychiatric disability, such as are available in psychiatric EDs. Others appear to object to separation of psychiatric rooms within the general ED. As one survey respondent wrote, regarding improvements in the treatment of psychiatric clients by emergency rooms, "Not have separate psych rooms all the way in the back, it's almost not even part of the regular ER."

Complaints regarding violations of either Title II or Title III of the ADA can be made to the Department of Justice. A complaint can be filed with the Disability Rights Section of the Department of Justice's Civil Rights Division. Its home page, www.usdoj.gov/crt/drs/drshome.htm, has information about how to file a complaint. (Note: the information regarding personnel on the home page may not be completely up to date.)

The Employee Retirement Income Security Act

The Employee Retirement Income Security Act (ERISA) provides for federal regulation of employee benefits, including pensions and health care.[42] When a health insurance or managed care company refuses to authorize either emergency room or follow-up treatment that the patient believes is covered under his or her insurance plan, ERISA provides a remedy for the wrongful denial of care.

Who Is Liable?

Generally, whoever makes decisions regarding denial of benefits under a health care plan is liable. Since ERISA covers employee benefit plans, a plaintiff would need to bring a claim against the benefit provider, which could be an insurance company, a health maintenance organization, and even an employer that is actively making benefit decisions. In order for a court to entertain litigation under ERISA, generally the client must first have appealed a denial of reimbursement through the managed care or insurer's grievance mechanisms.[43]

Requirements

The Employee Retirement Income Security Act provides that a civil action may be brought by a participant or beneficiary of an employee benefits plan, but the remedy is limited to (1) recovery of benefits due; (2) enforcing rights; or (3) clarifying rights to future benefits under the terms of the plan.[44]

Participants/beneficiaries may also seek injunctive relief for acts or practices that violate the terms of the plan. Also, since Congress based the structure of benefit plans upon trust law theories, plan sponsors are considered to be fiduciaries for the purpose of ensuring that benefits are used and provided to employees and beneficiaries. A fiduciary is a person in a position of trust with respect to the management of benefits for another, who has a duty to manage those benefits according to the terms of the trust or plan under which he or she was appointed. Accordingly, appropriate relief may be sought for a breach of that duty.[45] Still, a successful plaintiff can only expect to recover the benefit denied or the value of the benefit if it was obtained through other means. For example, if a health insurance company refuses to pay for a particular treatment or test in an ED or elsewhere, and the individual seeking the test or treatment believes it is covered by the insurance plan and pays for the test or treatment, he or she can seek to recover the cost of the test or treatment.

The Employee Retirement Income Security Act has a provision that expressly preempts all state laws that *relate to* any employee benefit plan.[46] Early court decisions held that the preemption included medical malpractice claims. However, recent case law has narrowed the preemption somewhat, holding that in limited circumstances, when treatment decisions were made by the same actor who made eligibility decisions, ERISA did not preempt actions for medical negligence.[47] In 2004, the Supreme Court clarified that "inextricably intertwined" decisions of treatment and plan eligibility applied only when made by the same individual, acting as both the beneficiary's treating professional and the determiner of eligibility.[48] This is unlikely to be a common occurrence.

Special Issues

Much of the tension in earlier years relating to managed care refusals to reimburse for emergency room care has been vitiated by Congressional passage of the reasonable layperson standard, which requires that benefit providers must reimburse for any emergency room visit that a reasonable lay-person would have believed was necessary under the circumstances.[49]

The most prominent case involving denial of admission to a person with psychiatric problems under ERISA is *Tolton v. Biodyne*.[50] In *Tolton*, a man with a psychiatric disability was refused inpatient care for problems relating to chemical dependence and suicidality by utilization review personnel at the benefits provider's office. After several visits to emergency rooms and admission to a residential treatment program, he committed suicide. His widow brought claims against Biodyne, the benefits provider, for malpractice, wrongful death, improper refusal to authorize benefits, and insurance bad faith. The district court, later affirmed by the Sixth Circuit, held that all of these claims were preempted under ERISA, even though the refusal of benefits was pursuant to utilization review.

Tolton was the first in a long line of cases involving denial of care to individuals with psychiatric disabilities, and its holding was typical of most of these cases. Claims of wrongful death,[51] breach of contract,[52] loss of consortium,[53] medical malpractice,[54] negligence,[55] negligent infliction of emotional distress,[56] intentional infliction of emotional distress,[57] negligent misrepresentation,[58] and negligent failure to train employees,[59] have all been brought against benefits providers for failing to authorize adequate care for beneficiaries suffering from psychiatric disabilities. All such claims have been held to be preempted under ERISA.

The Emergency Medical Treatment and Active Labor Act

This is the federal statute whose name is probably best known to ED professionals, although not necessarily in its application to people with psychiatric disabilities.[60] Emergency departments are often confused about the precise requirements of EMTALA, which is not surprising because of differing interpretations of the statute's scope and requirements by different federal courts. The Emergency Treatment and Active Labor Act is particularly confusing in its application to people with psychiatric disabilities because of its interaction with involuntary commitment requirements.

Who Is Liable?

The statute permits individuals to sue hospitals. Although an individual cannot sue a doctor or other individual under EMTALA,[61] the Department of Health and Human Services (HHS) can suspend a doctor's right to participate in the Medicare/Medicaid program and levy hefty civil penalties, $50,000 per offense. The Emergency Treatment and Active Labor Act allows individuals to collect any damages they are entitled to recover under state law as a result of the hospital's failure to comply with EMTALA.[62]

Requirements

The Emergency Medical Treatment and Active Labor Act has two basic requirements: first, anyone who "comes to the emergency department" must be screened for an emergency medical condition, which includes psychiatric conditions.[63] The definition of "emergency department" has been changed by the 2003 regulations. The new regulations' definition of "dedicated emergency department"[64] may ultimately include psychiatric units, if they routinely evaluate and treat patients for emergency psychiatric conditions who do not have scheduled appointments, or if they hold themselves out as available to provide emergency care on a 24-hour basis.[65]

Second, if an emergency condition is discovered, it must be "stabilized" before the person can be discharged or transferred. The act forbids the conditioning of treatment on ability to pay and forbids "dumping"—transferring patients to another hospital—except under certain conditions related to the patient's well-being rather than source of reimbursement. However, plaintiffs need not show that the hospital or doctor acted with improper motivation to prevail under EMTALA.[66] They must, however, be able to show that the hospital knew of the emergency condition; misdiagnosis is not actionable under EMTALA if the screening was performed appropriately.[67]

Recent regulations have clarified when EMTALA applies to people coming to a hospital in an ambulance after a series of court decisions reached different conclusions.[68] Regulations now provide that a person in an ambulance is considered to have "presented" to a hospital for emergency care if the hospital owns and operates the ambulance or if the ambulance is on hospital property.[69] People in an ambulance not owned or operated by the hospital have not "presented" to the hospital, and it can instruct the ambulance that it is on diversionary status without violating EMTALA. If the ambulance ignores the hospital's instructions, however, and delivers the patient to the hospital, the patient is considered to have "presented" to the hospital, which activates the hospital's responsibilities under EMTALA.

Special Issues

INTERACTIONS BETWEEN EMTALA AND CIVIL COMMITMENT LAW. Most EMTALA claims involving people with psychiatric disabilities arise out of the suicide between one hour and several months after discharge of a person seen by an emergency room.[70] One case involved a suicide in the emergency room itself.[71] Some ED professionals believe that this means EMTALA is violated if a person with a psychiatric complaint is allowed to leave an emergency room prior to the screening examination. However, this is not generally the case.

The requirements of EMTALA regarding screening and stabilization must be distinguished carefully. First, there is some doubt as to whether

EMTALA applies at all if neither the individual nor the family are seeking treatment for any condition; thus, a court questioned whether EMTALA applied in the case of an individual brought in by sheriff's deputies because they suspected him of being mentally ill or intoxicated when the individual himself sought no treatment.[72]

In general, an ED generally faces no EMTALA liability if a person leaves before being screened; however, if the hospital is aware that the person had a clearly emergent condition and left because of the delay involved in being seen, EMTALA liability may attach.[73] Some courts have expressed doubt that threats of suicide "without more" qualify as emergency conditions creating a duty to stabilize on the part of the hospital.[74] Guidelines to the federal regulations make it clear that simply expressing the intent to harm one's self or others by itself is not necessarily sufficient to create an emergency medical condition for the purpose of EMTALA. Rather, an additional layer of consideration requires the examining physician or mental health professional to assess the seriousness and dangerousness of the threat: "in the case of psychiatric emergencies, if an individual expressing suicidal or homicidal thoughts or gestures, *if determined dangerous to self or others*, would be considered to have an EMC [emergency medical condition]."[75] One state supreme court, interpreting a state law analogous to EMTALA, concluded that relatives' reports of suicidality were insufficient to trigger a duty to stabilize when the individual appeared completely calm and denied suicidality during the screening.[76]

The duty to stabilize and treat a condition arises at the point at which an emergency medical condition (in psychiatric terms, a determination that the individual is a danger to himself or others) is actually discovered through screening. A hospital has no duty to stabilize a condition that it does not detect.[77] Because a hospital has an obligation to provide treatment to stabilize the condition, it may be liable under EMTALA for discharging or transferring an individual determined by the hospital or its doctors to be a threat to self or others after screening without provision of adequate stabilization and treatment,[78] but only if the person sought treatment. If the individual refuses treatment, even if he or she has an emergency medical condition, EMTALA does not apply, as long as the facility has educated the individual about the need to stay for treatment.[79] One case involving the liability of a hospital that offered a woman admission, which she declined, is unclear because the hospital chose to defend on the grounds that she was stable, rather than asserting that she had refused treatment under the statute.[80] The Emergency Medical Treatment and Active Labor Act does not require forcible detention or treatment. Although several hospitals have pointed to their obligations under EMTALA to justify involuntary procedures such as catheterizations in the ED, courts have rejected this argument: EMTALA neither preempts state statutes or regulations requiring that informed consent must be obtained before treatment is provided;[81] nor does it preempt state emergency commitment statutes.

The definition of "stable" in the context of people with psychiatric emergencies is that a person is considered "stable" when he or she is "no longer considered to be a threat to him/herself or others,"[82] which at least one court has interpreted as setting a broader standard than simply a conclusion that the person is neither homicidal nor suicidal.[83] While a person can be stabilized for a period of time through the "the administration of chemical or physical restraints for the purpose of transferring an individual from one facility to another," "the underlying medical problem may persist and if not treated for longevity [sic] the patient may experience exacerbation of the EMC [emergency medical condition]. Therefore, practitioners should use great care when determining if the emergency medical condition is in fact stable after administering chemical or physical restraints."[84]

FAILURE TO RECOGNIZE EMERGENCY MEDICAL CONDITIONS IN PATIENTS WITH PSYCHIATRIC DISABILITIES. One of the most frequent complaints of people with psychiatric disabilities in the surveys related to the failure of hospital staff to take their physical and medical complaints seriously. If a hospital fails to appropriately screen in response to a patient's complaint and thereby misses an emergency medical condition, the hospital and the physician can be held liable under EMTALA. A number of cases involve complaints by relatives of an individual with psychiatric disabilities who died after an emergency room interpreted his or her dizziness, incoherence, or agitation as psychiatric symptomology rather than as symptoms of an ultimately fatal condition.

HOSPITALS UNDER CONTRACT WITH THE STATE OR COUNTY TO PROVIDE MENTAL HEALTH SERVICES. It is also unclear whether emergency rooms that have no mental health professionals on staff and no psychiatric facilities in the hospital have any duty to provide a mental health screening.[85] The Emergency Medical Treatment and Active Labor Act only requires screening and stabilization "within the capabilities of the staff and facilities available at the hospital."[86]

The Health Insurance Portability and Accountability Act

In 1996 Congress passed the Health Insurance Portability and Accountability Act (HIPAA).[87] One of the provisions of the act required HHS to recommend regulations protecting the confidentiality of patients' records to Congress. The statute provided that if Congress had not passed a statute enacting federal protections of patients' rights by August 21, 1999, HHS would promulgate regulations to protect patient privacy. Although Congress held hearings and considered several bills, none passed. In response to the statutory directive, HHS published regulations in the *Federal Register* on Dec. 28, 2000, along with almost 100 pages of commentary interpreting the regulations. The regulations were suspended by the incoming Bush administration, which published final regulations on August 14, 2002, that altered some (but by no means all) of the privacy protections drafted by the Clinton administration. The final regulations become effective on April 14, 2003, with some minor exceptions for small health care organizations, which had an additional year to meet the requirements. The regulations can be accessed online at www.hhs.gov/ocr in several formats. The regulations quoted below are found online at www.hhs.gov/ocr/part8.pdf. The quoted commentary, which precedes the regulations, is found online at www.hhs.gov./ocr/part2.pdf. Since many of the Clinton administration's provisions were left substantially the same, the commentary to those regulations should be influential.

Who Is Liable?

Individuals who believe that their rights under HIPAA have been violated by a "covered entity" (health care providers and health plans) may file a complaint with the Secretary of HHS within 180 days of the date of the violation.[88] The Department of Health and Human Services can, in its discretion, refer particularly egregious complaints to the Department of Justice for criminal prosecution and penalties.

Requirements

There are a number of provisions in the final regulation of particular interest to people with psychiatric disabilities. They include:

- the right to notice of the uses and disclosure of protected health information[89]
- the right of individuals to request restriction of uses and disclosures of protected health information[90]
- the right of individuals to access their own health records[91]
- the right of individuals to correct and amend their health records[92]
- the right of individuals to request an accounting of disclosures of protected health care information[93]
- the right of facilities to disclose protected health information for law enforcement or civil litigation purposes.

THE RIGHT TO ACCESS HEALTH RECORDS. The new regulations create a general right for an individual to access his or her own health records,[94] subject to a number of definitions and exceptions discussed below. Protected health information is defined quite broadly, and the commentary makes it clear that individuals "have a right of access to information used to make health care decisions or determine whether an insurance claim will be paid."[95] The comments also underscore that the right of patients to access their records is broad, and the limitations are meant to be very narrowly construed: "We intend to create narrow exceptions to the right of access and we expect covered entities to employ these exceptions rarely, if at all. Covered entities may only deny access for the reasons specifically provided by the rule."[96]

Because so many states restrict the rights of psychiatric patients to access their own records, the new regulations generally reflect an improvement over most current state practices. The new regulations preempt state regulations that are less protective of patient rights, but do not displace stronger state or Federal regulations.

EXCEPTIONS TO THE RIGHT OF ACCESS.   There are a number of exceptions to the right of access to records, categorized in a Byzantine manner. There are four exceptions listed to the general right of access to records. There are five additional categories which, although theoretically not exceptions to the right of access, provide grounds for unreviewable denial of access by covered entities. Finally, there are three categories where covered entities may deny access subject to appeal by the individual and review of the denial.

The four exceptions to the general right of access to records are: (1) psychotherapy notes; (2) information compiled in reasonable anticipation of or for use in a civil, criminal, or administrative action or proceeding; (3) where access is prohibited by the Clinical Laboratory Improvements Amendments of 1988;[97] or (4) where access is exempt under the regulations to the Clinical Laboratory Improvement Amendments Act.[98]

PSYCHOTHERAPY NOTES UNDER REGULATIONS.   Psychotherapy notes is actually a very limited category and does *not* refer to the individual's chart, with its progress notes, nurse's notes, physician's orders, etc. In fact, this exception probably rarely applies to clients of the state mental health system. Rather, psychotherapy notes are "notes recorded in any medium by a health care provider who is a mental health professional documenting or analyzing the contents of a conversation during a private counseling session or a group, joint, or family counseling session."[99] It is abundantly clear from the commentary that "psychotherapy notes" is intended to refer to a mental health professional's own personal notes of a therapy session. In fact, notes do not count as psychotherapy notes unless they are kept separate from the patient's medical chart.[100]

INFORMATION COMPILED IN ANTICIPATION OF . . . CIVIL, CRIMINAL, OR ADMINISTRATIVE PROCEEDINGS.   The commentary to the regulations clarify that this is intended to protect work product (attorneys' notes, memoranda, impressions, etc.) and discovery, while not impairing an individual's right to the underlying health information.[101]

GROUNDS FOR UNREVIEWABLE DENIAL OF ACCESS TO RECORDS.   The regulations create five areas where a covered entity may deny access to records without any opportunity for review.[102] The first area simply reiterates the categories described above under exceptions to the right of access. The other four areas where records requests can be denied with no right to review are (1) prisoners' requests to review their records;[103] (2) a research subject's request to see records from research, only if the consent form notified the subject that the right of access would be suspended during research;[104] (3) if protected health information is contained in records subject to the Privacy Act (more commonly known as the Freedom of Information Act) and the request would be denied under the Privacy Act;[105] or (4) if "information was obtained from someone other than a health care provider under promise of confidentiality and the access would be reasonably likely to reveal the source of the information."[106] Denials of access to health care information on any of these bases are unreviewable.

REVIEWABLE GROUNDS FOR DENIAL OF ACCESS TO RECORDS.   The right of a patient to see his or her chart can be restricted in one of three circumstances, and each of these circumstances is reviewable by an appeal process. A licensed health care professional may deny access if in the exercise of professional judgment it is determined that such access is "reasonably likely to endanger the life or physical safety of the individual or another person."[107] This exception is far more limited than that which appears in many state statutes, and the commentary is explicit that emotional endangerment or harm is not sufficient to trigger the exception: "Under this reason for denial, covered entities may not deny access on the basis of the sensitivity of the health information or the potential for causing emotional or psychological harm."[108] A health care professional must find 1) that the individual has exhibited suicidal or homicidal tendencies; and 2) that access to the records would reasonably result in murder, suicide, or other physical violence.[109]

SUBSTANTIAL HARM EXCEPTION.   The second reviewable exception is when the requested information makes reference to another person (except for a health care provider) and in the professional judgment of the licensed health care professional, the access would be likely to cause "substantial harm to such other person."[110]

PERSONAL REPRESENTATIVES' REQUESTS FOR RECORDS.   Finally, interestingly, if the personal representative of an individual makes the request, rather than the individual him or herself, the request may be denied if provision of access to records to the personal representative "is reasonably likely to cause substantial harm to the individual or another person."[111] The commentary makes clear that the drafters of the regulation did not regard it as a given that an individual's personal representative would always act in the best interest of the individual, and refers explicitly to domestic violence, and potential discord between personal representatives and individuals. If a licensed health care professional determines that it is not in the best interest of the individual to treat a personal representative as though he or she actually stood in the shoes of the individual, the health care professional may refuse access to the records.[112]

INDIVIDUAL RIGHTS IN THE PROCESS OF REQUESTING ACCESS TO RECORDS. The regulations discourage blanket denials of access, requiring that "the covered entity must, to the extent possible, give the individual access to any other protected health information requested, after excluding the protected health information to which the covered entity has a ground to deny access."[113] The regulations also require that an individual receive a timely response to an access request, including both the basis for any denial of access, and the name or title and telephone number of the individual designated by the covered entity to handle appeals and complaints. Finally, if the covered entity does not itself have the records, but knows where they can be found, it is required to inform the individual where to direct his or her request for access to the records.[114]

TIMELINESS OF RESPONSE. The covered entity is required to act on any request within 30 days of its receipt, unless the records are not on-site, in which case the covered entity gets 60 days to act. The covered entity may also give itself a 30-day extension, as long as within 30 or 60 days, as applicable, it gives the individual notice of the reasons for the delay and the date by which it will complete action on the request. The covered entity may only give itself one extension.[115]

OPTION OF A SUMMARY. Many people who have dealt with psychiatric clients' right of access to their records are familiar with the substitution of a summary for the actual records. However, under the HIPAA regulations, a summary may only be provided if the individual agrees in advance.[116] There is very little incentive for individuals to agree to this, since the regulation also allows the covered entity to charge for the preparation of the summary.

FEES. The hospital or other covered entity may charge a "reasonable," "cost-based" fee including expenses for copying, labor, and postage.[117]

FORM OF ACCESS. The hospital or other covered entity must provide access in the format requested by the individual, presumably including computer discs, if it is readily producible in that format. Otherwise, the covered entity must provide the information requested in a readable hard copy form, or whatever form is agreed to by the covered entity and the individual. The requirement that the information must be presented in readable form may present considerable grounds for argument in the future.[118]

PROCESS OF REVIEW DENIAL. This is one of the most problematic portions of the regulation. The review of a denial of access is to be conducted by a health care professional designated by the covered entity, and the sole gesture toward neutrality is the requirement that the reviewing individual not have been "directly involved" in the denial of the request. There is no designated time for this review to be completed, beyond the requirement that it be "reasonable."[119] This is why the commentary's explicit statement that exceptions to the right of access are "narrow" and denials of access should be "rare" is significant.[120]

Medicaid and Medicare

The Medicaid statute encompasses numerous federal requirements, which hospitals must meet in order to receive reimbursement under the Medicare and Medicaid programs. Overall, these are called conditions of participation (COPs). In 1999, the COPs were revised to include new standards relating to patients' rights, particularly in the area of seclusion and restraint.

Who Is Liable?

The Medicare and Medicaid statutes apply to facilities that accept Medicare and Medicaid reimbursement, including hospitals, freestanding clinics, and state agencies. In the case of private entities, such as private hospitals, there is no possibility of action in federal court by patients. However, complaints about either private or state facilities can be made to the regional offices of the Centers for Medicare and Medicaid Services (CMS), which can investigate and determine whether the regulations have been violated. In appropriate circumstances, CMS can threaten to cut off federal funding to the facilities if the offending practice is not remedied. This has happened recently in the case of state facilities for violations of regulations related to restraint[121] and patient safety.[122]

While courts have held that some parts of the Medicaid statute are privately enforceable against state agencies under 42 U.S.C. 1983, the U.S. Supreme Court recently held that rights conferred solely by federal regulation, which are not merely interpretations of a federal statute, are not independently enforceable by individuals in federal court.[123]

Requirements

The patients' rights section of the Medicaid regulations requires hospitals to inform patients of their rights,[124] have a grievance system in place,[125] protect patients' privacy and confidentiality,[126] and protect patients' safety.[127] Other rights that are of particular concern to people with psychiatric disabilities, such as the right to be free from unnecessary seclusion and restraint, the right to informed consent, the right to be free from abuse and harassment, and the right to access one's own records, are discussed in greater detail at pp. 98–100 *infra.*

REQUIREMENTS THAT PATIENTS BE INFORMED OF THEIR RIGHTS. The patients' rights regulations include the requirement that patients and their family members must be given information about their rights. This is not limited to hanging up posters in the lobby. In its *Interpretive Guidelines* and instructions to inspectors, CMS articulates its understanding that the alternative communication techniques mandated by Section 504 to communicate with deaf and blind patients will also apply to the provision of information about their rights.[128] In its *Guidance to Surveyors*, CMS emphasizes that surveyors must check to ensure that "[t]he hospital informs each patient of his or her rights in language that the patient understands..." If the patient is deaf or blind, the hospital must use "alternative communication techniques or aides ... or take other steps as needed to effectively communicate with the patient."[129] This can include "specialized programs" and "use of interpreters."[130] Significantly, CMS has designed "probes" that the inspectors are supposed to use in determining whether the hospital is complying with the COPs. One of the probes associated with the requirement that patients be informed of their rights specifically requires inspectors to determine, "Does the hospital have alternative means of communication such as written materials, signs, or interpreters to commune with patients when necessary?"

RIGHTS UNDER MEDICAID AND MEDICARE REGARDING COMPLAINTS AND GRIEVANCES. The grievance system must specify time frames for review of the patient complaints and responses to them. Responses to the patient complaints must be in writing, and must identify a hospital contact person, the steps taken to investigate the grievance, the results of the investigation, and the date of completion.[131] Finally, the *Interpretive Guidance* for surveyors testing compliance with the conditions of participation notes that when a patient files a grievance or complaint with a hospital, the resolution of the complaint must be communicated in a language and manner that the patient can understand.[132]

RIGHTS UNDER MEDICAID AND MEDICARE REGARDING SAFETY. The conditions of participation relating to patients' rights include a right to receive care in a safe setting.[133] In addition, in another part of the regulations, the hospital must agree to comply with federal and state laws relating to the health and safety of patients.[134] Significantly, the example used in CMS's *Interpretive Guidelines and Manual* to illustrate such a federal law is Section 504 of the Rehabilitation Act of 1973.[135]

RIGHTS UNDER MEDICAID AND MEDICARE REGARDING PARTICIPATION IN FORMULATING TREATMENT PLANS. Hospitals that participate in the Medicare and Medicaid programs must give patients, including emergency room patients, the right to participate in formulating their own treatment plans.

Special Issues

Of particular concern to psychiatric patients are the stringent requirements imposed by the regulations on the use of seclusion and restraint, and the right of the patient to access his or her own records, to informed consent, to formulate advance directives, and to have the hospital staff comply with those advance directives. These are discussed in turn below. In addition, the right to be free from discrimination on the basis of psychiatric disability is crucial. The conditions of participation include, in addition to the section on patients' rights, conditions relating to compliance with federal law, including a specific agreement to comply with various federal civil rights laws, including Section 504 of the Rehabilitation Act.[136] Thus, a hospital's failure to comply with the Rehabilitation Act's requirements regarding the provision of auxiliary aids, such as interpreter services to deaf clients, is a violation of its provider agreement with CMS, as would be any act of discrimination on the basis of psychiatric disability. The *Guidelines and Manual* are important because they are used by CMS inspectors to determine whether a hospital is in compliance with the conditions of participation.

RIGHTS REGARDING THE USE OF RESTRAINTS.   The new regulations require that a physician actually visit any patient in restraints within one hour.[137] The *Interpretive Guidelines* require that this visit be in person and not by telephone or any other remote methodology.[138] The visit is required even if the patient is removed from restraints prior to the physician's arrival.[139] These regulations were unsuccessfully challenged in federal court by a trade association of private psychiatric hospitals.[140] The regulations contain the familiar prohibition on the use of restraints "as a means of coercion, discipline, convenience, or retaliation."[141]

The restraints may only be ordered as a last resort, after other methods of behavior management have been exhausted.[142] "The decision to use a restraint is driven not by diagnosis, but by comprehensive individual assessment that concludes that for this patient, at this time, the use of less intrusive measures poses a greater risk than the risk of using a restraint or seclusion."[143]

Restraints must be removed "at the earliest possible time."[144] Each written order requiring restraints is limited to four hours or less, depending on age, and may only be renewed for up to 24 hours.[145] Each renewal must also include a written description of the patient's needs and the reasoning behind the continuing restraint.[146] New interpretive guidelines clarify that handcuffs, pepper spray, batons, Taser guns, and other weapons cannot be used to restrain a patient in EDs or in hospitals.[147]

RIGHTS RELATING TO ACCESS TO RECORDS.   The Medicaid patient rights regulations provide that a patient has a right of access to his or her records within a reasonable time frame[148] and that requests for records may only be denied on a limited basis.[149] If the patient is incompetent, the record should be made available to his or her representative.[150] The records must be provided in a "timely" manner, although "timely" is defined as 30 days (or 60 days under some circumstances).[151] Although reasonable fees may be charged to cover the cost of providing the records, these fees may not create a barrier to the individual's receiving his or her records.[152] There has been litigation in a number of states over the question of what constitutes a reasonable copying cost for record access.

RIGHTS RELATING TO INFORMED CONSENT. The conditions of participation require hospitals to give patients and/or their representatives the right to participate in their plan of care.[153] These regulations apply in the ED, as well as in the hospital. The regulations make clear what informed consent means in practice: "the right to be informed of his or her health status, being involved in care planning and treatment, and being able to request or refuse treatment."[154] Although the right to request treatment does not mean that a patient can "demand the provision of treatment or services deemed medically unnecessary or inappropriate"[155] the patient does have an explicit right to make informed decisions regarding his or her care,[156] including the right to have an advance directive respected by hospital staff[157] (see Patient Self-determination Act [PSDA], immediately following this section).

Emergency department physicians, however, routinely ignore the requirements of informed consent. There are many reasons for this. First, the rushed atmosphere of the ED is not conducive to the kinds of discussions that make true informed consent possible. Second, many physicians entertain the mistaken belief that informed consent requirements do not apply in the ED. A respected expert in the field recently wrote (in the context of obtaining consent for research purposes) that "the issue of patient consent is particularly difficult to resolve because the patient in crisis may, by definition, be unable to give informed consent."[158] It is legally incorrect that a patient in crisis by definition cannot give informed consent. Voluntary patients who cannot give informed consent are either unconscious or incompetent, and being in crisis is not synonymous with being incompetent. Nor is disagreement with a proposed treatment plan or disposition identical with incompetence. However, some patients do present in the ED with doubtful competence, discussed in the section on competence and informed consent at pp. 82–83 and 108–109. Some state laws permit involuntary treatment of individuals under legal orders of involuntary detention.

Patient Self-Determination Act

The PSDA[159] was passed by Congress in 1991 to ensure that health care providers inform their patients of whatever rights they have under state law to make decisions about their health care.

Who Is Liable?

Any facility that receives Medicare payments is subject to the requirements of the PSDA. Since, unlike the conditions of participation discussed above, the PSDA is part of the Medicare statute, rather than being found solely in regulations, it is possible that it could be enforced through a federal court action by a patient under 42 U.S.C. 1983.[160] In order for this to happen, the federal court would have to find that Congress intended that the PSDA create a federal right. Whether this is the case requires a complex statutory analysis that is beyond the scope of this book.[161] Even if the right is not enforceable through court proceedings, CMS, an office in HHS, enforces the requirements of the PSDA.

Requirements

While it has been noted that the PSDA generally does not create any new *substantive* rights, it does impose on emergency rooms and other health care centers new administrative requirements.[162] These include requirements to provide written instructions to patients about their rights regarding making decisions about their care, including their right to refuse care, requirements to document whether each patient has an advance directive, and requirements to educate hospital staff and the larger community about the use of advance directives.[163] Also, EDs are required to have written policies concerning the use of advance directives that patients can have access to and to not discriminate against any patient for having (or not having) an advance directive.

Special Issues

THE PSDA AND THE SUICIDAL PATIENT. The PSDA's requirement that all patients be provided with information about their right to refuse treatment, including life saving treatment, creates special issues when patients contemplating suicide come into the ED. Anecdotal evidence suggests that hospitals simply ignore the requirements of the PSDA in those situations, and no one has complained about this.

HOSPITALS THAT DO NOT COMPLY WITH THE FULL REQUIREMENTS OF THE PSDA. One scholar has noted that while the PSDA is not limited to end-of-life decisions, but covers all rights that the individual has to refuse treatment, "the information typically provided to patients (even in psychiatric institutions) is almost exclusively oriented toward end–of–life decisions."[164] In addition, both hospitals and EDs must comply with the terms of a patient's advance directive, but there is some anecdotal evidence that these are ignored, particularly in the case of psychiatric patients.

State Laws

Statutes Limiting Detention in the Emergency Department

As mentioned above, some states regulate by statute the amount of time an individual can be detained in an emergency room without being permitted to leave. For example, in Washington, if a person "is brought" to an emergency room and refuses voluntary admission and staff believe that he or she meets the commitment standard, the law permits an ED to "detain such person for sufficient time to notify the county designated mental health professional of such person's condition . . . but which time shall be no more than six hours from the time the professional staff determine that an evaluation by the county mental health professional is necessary."[165] In Maryland, a person with a psychiatric disability may not be detained more than six hours before the physician examination[166] and may not be kept more than 30 hours in the emergency room.[167] In Pennsylvania, any person taken involuntarily to a facility for psychiatric assessment must be examined within two hours.[168]

These statutes are often violated and rarely enforced. One attempt to enforce the statute in Washington reached the state's highest court on the issue of when the six hours began to run. The Washington Supreme Court held that the six-hour time limit began to run after the hospital staff determined that statutory standards for commitment were met and called the county designated mental health professionals, who are the gatekeepers in the Washington system, rather than when the individual arrived at the ED. Referring to the time gap between arrival at the ED and examination by hospital staff, the court held that the state Constitution created protections to limit that time, see above at pp. 83–84.

Although some states do regulate the amount of time an individual can be detained in an ED, no state has legislated on the allowable time between arrival and examination. Maine, for example, has legislation that creates a number of different time frames (no more than 18 hours between the filing of an initial detention order by emergency room staff and its endorsement by a judge[169] and no more than two days between evaluation and admission to a hospital ward[170]), but even Maine has no limit on the amount of time a person may be detained before he or she is actually examined by a physician. The lack of time limitation on involuntary detention of a person who has not yet been determined to be a danger to himself or herself or others raises constitutional questions that have yet to be resolved.

Some hospitals have developed policies that effectively limit the length of time that a patient can be involuntarily detained without assessment, and distinguish rapidly between patients who will be detained and patients who will be allowed to leave. The Bellevue Hospital policy is a good example of such a policy, permitting involuntary detention of individuals brought in subject to valid detention orders, but requiring prompt triage of other presenting psychiatric patients into emergent, urgent, and standard categories, according to a number of criteria. Patients who fall into the standard category can leave if they so desire, and patients who are emergent or urgent must be seen and assessed within a limited time frame.[171]

Patients' Bill of Rights

Almost all states have specific rights for persons detained because of mental illness. Some of these statutes apply in emergency room settings[172] while others statutorily exclude emergency room settings from complying with patients' rights requirements.[173] Lawsuits have been brought under patients' bill of rights statutes challenging the practice of forced disrobing in EDs,[174] pepper spraying psychiatric patients in EDs,[175] and the death of psychiatric patients in EDs.

Tort Claims

A tort is a legal term describing the breach of duty by one person to another. Torts are often divided into intentional torts, which in the ED context would include actions alleging battery, assault, false imprisonment, and intentional infliction of emotional distress, and actions challenging negligence, such as medical malpractice, or failure to obtain informed consent, which are typically based on the failure to exercise proper care.

Until the 1960s, hospitals were typically not held legally liable for errors committed by emergency room doctors, since those doctors were not employees of the hospital. Furthermore, neither hospitals nor physicians were held liable for deaths or injuries resulting from refusals or failure to treat patients in EDs. Two important court cases were decided in the 1960s that changed the face of hospital liability for emergency services. In 1961, for the first time, a state supreme court decided that a private hospital that held itself out as providing emergency services had a duty to accept and treat patients who had genuine emergency conditions.[176] In 1966, the Illinois Supreme Court decided *Darling v. Charleston Memorial Hospital*,[177] which established the basis for hospital liability for emergency room malpractice, regardless of the financial arrangements between the hospital and ED staff.

Although improper discharge cases generally receive the most publicity, they do not dominate the field of malpractice in the treatment of psychiatric patients in EDs. Emergency room malpractice cases can involve improper evaluation, failure to obtain informed consent, improper seclusion or restraint, injuries by hospital security guards, false imprisonment, or battery. Although liability for failure to warn is a much-discussed issue in psychiatry, it rarely comes up in the emergency room context, possibly because threats of violence to specific others in the context of an existing psychiatric crisis predictably result in commitment rather than discharge.[178]

Obviously, each state has different statutory law and different malpractice precedents, but some issues are common to all states.

Intentional Torts

False Imprisonment

A private ED or a physician or psychiatrist who prevents an individual from leaving the hospital without complying with the requirements of the law may be liable for false imprisonment. In order to be liable for false imprisonment, the emergency room and its agents must have lacked legal authorization to detain the individual. It is not only the failure to fill out the proper paperwork to detain a patient that may create liability for false imprisonment. If a certificate of involuntary commitment is incorrectly or incompletely filled out, this may be sufficient to make out a claim for false imprisonment.[179] In addition, seclusion within an ED without proper authorization can also constitute false imprisonment.[180]

The intent to falsely imprison is not required for liability on a false imprisonment claim; the claim only requires proof of intent to detain. Thus, when a doctor failed to follow new state requirements for commitment of a patient, the fact that he followed the older requirements and did not intend to violate the law was held applicable to a negligence claim, but not to one of false imprisonment.[181] By the same token, the fact that a physician followed the requirements of state law is a complete defense to a claim of false imprisonment.[182] While simply filling out the paperwork correctly is sufficient to bar a claim of false imprisonment, the physician's evaluation and substantive judgments must not have deviated substantially from those that would have been exercised by a reasonable physician or mental health professional in his or her position, or the physician could be liable for negligence or violation of the patient's civil rights.[183]

Assault/Battery

Assault and battery are claims that are frequently the subject of considerable confusion over the meaning of the law. First, they are both potential criminal charges, as well as civil tort claims, and their meaning may be different in the criminal and civil contexts. Second, the legal meanings of assault and battery differ substantially from the common understanding of the terms.

In law, a *battery* is a nonconsensual touching. A minor physical contact, if unwanted, can support a claim for battery. For example, when a security guard grabbed a visitor by the arm to walk him out of a hospital and held on to it for several steps a valid claim for battery was held to exist by the court.[184] Battery cases are brought against security guards for injuring or assaulting patients[185] but also against doctors for ordering medicine without informed consent,[186] and against nurses and others for re-straining patients.[187]

An *assault* in the law is an act that places a person in reasonable apprehension of imminent harmful or offensive bodily contact or physical harm.[188] Generally, assault and battery are pled together in complaints, since placing an individual in apprehension of unwanted physical contact is often followed closely in time by actual unwanted physical contact. Assault and battery claims are filed by patients in obvious cases, such as being injured or beaten by security guards, but also following forced medical procedures such as catheterizations,[189] and after unwanted contact with hospital security guards, including searches,[190] escorts, and altercations of various kinds.[191]

Intentional Infliction of Emotional Distress

Both treatises and patients' reports reflect that patients with psychiatric disabilities are often treated with hostility by staff in EDs. Sometimes, this treatment is felt to be so deliberate and injurious that patients sue for intentional infliction of emotional distress (IIED). In order to state a successful claim for IIED, a plaintiff must establish (1) intentional or reckless conduct by the defendant that was (2) extreme and outrageous (3) causing (4) severe emotional distress.[192] Courts have not been especially sympathetic to these claims when they are brought by emergency room patients. In *C.M. v. Tomball Regional Hospital*,[193] a minor girl came to the emergency room after she was raped. She was treated dismissively by the hospital staff there, who screened her in front of the entire emergency room waiting area, where 10–15 others overheard the conversation, including an acquaintance of the victim who told others about what had happened.[194] Despite her mother's pleas, the hospital informed the victim there was nothing they could do for her (because she had bathed) and refused to gather information in a rape kit. The mother testified that the victim was completely devastated by the loss of privacy and had to move because she could no longer go to school with those who knew about the incident.[195] Nonetheless, the court ruled that while the emergency room staff were "rude, insensitive, and uncaring . . . [their] conduct did not rise to the level of intentional infliction of emotional distress under prevailing standards."[196]

There have, however, been successful claims brought for IIED for treatment received while in a hospital. In *Hoffman v. Memorial Osteopathic Hospital*,[197] the plaintiff, who was suffering from neurological disease, successfully recovered for his IIED claim. He had fallen to the floor, and the emergency room physician had ignored his pleas for help and allowed him to remain on the floor for over an hour. Therefore, it is possible that the treatment received by some patients with psychiatric disabilities in the emergency room may rise to the level of intentional infliction of emotional distress.

Negligence

Tort claims alleging negligence are different from claims alleging intentional actions such as assault or false imprisonment. Negligence is the failure to exercise a reasonable duty of care owed to others. In the ED context, there are a number of specific claims for negligence. Hospitals can be negligent in the hiring and training of security guards or in the safety they provide to ED patients.[198] Malpractice is a form of negligence specific to professionals, in this case health care professionals.

Malpractice

Malpractice requires the establishment of duty arising out of the treatment provider–patient relationship. A team whose function was simply to assess patients to determine if they should be detained involuntarily, but that provided no treatment, had no duty of care to the patient.[199] If the duty of care exists, then a deviation from professional standards that causes injury to the patient is malpractice. The distinction between medical malpractice and other torts is significant, because many states require plaintiffs to fulfill various administrative requirements, such as obtaining a certificate from a doctor, or presenting their case to a panel, prior to filing a malpractice case in court. No such requirements attach to claims for false imprisonment, battery, or other intentional torts.

Although federal statutes such as EMTALA place a considerable burden on EDs, some state malpractice laws provide more favorable treatment for EDs than for other malpractice cases. For example, in Florida a successful malpractice suit against state and county EDs requires a showing of more than mere negligence. Rather, a plaintiff must show "reckless disregard" for the patient's well-being.[200] In addition, in malpractice cases against EDs, a number of states, including Florida and California, impose a specific requirement that testifying experts must have had "substantial professional experience within the previous five years while assigned to provide emergency medical services in a hospital ED."[201]

In order to deviate from standards of care, of course, those standards must exist and be the subject of reasonable consensus in the field. A survey of state malpractice cases makes clear that emergency medicine, as applied to psychiatric patients, has relatively few such standards. However, some basic standards appear to exist, as supported by case law and treatises.

A PSYCHIATRIST PERFORMING AN ASSESSMENT OF MENTAL ILLNESS AND DANGEROUSNESS IN AN ED IS HELD TO A STANDARD OF CARE FOR PSYCHIATRISTS IN GENERAL.   In most cases, a psychiatrist in an emergency room performing an assessment or examination is held to a standard of care for psychiatrists in general.[202] Courts have not recognized that a psychiatrist operating in the context of an emergency room setting should be held to a different standard and have refused to disqualify a psychiatrist from testifying in cases involving emergency rooms on the grounds that the psychiatrist has not practiced in emergency room settings.

In fact, in one case an appellate court reversed the exclusion of the expert testimony of a psychologist regarding whether a woman should have been discharged from an emergency room. The defendants had argued that the testimony should be excluded because the psychologist had neither emergency room experience nor a medical degree.[203] The court noted that the expert's testimony "concerned the limited area of the diagnosis and treatment of mental illness" and that, at most, his lack of a medical license "affected his credibility."

EMERGENCY ROOM PHYSICIANS EVALUATING A CLIENT PRESENTING WITH A PSYCHIATRIC ISSUE ARE GENERALLY NOT REQUIRED TO SEEK PSYCHIATRIC CONSULTATIONS, BUT WHEN THEY DO, THEY HAVE A DUTY TO REVIEW THE FINDINGS, PROPOSED DISPOSITION, AND RATIONALE OF THESE CONSULTANTS, AND FAILURE TO DO SO CONSTITUTES A BREACH OF THE STANDARD OF CARE.[204]   It may appear to be common sense that a consult, once requested, should be reviewed and considered, but a number of cases in which hospital defendants have done poorly have revolved around the combination of a failure to heed the concerns of a consultant or staff person who specialized in the assessment of people with psychiatric disabilities, and a bad outcome.[205] For example, in one case, a man who went to the ED after becoming suddenly paralyzed was assumed by the emergency physician to have psychosomatic problems because he had a history of panic attacks. Although the man and his wife insisted that these symptoms were different from those of a panic attack, after the man's blood work came back normal, the physician ordered a psychiatric consultation. The consult was conducted by a counselor, who told the physician that the patient was not suffering from a psychiatric condition. The physician called the counselor's supervisor, a psychiatrist, who concurred over the telephone that the symptoms did not sound like a panic attack. In the ensuing hours, the physician did not order an MRI or conduct any medical test to determine if there might be a medical source of paralysis. After a number of hours, the physician called a neurologist, who said he could not rule out any number of diseases that attack the nerves in the spinal cord. The emergency room physician still did not order any tests. The next morning, the patient was discovered unconscious, brain damaged, and in an irreversible coma. He was finally diagnosed with transverse myelitis, and after four months, life support was withdrawn and he died. The jury awarded $2,559,375.00.[206]

In addition to the opinions of their own staff, hospitals have some level of duty—how much is unclear—to attend to the opinions of professionals at a transferring hospital about the condition and symptoms of the patient.[207]

By the same token, however, when a consultation is sought and the consultant expresses the opinion that a patient is safe to go home or does not meet the legal standard necessary to be detained involuntarily, courts and juries also tend to defer to that finding in exonerating hospitals which then discharged the patient, even when the patient later commits suicide.[208] This was true in one case even when the patient's family member begged the hospital to detain him.[209]

THE DUTY OF AN EMERGENCY ROOM PHYSICIAN IS TO MAKE A DIAGNOSIS AND DETER-MINE A PROPER TREATMENT PLAN DIRECTED TO ENSURING THE PATIENT'S WELL-BEING AND SAFETY, BASED ON INFORMATION FROM AS MANY SOURCES AS AVAILABLE. THE FAILURE TO CONSULT WITH OR TALK TO READILY AVAILABLE RELATIVES OR OTHER SOURCES OF INFORMATION BEFORE MAKING A DECISION TO DISCHARGE MAY BE A BREACH OF THE STANDARD OF CARE.[210] No court has held that ED personnel have a duty to flush out informants, or even make telephone calls. But if an informant such as a spouse or relative is in the ED, and if that individual relays or could have relayed information relating to dangerousness, then the ED professional may breach a duty of care by ignoring the availability of such information. Of course, this information itself should be investigated; many people who bring relatives or clients to EDs have clear desires that the individual should be admitted and may shade their accounts to ensure that the dispositional alternative they prefer is chosen.

State mental health professionals are held to the same standard of care as private mental health professionals.[211] Many states grant statutory immunity to employees of the state for lawsuits against them in the performance of their state duties. Some state-employed doctors and psychiatrists have attempted to claim this immunity in negligence actions challenging decisions to commit or release patients. However, courts have not been sympathetic to these claims in general, reasoning that the duties of the physician arise from their profession as physician, rather than specifically from their roles as state actors.

This immunity for state actors should not be confused with statutory immunity granted by many states to all physicians when they are evaluating people to determine whether they should be detained involuntarily.[212] The language of these statutory grants of immunity varies, and in some states, such as Massachusetts, immunity is only granted for decisions to involuntarily detain or admit, and not for decisions to allow the person to leave. There are already too many pressures on ED personnel to over-detain, and the language of these statutes should be altered to expand immunity to any decision related to involuntary detention, including release.

Failure to Obtain Informed Consent

Emergency rooms can be noisy, chaotic places. The staff has a strong interest in calming patients who are frightened and agitated. However, the administration of medications to people with psychiatric disabilities in emergency room settings raises issues of informed consent. There are obviously times when medications can be administered without consent, and other times when it is both illegal and unethical to do so. This section attempts to distinguish these sometimes blurry boundaries.

The doctrine of informed consent is rooted deep in common law and in our respect as a society for an individual's right to control his or her own body. Case law has emphasized that the right to bodily integrity may be even more important than the state's interest in preserving life. Medical treatment performed without the person's consent amounts to battery. But consent is not all that is required. Informed consent requires giving the patient information about the nature of the proposed treatment, its benefits, possible risks, and alternative therapies. This is obviously difficult in the hectic pace of many emergency rooms. However, there is no blanket exception to the requirement of informed consent, simply because the environment of the emergency room makes it more difficult.

There are exceptions to the requirement of informed consent. They differ from state to state, and are often misunderstood even within the state in which emergency room professionals practice. There are two basic exceptions: the emergency exception and the exception relating to incompetent patients (which is not really an exception, as it simply transfers the requirement to obtain informed consent to another individual).

The emergency exception does *not* cover all treatment in emergency room settings. A clear analysis of what constitutes an emergency under this doctrine is crucial to understanding that psychiatric patients retain rights to informed consent in the emergency room. Despite the name, not all emergencies are created equal. The fact that an individual seeks medical or psychiatric treatment in an emergency room does not mean that he or she has waived the right to informed consent. Rather, the emergency exception to the doctrine of informed consent generally obtains "if and only if, the patient is unconscious or otherwise incapable of giving consent, and either time or circumstances do not permit the physician to obtain the consent of a family member."[213] The highest court in Massachusetts explicitly held that an emergency room physician's judgment that a procedure was necessary to save a competent patient's life was not sufficient to overcome the patient's right to informed consent, especially when her family also opposed the procedure.

Consumer Protection Laws

An increasing number of cases against hospitals and EDs are stating claims under broad state consumer protection statutes, which include the provision of medical services.[214] In one case, Yale New Haven Hospital was sued for claiming that its ED was capable of providing the highest levels of trauma care, when the plaintiff claimed that it was so understaffed that this claim amounted to consumer deception.[215] Some of these claims have been dismissed when the court finds that the consumer protection laws were aimed at physicians acting in a commercial or entrepreneurial context.[216]

Joint Commission on Accreditation of Health Care Organizations Standards

The Joint Commission on Accreditation of Health Care Organizations (JCAHO) is a national organization that undertakes to accredit many different kinds of health care entities, from hospitals to home health care. The joint commission has accreditation standards for entities providing psychiatric care (behavioral health care standards) and general hospitals (hospital standards). Many psychiatric hospitals seek accreditation under both sets of standards. The Joint Commission on the Accreditation of Health Care Organizations has promulgated accreditation standards in a number of areas that apply to both behavioral health care and acute care hospitals, including treatment and rights, responsibilities, and ethics.

Restraint

The commission's requirements related to the use of restraints are applicable to all EDs that use restraints for behavioral health reasons, regardless of whether they are emergency rooms in general hospitals or psychiatric emergency rooms.[217] However, only select standards apply outside the setting of a psychiatric unit.[218] The JCAHO defines restraints as "any physical or pharmacological means used to restrict a patient's movement."[219] It specifically recommends "security or sitters to monitor patients being evaluated for suicidal ideation" rather than seclusion or restraints.[220] The joint commission differentiates between restraints associated with acute medical or surgical needs and restraints used in the context of behavioral health.[221]

Restraint and seclusion for behavioral health reasons are "limited to emergencies in which there is an imminent risk of an individual physically harming himself or herself, staff, or others and non-physical intervention would not be effective."[222] Interestingly, JCAHO requirements specify that "the client's family is notified promptly of the initiation of restraint or seclusion";[223] depending on the client's relationship with his family, this may be a violation of HIPAA confidentiality requirements. All patients in restraints must be continually monitored, in-person, for as long as they are restrained.[224] "In-person" means that the observer must have direct eye contact with the patient. This can be done through a window or doorway, but cannot be done over a video monitoring system. Nor can the required physician examination take place over a video monitoring system. No restraint order can last longer than four hours, but after four hours, a registered nurse or other authorized staff member may re-evaluate the patient, and if he or she concludes restraints are still clinically necessary, can obtain an order from a licensed independent practitioner for a written or verbal order. A patient must be re-examined in person by a licensed independent practitioner after eight hours in restraint.

Seclusion

The use of seclusion in an emergency room setting as a standard policy to prevent psychiatric patients from leaving is prohibited by JCAHO standards, which permit seclusion or restraint "only in an emergency when there is an inherent risk of an individual physically harming himself or herself or others, including staff. Non-physical interventions are the first choice as an intervention, unless safety issues demand an immediate physical response."[225] The standards prohibit the use of restraint or seclusion for any other purpose; they require that staffing levels and assignments be set to minimize circumstances that give rise to the use of seclusion or restraint.[226] Unlike restraints, seclusion can be monitored by audio-visual means after the first hour. Other than this requirement, most of the JCAHO's requirements are identical for seclusion and restraint.

Like the CMS, JCAHO accepts complaints from patients for violations of accreditation standards and sometimes conducts spot investigations that result in the suspension of accreditation. Making a complaint to JCAHO is easy. There are complaint forms readily available on line at www.jcaho .org/general+public/public+input/report+a+complaint/qi_report_form_+ _2.doc. A complaint can be emailed to complaint@jcaho.org or faxed to 630-792-5636. (The Quality Incident Report form available online gives guidance as to how to present the complaint.)

Professional Standards

American College of Emergency Physicians

One major problem of emergency room treatment of people with psychiatric disabilities is that emergency room professional standards have not kept pace with federal, state, or licensing standards. Thus, the American College of Emergency Physicians (ACEP) standard regarding use of patient restraint in emergency rooms has no requirement that restraints should be ordered by a physician, or indeed by any mental health professional.[227] Under the ACEP policy, anyone, including a security guard, could initiate restraints. The ACEP policy has no requirements for observation, other than "periodic assessment." The policy does state that "the use of restraints should conform to applicable laws, rules, regulations and accreditation standards," which have at this point progressed to a much greater degree of detail than what is contained in the ACEP standards.

Behavioral Experts Standards

In an attempt to establish standards in the care of people with psychiatric disabilities in ED settings, a list of 52 distinguished experts in emergency treatment of people with behavioral disorders was compiled by Comprehensive Neuroscience, Inc. They were asked questions about assessment and the appropriateness of restraint, seclusion, and various medications in the care of people with psychiatric disabilities.

The expert consensus on use of physical and chemical restraints reflected a variety of positions. The experts endorsed the position that restraint is a last resort. Restraining a patient is appropriate if the patient presents an "acute danger to other patients, bystanders, staff or self." Restraint is only "sometimes" appropriate to prevent an involuntary patient from leaving the facility, and rarely or never appropriate to "prevent a voluntary patient from leaving prior to an assessment," to "maintain an orderly treatment environment," or because of a "lack of resources to supervise patient adequately."[228] However, the expert panel takes issue with CMS's definition of chemical restraint, finding that any medication provided for the treatment of a psychiatric disorder cannot be considered a chemical restraint, even if it is not part of an existing treatment plan.

American Psychiatric Association Task Force on Psychiatric Emergency Services

This useful report was recently published, and notes the lack of standards currently guiding the provision of psychiatric emergency services, as well as the difficulties in financing and reimbursement that face psychiatric emergency services. It canvasses the entire range of emergency services, from traditional EDs to mobile crisis units, and proposes standards in a number of different areas, including staffing, space, medication, and medication storage, for each of the different models of psychiatric emergency services. It is not as oriented to treatment as the behavioral experts standards discussed above, nor as detailed on ED policies and practices in areas affecting patients' rights as the standards and recommendations in appendix A, but serves as a useful complement to both. The task force report, which has been referenced throughout this book, is discussed in more detail in the next chapter.

6

Solutions to Problems in Emergency Department Treatment of People with Psychiatric Disabilities

This book began with the story of Linda Stalker and her experience at the Baystate Medical Center emergency department (ED) in Massachusetts. Her story was chosen because it was typical of the myriad problems facing people with psychiatric disabilities in EDs, including restraint, disrobing, use of security guards, and escalation of the individual's original difficulties.

However, the response from Baystate Medical Center to Linda Stalker's problems was anything but typical. Baystate no longer follows an automatic policy of removing the clothing of psychiatric patients. It has adopted a psychiatric advocate program that has reduced seclusion and restraint rates substantially. It has changed the ED environment to attempt to make it more comforting and less threatening to people in psychiatric crisis. This chapter looks at how Baystate and other EDs have tried to solve the problems outlined in this book. And, because no matter how many changes are made by EDs, they are still by their very nature not optimal environments for people in psychiatric crisis, this chapter also examines the many alternatives to EDs for people in psychiatric crisis, examining different models, funding, and feasibility. This chapter begins with the rest of Linda Stalker's story.[1]

Linda Stalker's treatment at Baystate Medical Center had a context unknown to her but familiar to many ED staff. Twenty years previously, a psychiatric patient who left without getting help returned to the ED waiting area and stabbed a boy to death. He tried to get into the ED itself, but a cardiologist held the door shut. After that, "the pendulum swung. It went from 'Let's be nice to the patients' to 'Let's protect us first.' "[2] Emergency departments where such tragic incidents take place often react by adopting policies and practices that may hurt and damage thousands of patients for decades afterward. Baystate recognized the legacy of that experience on its policies and moved forward.

It is very important to this story that Deb Provost, the head of the ED at Baystate, had only recently assumed her duties when she was confronted with the complaint about Linda Stalker's forcible disrobing. Because she was new, she did not have the inevitable emotional connections to the stabbing at Baystate. She says, "I was free to ask why are we doing this?" Even so, as she admits, "we were not that eager to change." The first reaction of Baystate staff when challenged by state licensing and mental health agency officials about Linda Stalker's experience of mandatory disrobement was "we have to do that; that's our policy." The policy was necessary, they felt, to keep patients and staff safe. For many hospitals, that is the immediate response to complaints about policies, such as disrobing, even though disrobing is far from a universal requirement across EDs.

Linda Stalker did not complain directly to Baystate. Very few patients who expect to revisit hospital EDs have the courage to complain to the places where they will return in crisis and need and where they feel vulnerable to staff hostility and resentment. Linda Stalker wrote to an advocate at the Massachusetts Department of Mental Health, who contacted the licensing division of the Department of Mental Health. The licensing division turned to its counterpart at the Department of Public Health, which licenses Baystate Hospital. The joint visit from the Department of Mental Health and the Department of Public Health licensing divisions was the first time that Baystate Medical Center knew that Linda Stalker had complained.

After some initial resistance to changing policies, however, Baystate staff, led by Ann Maynard, the chief ED nurse, and Deb Provost, decided to follow the principle of "Let's look at it through the patient's eyes." And what they saw when they did this was that their beliefs about safety were at odds with what felt safe to a patient. "In my mind," says Ann Maynard, "I was thinking 'I'm just making you safe' . . . But then a person who came in because they just needed to talk to someone, we end up wrestling them to the ground."

Today, Baystate Medical Center does not require all psychiatric patients to disrobe. Patients are asked to disrobe only if safety concerns are presented and specifically documented by the primary nurse or physician. Even in those situations, the patient can never be completely stripped—underwear and socks may be kept on—and the clothes must be returned as soon as there is no safety risk. Baystate's ED employs psychiatric advocates who talk to psychiatric clients about their needs. All ED staff receive training in de-escalation. Baystate has developed a chart audit tool that permits educational feedback to staff. The staff has made environmental changes to the unit— changing paint color and other actions designed to create a more calming environment. Duration of restraints has dropped to a median of two hours, still too high for Baystate staff who are working to reduce it further. The staff has received letters from patients and family members who appreciate the changes. Linda Stalker appreciates the changes, but she still avoids Baystate because years later the trauma of being stripped by guards remains vivid in her mind.[3]

Improving the environment at EDs for psychiatric patients is something that ED staff can do and are dedicated to doing. What they often cannot do is solve the problems that bring the people to their door in the first place. Thus, before any discussion or analysis of improvement in ED policies and procedures, the crucial point must be underscored that problems in EDs rarely have either their origin or solution completely within the ED or even the hospital.

Focusing on Emergency Departments Alone Will Never Be Sufficient to Solve Systemic Problems

Emergency departments are the canaries in the mineshaft of community mental health. While some improvement of EDs can be accomplished simply with changes in the ED itself, as discussed below, many of the problems facing EDs, like the crises that bring a person to the ED, have their origin in community systems or funding streams over which ED staff have little or no control.

When the community mental health system does not have a continuum of 24-hour, seven-day crisis services for people with psychiatric disabilities, substantial, unnecessary, and expensive use of the ED (or the criminal justice system) is inevitable. In a system with adequate case management, hot and warm lines, respite care, and well-trained, flexible community providers, use of EDs by people in psychiatric crisis could be expected to drop substantially.

This is true for a variety of obvious and less obvious reasons. First, in a system where crisis alternatives existed and were open around the clock, there would be less use by people who come in voluntarily for help because they have nowhere else to go and no one available to talk to about their panic, desolation, or despair. Perhaps more subtly, there would be less use of EDs by community providers who use the ED as a *de facto* respite from difficult clients or as a form of last resort conflict resolution, or police, who may see it as a humane alternative to a holding cell.

Therefore, both policymakers and advocates who seek transformation of ED practices must begin with an assessment of the external pressures on the ED and what community mental health needs it is expected (usually inappropriately) to meet. Mental health agencies, themselves strapped for funds and prey to loss of Medicaid funds, often make cuts that directly impact EDs, without consulting EDs on working jointly to minimize the impact on both the agency's clients and the EDs.

On the other hand, the fact that the system has to be changed does not mean that there is no reason to alter practices at the ED level. Nor does it mean that EDs should be as passive and reactive as they have historically tended to be in the face of increasing demands. When individual hospitals and EDs decide to try and improve their services, they are able to achieve a great deal. When emergency physicians or hospitals decide to unite and take action, they are able to achieve significant social change. There are numerous examples of this, from legislation in Arizona restricting the ability of managed care organizations to limit ED reimbursements to transformation in the treatment of rape victims, illustrating that EDs and their staff can be a powerful engine for social change.

Solutions to Problems Facing Emergency Departments Do Exist

Licensing and Accreditation Agencies, and the Hospital Itself, Must Change Performance Evaluations of Emergency Departments and Their Staff to Reflect Differing Requirements in the Evaluation and Treatment of People with Psychiatric Disabilities

There is currently no widely accepted evaluation instrument to assess how well or poorly EDs meet the needs of patients with psychiatric disabilities. There are several reasons for this. First, patients with psychiatric disabilities constitute a very small proportion of the case load in most EDs. In any given hospital ED, psychiatric patients may constitute 3–10% of the case load; depending on the source, the national average has been estimated as between 3 and 5%. However, there is no widely accepted evaluation instrument in use even among psychiatric emergency services, where people with psychiatric disabilities are the only patients treated by the service.

Second, it is difficult to develop evaluation instruments in a context where many standards of assessment and care are themselves uncertain. Although using outcome measures would avoid this particular problem, and outcome measures are generally considered superior to process measures, judging the quality of care for psychiatric patients in EDs based on outcome is universally agreed to present "a formidable task."[4] This is true from a measurement and a causality perspective. Many of the criteria for successful treatment of psychiatric crises are highly subjective and would require follow up to determine definitively. It is hard to measure reduced anxiety, agitation, or suicidality in the context of a busy ED. Unless an ED is in a small community or works with community providers it cannot get the kind of follow-up information necessary to measure successful outcomes. Simply not seeing a patient again does not indicate successful treatment; it may, for example, indicate suicide. Causality is difficult to impute: it is more difficult to conclude that a suicidal patient would have killed himself but for the intervention of the ED than to understand that ED intervention in a case of a heart attack made the difference between life and death. This is especially true if a longer perspective is taken in judging success in ED interventions. Involuntary inpatient hospitalization of an apparently suicidal patient may be "successful" at preventing immediate suicide but, as Doctors Dawson and MacMillan suggest, leave the patient so traumatized and untrusting as to increase the overall chance that the individual will commit suicide later on.[5]

One way of measuring outcome might be to measure patient satisfaction, but again, patient satisfaction in the context of psychiatric crises may not, in the first instance, seem to necessarily equate with quality care: a patient may disagree with a clearly warranted decision to involuntarily detain and be highly dissatisfied as a result. Or a patient who wants an inpatient admission may disagree with an appropriate decision to refer to outpatient treatment.

Third, there is the question of what is practically possible. Chart audits, the most common and inexpensive means of quality assurance, tend to have low content validity and provide inadequate documentation to readily examine many quality-related issues. However, as one author pointed out, chart audits performed during the patient's stay and within 24 hours thereafter have a much more marked impact on performance.[6] Checklists may be useful[7] in many ways, but they cannot measure either patient satisfaction or outcome.

However, there is a crucial need for a specific instrument to measure quality of care to people in psychiatric crises, or at the very least to exclude the care of patients in psychiatric crisis from standard measures of successful EDs. The reason for this is that many of the traditional criteria used to determine whether an ED is successful operate *against* the delivery of high quality care to people in psychiatric crisis, or else are not readily transferable to the unique medico-legal context of psychiatric crisis. This places well-intentioned professionals in the ED in a difficult, if not intolerable, bind.

Speedy Disposition Is Not Necessarily a Measure of Quality ED Care in Psychiatric Crisis

In many cases, ED staff members feel pressure to make dispositional decisions when delay might mean the difference between discharge home and inpatient hospitalization, perhaps at a state institution far from home and the person's community supports. For medical patients, inpatient hospitalization is often desired and does not carry a burden of stigma. For psychiatric patients, even a brief record of inpatient hospitalization may make it more difficult to obtain certain kinds of employment or maintain custody of their children.

But a speedy disposition, regardless of its quality, is a highly rewarded outcome, even if staff members believe that it will simply result in the return of the patient in a few days or weeks. The percentage of "boarding" patients is a statistic that characterizes a flawed ED. The solution to this—a small number of crisis beds available to ED staff—has been implemented in many places and is discussed below. But if the ED does not have crisis beds at its disposal, then it may make unwise discharge or clinically inappropriate admissions decisions, simply to move the patient out of the ED.

The Number of Patients Who Leave without Being Seen Is Not Necessarily a Measure of Quality Emergency Department Care for Psychiatric Crises

Emergency departments are often evaluated negatively based on the number of patients who leave without seeing a doctor. This measurement assumes the freedom of the patient to make that decision and leave. Because EDs have the ability to hold psychiatric patients against their will, however, any measure of how many patients left without receiving assessment or care will not make much sense in the psychiatric arena. Generally, such patient departures signal excessive delays. But delays can and do exist with psychiatric patients who are not free to vote with their feet. Furthermore, the pressure created by this particular benchmark may create an incentive to involuntarily detain patients who might not otherwise qualify under the state statute.

Recidivism Is Not Necessarily a Measure of Quality Emergency Department Care in a Psychiatric Crisis

Another example of a criterion used to negatively evaluate EDs is recidivism, if a discharged patient returns to seek care within a few days after discharge. In the case of psychiatric patients, voluntary return to the ED may be an extremely positive sign that the individual recognizes the need for assistance and takes the responsibility to seek it. Or, it may have nothing to do with the quality of ED treatment and everything to do with events in the individual's life. Finally, an individual's return to the ED may or may not be voluntary, and the number of social problems that are solved by returning an individual to the ED may not be a reflection on the quality of care he or she received.

Compliance with Aftercare Is Not Necessarily a Measure of Quality Emergency Department Care in a Psychiatric Crisis

Patient compliance with aftercare is another sign that is often used to measure the success of ED treatment. For psychiatric patients, as for a number of other groups of patients, it is not clear whether this criterion fairly measures the performance of the ED. Some patients are poor, have transportation difficulties, or cannot follow up with aftercare; others choose not to do so for a variety of reasons, including fear that exposure to the mental health system may lead to loss of their children or loss of employment. Especially for patients brought involuntarily to the ED in the first place, follow up with aftercare is not a fair measure of the quality of services provided in the ED.

Other Commonly Used Criteria of Quality Care in Emergency Departments Do Not Apply to Psychiatric Treatment

Finally, some commonly used criteria to evaluate medical or ED success, such as patient mortality, are more complicated in the case of people in psychiatric crisis. Mortality after arriving at the ED is rare—in a study of 2231 visits to the ED for psychiatric reasons, only one patient died after arriving at the hospital.[8] Mortality after discharge may be difficult to measure, and clear linkage to poor care in the ED is not as clear as in the case of many medical conditions. Some kinds of mortality—suicide immediately after discharge—may measure failure of ED treatment, but after some period, there may be little nexus between ED treatment for psychiatric conditions and mortality, even suicide.

What Are Appropriate Indices of Successful Emergency Department Treatment of Psychiatric Crisis?

Objective criteria do exist to at least partially determine whether EDs are adequately responding to the needs of patients in psychiatric crisis. As noted earlier, adequate medical examinations and cognitive evaluations are crucial.

The American Psychiatric Association (APA) Task Force on Psychiatric Emergency Services developed a series of standards to apply to different settings, from hospital-based emergency services to mobile psychiatric services. These include standards for assessment, treatment planning, medication use and safety, seclusion and restraint, aftercare, space and equipment, staffing, medical records, leadership, quality improvement, and ethics and patients' rights.[9]

The Center for Public Representation has developed a set of standards for hospital-based emergency services that are, for the most part, complementary to the standards of the APA. They provide more detail in the area of patient treatment and patient rights, including standards in the areas of informed consent, seclusion, restraint, security guards, advance directives, accompaniment, maximum hours of detention, forced disrobing, medical assessment, medical clearance, crisis plans, and trauma-informed treatment. These standards can be found in appendix A.

It would be relatively easy to use a combination of the APA and the Center for Public Representation standards to develop an instrument that recorded the occurrence of certain objective factors on which consensus could be developed. For example, reducing the use of seclusion and restraint has been identified as a priority by the Center for Medicare and Medicaid Services and the Joint Commission on Accreditation of Health Care Organizations (JCAHO), and standards relating to the use of seclusion and restraint appear in the APA and the Center for Public Representation standards, as well as in other articles regarding measuring quality in psychiatric emergency services.[10] One measure of the quality of an ED might be continuous progress in reducing the use of seclusion and restraint (it would be unfair to set specific targets because different hospitals deal with very different kinds of patients).

Another measure might be patient satisfaction. Although the role of patient satisfaction is, as mentioned above, a difficult one to factor into the measurement of the success of an ED in treating people in psychiatric crisis, both the APA task force and the Center for Public Representation underscore the significance of measuring patient satisfaction and the delicacy of the process required to do so. The APA task force provides that

> There is a process for measuring patient satisfaction. This process includes an opportunity to obtain detailed information about patient concerns that is gathered in such a way that patients do not experience concern about being honest (e.g., interviews done by former mental health patients, anonymous surveys that are mailed back).[11]

Results from surveys conducted by the Center for Public Representation and the State of Connecticut Office of Protection and Advocacy for Persons with Disabilities suggest that measures of patient satisfaction could be extremely useful and that concerns about patient dissatisfaction related to involuntary detention are exaggerated. Complaints about poor care in EDs centered on disrespectful treatment, hostility, or unprofessional attitudes toward psychiatric patients, and refusal to take medical complaints seriously, while praise of EDs centered around respectful treatment and empathy displayed by staff. Providing patients with a mechanism for feedback, either through surveys or through a patient ombudsman, could be an important way to measure treatment in the ED, and to improve it in ways that would cost little and make an enormous difference.

Develop Alternatives to Traditional Emergency Departments

The unnecessary use of EDs is expensive and often unsatisfying for people with psychiatric disabilities. It comes about because police know about EDs and because EDs cannot turn anyone away, while most other mental health service providers are not open at night and on weekends. In addition, many less expensive alternatives to emergency room treatment are not reimbursable, while, ironically, ED treatment (sometimes even in the case of non-emergencies) usually is reimbursable, if the patient has insurance. Everyone—from patients to the EDs to insurance companies to social service agencies—is eager to prevent the use of EDs for psychiatric crises and to create alternatives that would be more helpful to people in psychiatric crisis.

Financing Issues Related to Alternatives
to Traditional Emergency Room Care

There is clearly a need to develop alternatives to traditional emergency room services for people in psychiatric crisis. Alternatives are preferable to most people with psychiatric diagnoses,[12] are less costly, and appear to be more effective (although "effectiveness" may be hard to accurately measure when it consists of preventing visits to emergency rooms or admissions to inpatient units).

In order for alternatives, such as family-based crisis homes or crisis hostels, to be feasible, they must be more broadly reimbursable than they are now. Currently, state and county mental health systems and private foundations bear the lion's share of funding for alternatives to emergency room treatment. Given the huge costs associated with emergency room care, this is not an effective utilization of social resources. Some entities have utilized various options available under Medicaid to bill for services provided by these alternative settings. Medicaid permits billing for crisis services or rehabilitation services. However, in order to receive Medicaid reimbursement, the alternative setting must be professionally staffed—a feature that increases costs and that some self-help groups strive to avoid.

Managed care organizations that negotiate capitated cost contracts with states have more flexibility in service delivery and can create effective crisis alternatives. The La Junta, Colorado, model discussed below was developed by Value Options pursuant to a contract with the State of Colorado. States negotiating contracts with managed care organizations for acute and crisis care should include a number of alternative models for crisis care.

Limitations on Alternatives to Emergency Department Care

One difficulty with these alternatives is that they do not include the medical examinations performed in the emergency room, which may reveal medical causes for the psychiatric distress. Thus, in some cases, ED alternatives may be used to ensure speedy dispositions following medical clearance at an ED rather than diversion from an ED.

In addition, alternative facilities cannot and should not be used for purposes of detoxification. Some patients are so intoxicated that they need to have immediate medical availability and monitoring services. Therefore, the alternatives discussed below cannot meet the needs of people with psychiatric disabilities who present to emergency rooms in a state of extreme intoxication.

Finally, in order for alternatives to be used to the maximum extent, police will have to be alerted to their existence and persuaded to take people there rather than to emergency rooms. This means, as a practical matter, that the location of these alternative settings needs to be determined in part with the convenience of police in mind. This consideration is absolutely key; in a presentation regarding development of emergency room alternatives in Seattle, the architects of the crisis triage unit emphasized the importance of ensuring that arrangements diminished rather than increased the work of the police.[13]

Although there are literally thousands of community residential alternatives to traditional hospitals and institutions in the United States today, and hundreds of peer-run or innovative alternatives to traditional community mental health services, many, if not most, of these programs rely on traditional crisis services—usually the ED—when their clients experience psychiatric crises. Simply stated, there is little incentive for individual providers to develop tools to help people in their most difficult times when a separately funded entity is already mandated to do so, no matter how much overall social benefit would be derived from the development of such alternatives.

As noted above, alternatives to the use of EDs by people in psychiatric crisis come in two basic forms: prevention/diversion, or programs that try to handle or prevent psychiatric crises without visits to the ED; and dispositional alternatives, which essentially use the ED as a routing system for diversion to more specialized psychiatric crisis services, freeing up needed ED beds. A well functioning community mental health system will have a number of safety nets in place to assist people in psychiatric crisis; the better they function, the fewer visits to the ED.

Prevention/Diversion

Hot Lines/Warm Lines

A hot line is a telephone number that can be used by people in crisis, often people who are suicidal. Hot lines are established and funded by federal,[14] state, county, and private organizations, and have different policies. For example, some hot lines limit the length of calls to 10 minutes. Despite many people's impressions to the contrary, hot lines are not obliged to maintain confidentiality. Many hot lines call either mobile crisis units or the police, often without telling the individual, who is then surprised when police or ambulances show up at the door, often with lights flashing. Hot lines also often operate in conjunction with mobile crisis teams, dispatching teams when it is judged that the caller needs in-person intervention. Sometimes the person is informed that the mobile crisis team is coming and sometimes not.

The experience of the State of Maine reflects both the successes and failures of hot lines. The state subcontracted with an experienced non-profit organization to establish a hot line to serve a specific population of psychiatric clients who had suffered early childhood physical and sexual abuse.

The hot line was available 24 hours a day, seven days a week. Anecdotal evidence suggested that its availability lowered rates of hospitalization and visits to the ED, but no research has been done to validate the claim.[15] This hotline was funded entirely by state funds.

However, the use of the toll-free "crisis line" established by Mainecare (Maine's Medicaid system) has been less successful, and the lack of success is related to Medicaid funding requirements. When an individual calls this crisis line, he or she is connected to a crisis team in the area, and the crisis worker makes a decision whether to call the police or send in the mobile crisis team. In order to bill Mainecare, the crisis worker must make a "provisional" diagnosis under the *Diagnostic and Statistical Manual of Mental Disorders*. Under Maine law, only the highest level of social work licensure, or psychologists, psychiatric nurses, and psychiatrists are allowed to make such diagnoses. Unfortunately, because of cost concerns, the crisis workers need not be licensed, or even be high school graduates.[16] Many calls to the crisis line in Maine are simply referred to the police, a fact unknown to most callers.

"Warm" lines are specifically designated as "pre-crisis" telephone availability, intended to provide support and avert crisis. Unlike hot lines, warm lines often do not limit the time a caller can take and are more typically operated by peers—people who have experience with many of the problems of the callers. Warm lines generally are open seven days week, but not on a 24-hour basis. They are usually staffed after regular business hours, from early to late evening.

Warm lines tend to remove pressure from hot lines by creating capacity to handle non-emergency calls. According to Professor Christopher Pudlinski, who has studied warm lines and their operation for over 15 years, they typically cater to a small group of frequent callers, and, as opposed to hot lines, often result in a continuing and therapeutic relationship between the caller and the peer counselor. These services cost very little compared to the cost of EDs: start-up costs for a warm line can be as little as $7500–8000 per year (when space and the phone line is provided in a local peer clubhouse or community mental health center). However, funding for warm lines is problematic; often groups receive initial start-up grants of up to $25,000 from federal, state, or local governments and then close down after the grant period of two to three years expires.

Mobile Crisis Teams

Mobile crisis teams take many forms, but their primary mission is basically the same. Almost all such teams provide crisis intervention services for those experiencing extreme emotional distress or a severe mental health crisis in their own home or in a non-hospital environment. While the service may be limited to crisis intervention and counseling, sometimes a package of services is offered including on-site assessments, linkage and referral, in-patient or out-patient care arrangements, and crisis follow-up. Often the teams are associated with and dispatched through a crisis "hotline" service that is available around the clock, or perhaps just during peak crisis times (e.g., nights and/or weekends). The hallmark of mobile crisis teams, unlike assertive community treatment teams, is that they respond to crisis, rather than having an ongoing relationship with the client.

Mobile crisis services may be part of a larger state or private non-profit mental health center, or simply a stand-alone agency providing contracted services. Staff members generally are state licensed mental health professionals or the equivalent. Fees for mobile crisis services range from free or nominal (e.g., $35) to more significant amounts that are cost based and typically billed to private or state health care insurers. However, most mobile services, regardless of billing practices, will not refuse to assist a person in crisis who does not have the ability to pay for the service.

A key feature that distinguishes mobile crisis services is how potential clients gain access to the service. In some cases clients must go to the ED in order to access mobile crisis teams. This is generally the case if the mobile crisis service requires a medical screening to be completed before conducting a mental health screening. Still others require referrals from either an ED or from the police as a safety precaution. Mobile services that respond directly to individual requests may be more at risk, but their service is most likely to divert potential ED patients. Below two mobile crisis services are discussed to illustrate differences.

Many states and counties have mobile crisis teams. In California mobile crisis services are mandated by state law. Some mobile crisis teams essentially limit their work to evaluation to determine whether an individual should be hospitalized, rather than providing treatment or a continuing relationship with the client. For example, the Department of Alcohol, Drug, and Mental Health Services in Yolo County, California, has contracted with a private non-profit called Suicide Prevention and Crisis Services (SPCS). For 18 years SPCS, based in Davis, California, has staffed a crisis hotline and provided mobile crisis services to a county population of about 200,000. The mobile team, all licensed mental health professionals, is usually called by the police or the hospital ED. The team, whose primary purpose is to conduct psychiatric evaluations for either voluntary or involuntary hospitalizations, responds to 75–95 calls each month during peak crisis times (nights and weekends). Services are billed to private insurers or Medi-Cal, unless the client is indigent with no means of payment.

Henderson Mental Health Center (HMHC) is a private non-profit that has served Broward County, Florida, for nearly 52 years. The center has 11 locations in and around Ft. Lauderdale and offers services every hour of the day every day of the year. Henderson Mental Health Center's goal is to provide immediate intervention for people in psychiatric crises to stabilize acute situations and prevent costly hospitalizations. Clients typically access the mobile response team, all licensed mental health professionals, via a self-referral telephone request and screening process. No prior medical screening is required and police may or may not be involved. Services are available on a sliding fee basis and Medicare, Medicaid, and private insurance are accepted. In contrast to the Yolo County mobile service team, described above, HMHC does not limit its mobile community outreach services to hospital commitment evaluations. Nor does it rely on EDs for client referrals. Henderson Mental Health Centers offer a full range of psychiatric services that are expressly designed to reduce costly hospitalizations.

Research on the effectiveness of mobile crisis teams is sparse,[17] and has yielded conflicting results. One study that compared state hospital admissions for counties with and without mobile crisis teams in Massachusetts, controlling for a number of different variables that might affect hospital admission, did not show any difference in admissions.[18] Another study showed a drastic decrease in hospital admissions after the introduction of a mobile crisis team—a trend that was reversed when the psychiatrist on the team left.[19] The authors hypothesize that the psychiatrist's ability to prescribe and administer medications on the spot may have made the difference in reducing hospital admissions.

Community Treatment Teams

Although programs based on the Assertive Community Treatment (ACT) model have a mobile component, their mission and mode of operation are quite different from the mobile crisis teams. ACT teams are by definition available 24 hours a day. Community treatment teams, such as the one started about two years ago by the Allegheny County Bureau of Mental Health, which services the greater Pittsburgh, Pennsylvania, area, are organized to offer consumers treatment and case management services in the community, typically at their residence, on an ongoing basis, not solely in times of crisis. Allegheny County has four such teams, and each team covers about 60 consumers. Each team has up to 10 staff members that collectively offer a diverse skill mix, including for example psychiatrists, psychiatric nurses, psychologists, case workers, and representatives from the bureau's peer network. Although the program is too new to assess with hard data, qualitatively it appears that the program is effective in minimizing the need for emergency visits to area hospitals by consumers in the program.

Crisis Residential Services

CRISIS HOSTELS.   Southeast Mental Health Services in La Junta, Colorado, has established crisis services based on the recovery model. Changes to the traditional model of mental health services include the establishment of a 24-hour/seven-day crisis hostel, with no predetermined threshold of psychiatric or emotional distress required. Only felons, active substance abusers, and those requiring medical care are screened out. This program has won awards for its superior effectiveness, both from the point of view of the consumer and for lowered costs. Consumers who have the ability to pay are only charged about $13 per day. Those covered by Medicaid stay free, as their costs are covered by state (Medicaid) capitation payments. Typical stays run the gamut, including short stays, such as a "drop-in" or an overnight, or longer multiple-night (3–7 days) visits. The duration is tied to the consumer's individual needs and circumstances.

The facility, which is actually attached to the mental health center, has 11 beds. It was originally a long-term care facility, but was converted about three years ago. The staff, which covers the three traditional eight-hour shifts, is comprised of a mix of peers and others who receive on the job training. Commonly, consumers are referred to the hostel through the center's crisis hotline services. The center provides pick-up services, which are often prearranged through the police or hospital EDs. This service is more significant than it may seem, since the center covers six rural counties in Southeast Colorado spanning nearly 200 miles.

Outcomes have improved since the establishment of the crisis hostel, among other recovery-based reforms in the rural Colorado mental health system. These outcomes are measured in terms of client satisfaction, community integration, full-time employment or education, and reduction in symptoms.

FAMILY-BASED CRISIS HOME. The private non-profit mental health center in Wisconsin's Dane County has successfully operated a Crisis Home Program, based on a family care model, for over 15 years. The program serves an urban/suburban area with about 450,000 residents. Within that community, 13 families with spare bedrooms offer alternatives to hospitalization for psychiatric clients experiencing a crisis. The clients, who are called "guests" and treated as such, stay on average two to three days per visit. The host families receive intensive training and their houses are licensed as adult family homes. The cost of stay in a crisis home is $100 a night, compared to a $700 cost for a night at the hospital. The program is funded by up-front funding from Dane County. However, any monies recovered by billing Medicaid are returned to the county.

Since clients effectively become part of the family, personal connections are often made: one guest who stayed with a family during a crisis period came back to help install a computer and others stay in touch with their host families. Because of this program, hundreds of people each year are able to stay in the community and avoid the expense, trauma, and stigma of hospitalization.

An early study of a similar family crisis home program showed that 80% of patients considered for inpatient treatment were successfully diverted to the program at considerable savings.[20] Eligible patients did not have a history of violence toward others, arson, or theft and were judged capable of functioning in an open psychiatric unit. Patient satisfaction with the program was very high (94%) and over three-quarters thought that the stay helped them avoid hospitalization.[21] In addition, staff and patients alike reported significant improvement in the patients' clinical functioning.[22]

CRISIS APARTMENTS. Transitional Resources (TR), a non-profit provider of mental health services, has served the Puget Sound area in and around Seattle, Washington, for nearly 25 years. Their mission is to provide short-term residential crisis care to divert individuals from unneeded psychiatric hospitalization. One approach to accomplish the mission involves short-term (three to five days) extensive 24-hour supervision and support in a "crisis apartment" for individuals who can be stabilized in an unlocked setting. Exclusionary criteria include alcohol/drug intoxication, assaultiveness, and the need for significant medical management. The "guest bed" is in one of a collection of studio apartments that are typically utilized for residential clients, most of whom are former state hospital patients. Consumers participate in the home-like milieu; receive one-on-one support from mental health professionals, including medication monitoring; participate in treatment groups; assist in household chores; and are linked to necessary support services after discharge.

Although TR's crisis apartment is a hospital diversion program, most of their clients, nonetheless, are referred by hospital EDs following a medical screening. That clients typically are processed through an emergency ED is not a TR program requirement. Rather, TR considers ED referrals a consequence of mental health care funding streams, which currently favor hospitals, including EDs. Direct client access to TR's crisis apartment program would necessarily require future changes to divert the funding stream from hospitals into community-based diversion programs.

SHORT-TERM RESIDENTIAL TREATMENT PROGRAMS. A number of communities have successfully created short-term residential treatment programs as alternatives to inpatient hospitalization. These programs also reduce reliance on EDs for people in acute psychiatric crisis.

One program, Short-Term Acute Residential Treatment (START) in San Diego, California, has six residential facilities with a total of 77 beds.[23] It serves 3000 adults annually (about half of the voluntary, public acute care services in San Diego County). The "core principles of the program are based on psychiatric rehabilitation."[24] Although the program accepts acutely suicidal and/or psychotic clients, the facilities use neither locks nor restraints. A carefully designed research project reflected that the clients admitted to the residential programs were similar in degree of disturbance and social functioning to the clients admitted to psychiatric hospitals, and that they showed similar levels of improvement at discharge and comparable satisfaction with the programs. The short-term residential treatment programs, however, operated at a cost of $186 per person per day in 1998, while the hospital programs cost $395 per person per day.

PEER-OPERATED HOSPITAL DIVERSION HOUSE.   The Power to Enable and Organize the Psychiatrically Labeled (PEOPLe), Inc., in Poughkeepsie, New York, provides a unique residential program called Rose House for consumers who may not be in acute crisis, but nonetheless need a safe environment to work through difficult emotional situations. Rose House serves residents of Ulster and Orange Counties. The program was initially developed as a diversion from a hospital ED or in-patient care. It differs from the residential treatment program described above in that the staff members are essentially peer advocates, since all have had personal experience with mental health treatment or coping issues. In addition, the acuity of residents may not be as high as those in some of the residential treatment programs described above. The length of stay is shorter, and there are fewer beds at the house. The program philosophy differs from the crisis residential programs described above in that it explicitly does not focus on mental health treatment provided by professionals.

Program offerings include Wellness Recovery Action Plan (WRAP) education, support groups, self-help books and CDs, as well as professional art equipment, musical instruments, and hobby and craft items. These are offered for the purpose of engaging people in enjoyable activities rather than giving them time to become self-absorbed in crisis behavior or thoughts. There are six staff members, including a mix of full- and part-time employees who provide care 24 hours each day and seven days a week. The program is funded completely by the State of New York.

Consumer visits, which typically average five days, are funded by the state and free to the consumers. The house has four beds, and plenty of personal amenities are provided. The cost of the program, as of 2005, is approximately $300 per person per day, compared to hospitalization, which averages $1100 per person per day. Consumers are either self-referred or they are directed to the house by area mental health providers. The program director indicated that considerable effort is expended within the community to communicate the program as an alternative to hospital care. Since opening in 2001, the program has shown an 85% success rate, with success defined as avoiding hospitalization in the year following use of the program. Participants in the program are followed up at intervals of one, three, and six months and one year. The program is currently raising funds to purchase another house and replicate the Rose House model in Dutchess County.

Walk-In Crisis Services

COMMUNITY MENTAL HEALTH CENTER.   El Paso Community Mental Health and Mental Retardation Center, a state-funded facility, provides mental health and mental retardation services for El Paso County, Texas. Crisis services, available 24 hours every day, include a walk-in program, telephone counseling, and crisis intervention. Walk-in clients who are experiencing emotional distress or a severe mental health crisis receive immediate face-to-face counseling and intervention. Services may include brief intervention, crisis counseling and support, and/or referral for individual counseling or long-term treatment. The center's staff includes master's level qualified mental health professionals. If needed, a psychiatrist is also available to administer medications or provide psychiatric intervention. While a mix of clients is served during the day (8 AM to 3 PM), only emergency assessments and evaluations are conducted after 3 PM. Since clients are mostly self-referred, the walk-in service is generally not in addition to, but rather in place of, a visit to the hospital ED.

PEER CENTERS. Allegheny County's Bureau of Mental Health Services offers an extensive array of mental health services in the greater Pittsburgh, Pennsylvania, area, which includes roughly 1.2 million people. One of these services is a Peer Support and Advocacy Network. Through the network, adults with mental illness help each other with support, assistance, and socialization.

Allegheny County is divided into nine "bases," or geographic service areas, all or most of which have peer- or consumer-operated drop-in centers. While these centers have professional staff present, the level of staffing is not such that the centers would be considered crisis centers. Rather, the drop-in centers primarily offer peer-to peer-support and advocacy services. Consumers can avail themselves of these services either through the drop-in centers or by telephone. In both cases, they interact with and receive assistance from peers who have direct experience with mental health issues.

Dispositional Alternatives

Some hospitals have developed a hybrid emergency/inpatient psychiatric unit, either within or adjacent to the hospital, where people with acute mental health (and often substance abuse) problems can receive treatment. The treatment period is longer than an emergency room stay but shorter than an inpatient stay. These units go by different names, but their purpose is to triage people with psychiatric disabilities or substance abuse from other ED patients, and give them short-term acute treatment in order to facilitate discharge rather than a longer-term admission to an inpatient psychiatric unit.

The anthropologist Lorna Rhodes studied one such nine-bed unit, and starkly portrayed the difficulties associated with working "in an environment of diminished resources and uncertain community" where staff "found themselves at the intersection of the urgent and often conflicting needs of the patients, the patients' families, the hospital, and the city."[25] In other words, she found the same problems that plague ordinary emergency rooms:

lack of suitable discharge options, unwillingness of reimbursing agencies to pay for care, and patients with complex medical and psychosocial problems. The patients on the acute psychiatric unit she describes have very different situations and problems, "but they share one characteristic: no one wants them."[26]

This problem is hardly unique to the acute psychiatric unit in Lorna Rhodes' study. Dr. Robert Okin has pioneered another such unit with better results in San Francisco, California, where the Department of Public Health has paid for housing at five residential hotels and one low-maintenance nursing facility.[27] The housing costs about $140 a night, compared with $731 a night in a San Francisco General acute care ward. This program has received a number of awards and has reduced repeat usage of San Francisco General's emergency room by certain groups of patients.

A variation of the acute short-term in-patient unit is a relatively new Mississippi acute partial hospital program. This program, like the short-term in-patient program, is designed to avoid long-term hospitalizations, but it relies on a heavy outpatient component. Patients are brought each day to an outpatient clinic for no more than 30 days. The clients receive extensive treatment in a highly structured environment. There is a family therapy component as well, since the patients return home at the end of each day. The program is considered appropriate for patients in the early phase of a potentially chronic mental health condition. Early intervention may preclude repeated visits to the ED and/or inpatient services.

Although there is an enormous need to expand the field of crisis alternatives to save money and ensure more appropriate treatment of people in psychiatric crisis, there will always be a place for the traditional ED for a number of reasons. First, prevention/diversion programs generally have a number of eligibility restrictions—the person must seek assistance voluntarily, or not be intoxicated—which, while understandable, still leave traditional EDs to deal with involuntary or intoxicated patients. Second, as emergency psychiatrists point out repeatedly, medical problems mask as, or co-occur with, or exacerbate psychiatric crises often enough that crisis alternatives can never fully replace traditional EDs. Prevention/diversion crisis alternatives are difficult to fund, in part because it is difficult to research their effectiveness (although no attempt has been made to research the effectiveness of an ED as compared to the alternative). Even the strongest advocates of community mental health services and alternatives recognize that there will always be a role for the ED in treating people with psychiatric disabilities. The late Dr. Loren Mosher, a respected innovator in community mental health, depicted the proper role of the ED as

> backup for community crisis intervention teams when they are
> uncertain of the proper disposition for a person seen in the community or the clinic. The emergency department can provide experienced consultants, rapid medical diagnostic tests (e.g., for

drugs), a longer period in which to evaluate the patient, and time to test whether or not a positive response will occur to removal from the site of the original crisis. To allow this we recommend that there be one or two crisis beds, available for up to 48 hours, in the emergency room. Basically, the emergency room should serve as a second triage point (after initial triage by the community team) for a selected subset of difficult cases.[28]

However, there is room for argument that the community mental health service providers, who know their own clients better than ED staff, should receive the training necessary to help the "difficult cases," and that only when medical etiology is suspected or intoxication is acute would it be appropriate for experienced community mental health providers to resort to the ED. And if community mental health was indeed available 24 hours a day, seven days a week, EDs would very likely not receive as many voluntary visits from people in psychiatric crisis.

Existing Emergency Department Practices Toward People with Psychiatric Disabilities Can Improve

Principles to Guide Emergency Departments in Improving Treatment of People with Psychiatric Disabilities

Although the community mental health system needs to be strengthened, and alternatives to EDs added, if the most meaningful change is to come about, there are still a number of changes that EDs can make on their own. These will, like the work of Baystate, make an enormous difference to individuals in psychiatric crisis.

The Center for Public Representation, working with a national board of experts in mental health, ED, licensing, legal issues, and managed care, has developed specific sets of findings and recommendations for ED improvement, as well as recommended standards for adoption by EDs. These recommendations were developed pursuant to a statement of four core values that EDs should strive for in their treatment of people with psychiatric disabilities:

1. Emergency department care of people with psychiatric disabilities should be patient-centered, that is "care that is respectful of and responsive to individual patient preferences, needs, and values and ensuring that patient values guide all clinical decisions."[29] Patient-centered care is an independent value, in and of itself.[30] Patient-centered care includes consciousness of and respect for cultural differences.

2. Emergency department care of people with psychiatric disabilities should seek to minimize coercion, increase choice, and reduce or eliminate the use of force.

3. Emergency department care of people with psychiatric disabilities

should be individualized and enhance a patient's perception of safety. Emergency departments should not assume that interventions intended to ensure patient safety enhance either patients' perceptions of safety or actual safety.

4. Emergency department treatment of people with psychiatric disabilities should respect a person's dignity, including attention to basic needs, such as food, hydration, and hygiene.

The first 12 findings and recommendations are summarized here and reproduced in full at appendix A. Obviously, the principles described above overlap in practice. Recommendations relating to patient-centered care may also involve treating a patient with dignity and respect and involving a patient in choices about his or her care. Thus, grouping individual recommendations under any given principle is arbitrary, to some extent. Nevertheless, the recommendations fit well under these four general categories.

Recommendations Relating to Patient-Centered Care

INAPPROPRIATE ASSESSMENT AND TREATMENT OF MEDICAL COMPLAINTS. One of the most common concerns voiced by people with psychiatric disabilities who responded to surveys about their experiences in EDs was that a psychiatric diagnosis or report that they took psychotropic medications predisposed ED staff to disbelieve or minimize medical complaints. Many recounted stories that, if true, would constitute bad medical practice, violations of the Emergency Medical Treatment and Active Labor Act, violations of the anti-discrimination provisions of the Americans with Disabilities Act (ADA), or all three. Both the breadth of the problem—the entire range of medical complaints suffered by people with psychiatric disabilities—and the depth of its source, stigma and the tendency to discredit or disbelieve people with psychiatric disabilities, make this problem difficult to remedy. Recommendations are made that encompass quality assurance/risk management chart review and increased staff training.

ACCOMPANIMENT. Many EDs already encourage friends or family to accompany a person to an assessment room, but some EDs require family to remain in the waiting area. Several informants for this book who requested anonymity reported that the reason for this practice was that facilities that restrain or lock a psychiatric patient into the assessment room do not wish to do so in the presence of family members or friends. The presence of another person may assist in keeping a person calm, and a person who serves as an intermediary between ED staff and the individual in psychiatric crisis may be invaluable. In addition, the person can provide collateral information or confirmation if necessary, thus assisting in assessments. The recommendations both recognize the need to ensure that the individual desires accompaniment (many people are brought to hospitals by people with whom they are actively in conflict) and that hospitals may need to limit the number of persons who accompany the individual for reasons of safety and facility management.

MEDICAL CLEARANCE. An issue that is frequently raised by ED professionals is the requirement by many inpatient psychiatric settings of excessive (from the ED perspective) testing as part of the medical clearance process. Individuals with psychiatric disabilities report that their refusals of blood tests or toxicology tests are not accepted by ED staff members, who need the results of such tests to accomplish transfers, and sometimes results in the use of force, including forced catheterizations. The recommendations conclude that there is simply no such thing as standard medical clearance that applies equally to all patients—old or young, strangers or well known to the staff, intoxicated or sober—but that there are certain very basic assessments well recognized by all: vital signs, medical history, visual examination, and mental status exam. Beyond that, the recommendations suggest that toxicology screening be considered and that professionals document their reasons to either order or forego a test.

ADVANCE DIRECTIVES. All EDs understand the concept of a "do not resuscitate" order or "DNR." By contrast, while many ED staff have heard of advance directives, they are not entirely clear about their application to ED situations, especially in the case of people with psychiatric disabilities. The recommendations reiterate that people with psychiatric disabilities are presumed competent to execute advance directives, and that hospitals must inquire about whether an individual has an advance directive or health care proxy.

An advance directive generally has a broader scope than a DNR, which concerns only end-of-life decision making. Health care proxies and advance directives, on the other hand, relate to the spectrum of health care treatment, and take effect if an individual is deemed incompetent to make his or her own health care decisions. Many psychiatric advance directives concern psychiatric treatment, either expressing the competent individual's preference for treatment even in the face of incompetent refusal (a so-called "Ulysses contract") or competently refusing certain kinds of treatment, e.g., electroconvulsive therapy[31] or specific psychotropic drugs.[32] Advance directives by people with psychiatric disabilities have been upheld by the courts.[33] When Vermont passed legislation limiting the advance directives of psychiatric patients under commitment orders, this attempt was struck down by the federal courts as discrimination on the basis of psychiatric disability in violation of the ADA.[34]

Advance directives specifically for people with psychiatric disabilities are readily available[35] and may become more widely used in the future. The law already requires EDs to determine whether an individual has an advance directive (see the section on Patient Self-Determination Act above, at pp. 100–101). If, at the time of an ED visit, an individual is deemed incompetent, and the basis of that judgment is carefully documented, the individual's advance directive should be respected, and attempts should be made to immediately contact the designated health care proxy.

CRISIS PLANS.   Crisis plans, unlike advance directives, are primarily developed by people with psychiatric disabilities to assist them and those who care for them when they are in crisis. An advance directive may be a component of a crisis plan. Social workers and staff who care for people with psychiatric disabilities in EDs should be aware of crisis plans. Some well known models of recovery plans, such as the WRAP, contain sections dealing with both crisis and post-crisis planning. Other treatment models such as dialectical behavior therapy (DBT) also rely on developing crisis plans.

The WRAP crisis plan includes classic components of an advance directive and health care proxy (naming preferred and unacceptable medications and treatments) but also helpful supplements (explaining why the medications and treatments are preferred or unacceptable) and more concrete approaches to managing the individual's life during a crisis ("things I need others to do for me and who I want to do it"). Information that would be particularly helpful for ED staff in a crisis plan includes "home/community care/respite options," as well as an "information for the physician" sheet, which can be filled out by the patient in writing or orally and includes a checklist of symptoms (changes in appetite, sleep patterns, ability to concentrate, recent headaches, numbness, coordination changes, stressful life events, etc.). The crisis plan and information for the physician are useful guides and can be downloaded online at www.mentalhealthrecovery.com/pdfs/crisisplan.pdf.

If a patient has such a plan, the patient should be asked whether it should be in his or her ED record; if the patient does not have such a plan, ED staff should be able to provide the patient with information about such plans and about any peer groups in the area as part of his or her referral.

Recommendations Relating to Decreasing the Use of Force and Coercion and Enhancing Choice

RESTRAINT AND SECLUSION.   Emergency departments' position on the use of restraint and seclusion is similar to the position of psychiatric hospitals a decade ago: the use is regrettable but inevitable, caused entirely by the patient, whose symptoms lead to behavior that is dangerous and out of control. This perspective has radically shifted at the hospital level in the last 10 years, with a number of psychiatric hospitals phasing out the use of restraint and seclusion entirely. The Commonwealth of Pennsylvania, which led the way in reduction of seclusion and restraint, plans to end all use of restraint and seclusion in its psychiatric facilities by January 1, 2006. Danville State Hospital has not used restraint in over four years and no longer even has a restraint policy, even though it has a number of forensic patients and others from the criminal justice system with a history of violent behavior.

Emergency departments have less space than many state hospitals, and the people they see may (or may not) be strangers to them or high on a variety of legal and illegal intoxicants. However, more than one ED professional interviewed for this book acknowledged that restraint and seclusion are used in a variety of inappropriate circumstances in EDs: because of staff shortages, because a patient escalated after attempts to remove clothing or personal valuables, or after a patient had been waiting more than eight hours on a gurney to be seen by a psychiatrist who did not want to come in on the night shift. Emergency departments have found that they can reduce the use of restraints and seclusion by simply focusing on reduction as a high priority in the ED or, like Baystate, by adopting a psychiatric advocate or sitter program, or through a number of other creative means.

The proposed standards designate the use of restraint by an ED as a sentinel event, requiring root cause analysis and debriefing of staff. They emphasize that any time a patient is not allowed to leave a room, including an assessment room, that legally constitutes seclusion for which appropriate patient protections and documentation must occur.

INFORMED CONSENT. Although ED treatises and the law underscore that ED staff must obtain informed consent for all proposed tests, treatments, and procedures, this often simply means that a patient signs a form. Sometimes even that formality is foregone if the ED is rushed and the patient is insistent. The recommendations are not as much concerned with formalities as with overt, forcible administration of unwanted tests and procedures, such as toxicology screenings. They also emphasize that force, including restraints, may not be used under any circumstances to perform procedures, tests, or screens on a non-consenting, unwilling patient without a court order from a court of competent jurisdiction, unless a professional specifically documents that the patient is at risk of death or serious medical injury if the specific test being ordered is not immediately conducted.

In addition, police are often involved in ED assessments of people with psychiatric disabilities, and the treatment functions may become blurred with criminal justice requirements. The standards underscore that no procedure should be performed solely at the request of police upon an non-consenting, unwilling patient. The fact that the procedure may be medically justifiable does not, by itself, suffice to overcome the refusal of a competent patient.

Finally, the standards establish that screenings and tests cannot be administered to a competent and refusing patient simply to accomplish that patient's transfer to an admitting inpatient unit. The fact that a psychiatric hospital or ward requires a toxicology screening in order to admit a patient is not a sufficient medical justification to overcome the refusal of a competent patient.

MAXIMUM HOURS OF DETENTION IN EDs (INVOLUNTARY PATIENTS). Some patients are brought by police or ambulance to EDs for assessment under statutory schemes that permit their involuntary detention pending assessment. Despite the fact that the statutes have narrow criteria for such involuntary detention, criteria that would indicate that the person's psychiatric condition is emergent or at the very least urgent—generally imminent danger to self or others—detained individuals are often kept waiting for assessment for many hours. Sometimes the individuals are kept in seclusion or restraint pending assessment. The standard proposes that an individual should not wait more than a maximum of three hours for assessment, and individuals in seclusion or restraint must be assessed within one hour, as currently required by federal regulations.

Enhancing Patient Feelings of Safety

One of the most crucial lessons for ED staff is that practices that make them feel safe, or that they believe should make their psychiatric patients feel safe, often result in escalating anxiety and fear for people in psychiatric crisis. These may lead to a kind of iatrogenic psychiatric crisis, caused or aggravated by ED practices that do not have a similar impact on other ED patients. These crises, in turn, generally lead ED staff to use force.

DISROBEMENT. Sometimes when individuals in psychiatric crisis are asked to remove their clothing in EDs, they become frightened and refuse. In many EDs, efforts to persuade such individuals quickly give way to calls for security. Security guards hold down the individual—who may have a history as a victim of rape and assault—and forcibly strip him or her of clothing. Individuals who endure this experience, such as Linda Stalker, report that the pain and damage of the experience stays with them for years. Yet ED staff interviewed for this book almost universally expressed surprise at the pain a policy they often automatically implement causes individuals with psychiatric disabilities. These automatic policies must change, particularly when resistance or refusal leads to forcible stripping by security guards of people who may well be victims of rape or childhood sexual abuse. The proposed standards would eliminate any policy that automatically required a psychiatric patient to exchange street clothes for a hospital gown or Johnny. Under the proposed policy, a voluntary patient who refused to remove her clothing could not be forcibly stripped, and a professional clinical assessment that the benefits of forced stripping outweighed the potential medical and emotional damage would be required prior to mandatory disrobement of an involuntary patient.

SECURITY GUARDS. Hospital deployment of security guards is an area where people with psychiatric disabilities may have distinctly different needs and reactions than people who come to EDs for medical conditions. Russell

Colling, an expert who works on health care security with JCAHO, has noticed that people with medical conditions prefer uniformed security guards, because they feel safer, while people with psychiatric disabilities tend to feel much more threatened by uniformed security guards. Survey responses by people with psychiatric disabilities confirmed Mr. Collings' impression, with many drawing parallels to police or people in military uniforms. "Uniforms 'register' as military or paramilitary, people who not only have authority to kill but whose authority is ultimately discretionary and seldom successfully challenged."[36]

The proposed recommendations suggest that hospitals use distinctive clothing, but not police uniforms, for security guards. As Steve Miccio, executive director of PEOPLe, Inc., notes, "the perception is that a formal uniform is somewhat intimidating and incites a response of danger or violence. The 'softer' look of distinctive clothing humanizes the approach. This way a patient knows the role of the individual as a hospital employee with a perceived reduced threat of forced treatment. It can be effective in reducing anger or fear."[37] Security guards also should be trained in de-escalation and in interacting effectively with people in psychiatric crisis. This is especially true for security guards who are given a role by the hospital in implementing seclusion or restraint.

TRAUMA. Emergency department staff members recognize that a substantial number of the people they see, especially people with psychiatric disabilities, have trauma histories. They don't think that EDs can help patients with these fundamental, long-term issues; nor do they recognize the ways in which ED policies may exacerbate or re-traumatize individuals who have been raped or abused in the past.[38] This is particularly ironic, since EDs worked successfully with women's rights groups to revamp previously traumatizing and insensitive practices in treating rape victims, and many of the same techniques are suggested for use with people whose psychiatric disabilities derive in part from prior experiences of rape and sexual abuse. Since many people in crisis may not be in a position to reveal past histories of sexual abuse, the recommendations suggest certain "universal precautions," which involve treating all patients as though they had trauma histories. These "universal" procedures include maximizing information given to the patient, giving the patient choice whenever possible, assuming a collaborative and respectful stance, and minimizing coercion. Examples of these practices include asking a patient's permission before taking blood or vital signs or before touching a patient (except in an emergency), addressing a patient by her last name rather than her first, explaining why certain procedures are being followed, and being sensitive to gender preferences in staff–patient interactions.

In addition, the recommendations suggest that ED physicians and psychiatrists carefully weigh a patient's trauma history when making recommendations relating to medication and inpatient admissions. Research shows that because control is so important to many trauma victims, inpatient admissions may be less therapeutic for them than for other patients. In addition, some patients' flashbacks may be misinterpreted as psychoses and treated inappropriately with antipsychotic medications. In some cases, antipsychotic medications may be very appropriate treatment for people with trauma histories; the recommendations merely concern the importance of taking the trauma history into consideration in making the recommendations.

Recommendations Relating to Treating a Person with Dignity

The expert panel assembled by the Center for Public Representation is in the process of developing standards and recommendations relating to treating patients with dignity and caring for their basic needs. Many survey respondents report waiting in assessment rooms without access to food, water, their medications, or toilet facilities, and (ironically) without providing them with their prescribed medications to meet medical and psychiatric needs. Some episodes of agitation can be traced to an individual's need to smoke, or the fact that the ED temperature is cold and the person's clothing has been taken away, and no blankets are available. The lack of available pay phones, or even the failure to stock hospital gowns in extra large sizes, has caused survey respondents considerable pain. Hospital policies of taking away all belongings have also caused agitation and even heartbreak, with one woman writing at length about the loss of a cross on a gold chain that was her only remaining belonging from her deceased mother. Anecdotal evidence suggests that EDs that employ psychiatric advocates or "sitters" or otherwise have staff whose responsibility it is to focus entirely on psychiatric patients attend to these problems more quickly than those where psychiatric patients are part of a mix of medical patients whose problems are generally perceived as more urgent.

Increase Funding for and Improve Research Related to Emergency Departments and People with Psychiatric Disabilities

One of the reasons for the absence of standards or conflicts in standards is that there is a paucity of research in the field of what constitutes adequate assessment, appropriate treatment, and good outcomes for people with psychiatric disabilities in crisis. There is also very little research on these topics relating to special populations, such as individuals with dual diagnoses, trauma histories, or linguistic barriers.[39] Most research on emergency services is descriptive in nature.[40]

There is a great deal of anecdotal evidence that retention and admission decisions are being made in the shadow of fears of legal liability, even when states grant decision makers immunity from suit for such decisions. Thus, there is a need for development of a validated instrument or rating scale that objectifies contingent suicidality[41] and gives ED physicians and psychiatrists some measure of assurance if they take the perceived risk of refusing to admit a patient who threatens to commit suicide if he or she is not granted a bed on an inpatient unit. Furthermore, there is a need for "well-designed studies to provide empirical support for alternative forms of psychiatric treatment"[42]: research on the cost-effectiveness of alternatives to standard ED evaluation and treatment of people with psychiatric disabilities, including Programs in Assertive Community Treatment (PACT) teams, family-based crisis homes, crisis apartments, and peer support in an individual's own house. This research is necessary to persuade the government and insurance companies to reimburse these alternatives, which in turn is essential if they are to take root and flourish.

Ultimately, however, for EDs to be able to treat people with psychiatric disabilities in sensitive ways that actually serve to alleviate rather than exacerbate crises, and in order for alternatives to flourish, EDs must be made less convenient—economically and otherwise—for those who use them inappropriately. These are not, for the most part, people with psychiatric disabilities. Identifying and controlling the inappropriate use of EDs is the underpinning of all efforts to transform the culture of psychiatric emergency services. This principle, and its consequences, is considered in the conclusion.

7

Conclusion

Although headlines declare that emergency departments (EDs) are in crisis, in reality EDs have been in crisis since the 1980s, when they first emerged in their modern form. From the budget and funding shortfalls of the 1980s, accompanied by the mandate of the Emergency Medical Treatment and Active Labor Act (EMTALA) that no patient be turned away, and the advent of managed care, to the current nursing shortage and heightened concerns about how EDs would cope with massive natural disasters or terrorist attacks, EDs have always operated under tremendous pressure.

Providing crisis care for people with psychiatric disabilities brings an overlay of additional issues: insufficient time; inadequate space; lack of expertise in assessment or treatment; vanishing dispositional alternatives; increasing numbers of individuals with complex combinations of medical, psychiatric, and substance abuse disorders; misunderstandings of legal requirements mixed with fear of liability; and frustration with frequent visitors demanding help that ED staff seem unable to provide all add to the pressures experienced by ED staff. The inherent tension between the trust and time necessary to help people in emotional crisis and the scarcity of time in EDs, as well as the legal mandate to file involuntary commitment petitions against individuals perceived as dangerous, means that EDs are often not the best place for frightened, psychotic, and suicidal people to get help or weather their crises. A number of people with psychiatric disabilities reported in surveys that they were terrified of returning to EDs, and that they went to considerable lengths to avoid an ED because they were afraid of being restrained, stripped, or involuntarily committed. Society pays the bill for expensive services when they do go or are brought against their wills. Sometimes the memories of past experience may create sensitivities for both the individual and staff, which in turn create their own momentum of escalation, force, and repetition of the original negative experience. It is a lose–lose situation for all concerned, and it has not changed in two decades.

The 1980s did have one advantage over the present day: the centrality of crisis services to the provision of public mental health care was generally acknowledged by psychiatrists, policy makers, and advocates, and the development of crisis alternatives to EDs was considered a necessary response to the problems inherent in EDs. By contrast, in the 21st century, the President's New Freedom Commission on Mental Health released a major policy report on mental health with very little attention given to either EDs or crisis services. The Joint Commission on the Accreditation of Health Care Organizations hosted a multi-day conference about ED overcrowding without a single presentation focused on psychiatric patients.[1] The Institute of Medicine issued a report intending to revolutionize the framework of health care provision in this country that includes relatively little about EDs and even less about people with psychiatric disabilities.[2]

There is a striking disconnect between the urgency of the problems facing EDs and the silence and inaction of policymakers. Even in the health and mental health fields, minimal research or funding for major service transformation is devoted to ED treatment or crisis care for people with psychiatric disabilities. There are a number of reasons why these difficulties continue to remain unsolved and largely unaddressed.

First, the treatment of psychiatric clients by EDs is not subject to oversight or monitoring by the federal or state agencies primarily concerned with mental health. Emergency departments serve a crucial function in the mental health system, providing assessment, treatment, and referrals for millions of people with psychiatric disabilities each year, yet they are isolated from both the public and private mental health systems. State mental health agencies oversee state psychiatric facilities, license private inpatient psychiatric hospitals or wards, and regulate community residential facilities. They do not generally oversee, license, or regulate EDs in their treatment of people with psychiatric disabilities. In fact, EDs are generally not monitored, regulated, accredited, or overseen by any agency focused specifically on, and having expertise in, mental health issues.

Second, the incentives created by the licensing and certification agencies that *do* oversee and monitor EDs often run precisely counter to appropriate treatment of people with psychiatric disabilities, by emphasizing swift and efficient assessment and disposition. Within EDs, people with psychiatric disabilities are marginalized and isolated. They make up a small proportion of people seen in the ED, but take up time and energy disproportionate to their numbers. They are perceived (usually correctly) as people for whom it will be difficult to find appropriate dispositions and referrals and (usually incorrectly) as sources of increased legal liability if they are simply discharged. Thus, for EDs that measure their success by swift disposition, psychiatric patients whose discharge is often accompanied by liability concerns may be perceived as a drag on the disposition statistics.

Third, the current situation serves the interests of actors more powerful than either individual EDs or the psychiatric clients they serve. For secondary utilizers of EDs—providers of mental health services, state mental health agencies, state departments of medical assistance, and police departments, all of whom are themselves overburdened and underfunded—the mandate that EDs be accessible 24 hours a day and impose no eligibility requirements means that EDs "solve" both individual and systemic problems with little, if any, downside to the secondary utilizer. Providers of mental health services and mental health agencies often send their clients to EDs without paying for the services provided there, thus achieving cost-free relief of the difficulty of coping with challenging clients. State public health agencies can cut Medicaid services, knowing that EDs will be forced by EMTALA to pick up at least some of the service costs, even if the services could be provided more beneficially and inexpensively in other settings. State mental health agencies can skimp on crisis services and even on community based services, knowing that EDs are required to respond to those needs. However inefficient and expensive this is for society in general, the scarce dollars don't come from the secondary utilizers, and so the inefficiency and burden on society, EDs, and people with psychiatric disabilities continues.

On one level, the solution to these problems is easily articulated. Most people in psychiatric crisis would undoubtedly prefer community and peer-run alternatives to EDs. Most EDs would clearly prefer that people with psychiatric disabilities avail themselves of these alternatives when they are in crisis. But alternatives—even those proven to be successful—are insufficiently funded and are often the first to be cut in hard times. Alternatives are not funded in part because they are not reimbursed by either the federal government or most insurance carriers. Often, successful crisis alternatives are solely funded by state dollars. They are not reimbursed by the federal government or by insurance carriers because Medicaid and insurance companies require both proof of effectiveness and credentialed providers. Many effective and inexpensive alternatives involve peer-run services, where the absence of credentialed staff dooms most reimbursement opportunities. Other alternatives, such as mobile crisis units, are caught between the tension of insufficient funding to pay credentialed staff and the threat of losing reimbursement without such staff members. For the most part, alternatives are not proven effective because they are not researched, and they are not researched because there is little demand for such research, even when EDs are operating over capacity and holding people with psychiatric disabilities for days, sometimes locked in tiny rooms, sometimes in restraints.

There is, however, a reason that is never articulated for the continuing social reliance on EDs to treat people in psychiatric crisis, no matter how inefficient, expensive, damaging, and ill-suited EDs are to perform this function. The secondary utilizers are once again the missing piece in this puzzle.

The emperor of the ED has costly, impractical, and almost non-existent psychiatric treatment clothing. Emergency departments, where people in acute emotional distress need the most psychiatric expertise, are unlike psychiatric wards and mental health community treatment centers in so many ways: the lack of expertise in mental health issues; the frequent presence of police, including sometimes police that restrain or even Taser psychiatric patients; the uniformed and sometimes armed security guards; the requirements of clothing removal; the frequent use of force rather than persuasion because there is no time to talk to anxious or delusional or frightened people; and the assessments of dangerousness or suicidality accomplished in 10 to 15 minutes or less.

The reason that no one talks very much about the lack of the emperor's psychiatric treatment clothing is because secondary utilizers see what they need to see: that EDs wear the daily uniform of detention, restraint, and social control. This is not to imply that ED staff desire or embrace the role that has been thrust upon them: they emphatically do not. General medical EDs and their staff repeatedly and vociferously disclaim expertise in assessing and treating people with psychiatric disabilities. The discomfort of ED staff with psychiatric patients is often a thinly disguised discomfort with the function of social control, an acknowledgement by caring health professionals that they do not have the time or expertise to provide the actual care needed by people in psychiatric crisis and a frustration that they are expected to do so.

Emergency departments are also the gatekeepers of involuntary commitment. The secondary utilizers of EDs—family, treatment providers, and police—often would not use alternatives to EDs that did not have the power to detain because, from their perspective, the primary function of EDs may not be treatment but detention. For many secondary utilizers, the two functions are desirable and inextricably intertwined. It is not coincidental that the only alternatives to ED treatment that have gained popularity, general reimbursement, and increasing utilization—psychiatric emergency services and mobile crisis units—generally include staff who have the ability to involuntarily detain people.

The recognition and articulation of the significance of this social control function—and the degree to which it is abhorred and resisted by both people with psychiatric disabilities and ED staff—is crucial to any discussion of the role of EDs in treating people with psychiatric disabilities. Because the social control function of EDs is not recognized, standard legal and policy protections that protect people subject to recognized social control and deprivations of liberty simply do not exist in EDs.

For example, while the process of involuntary civil commitment is heavily regulated, with strict time limits on every step of the process, in many states, legal protections do not exist on the length of time an ED may involuntarily detain an individual without filing statutorily required petitions or certificates, even though EDs engage in this practice on a daily basis. While state hospitals and psychiatric hospitals have made reduction and elimination of seclusion and restraint a priority and publish on the subject regularly, publications relating to projects to reduce restraint and seclusion in EDs can be counted on one hand. Legal protections relating to informed consent and forced medication are not routinely enforced in ED settings. Because the social control function of EDs is not recognized, many people in the mental health system are unaware of ED policies that require psychiatric patients to remove their clothing and authorize security guards to strip them if they do not or of forced catheterization practices that would not be permitted in most psychiatric hospitals, psychiatric wards, or community mental health centers. Although most state mental health agencies are familiar with protection and advocacy programs and their mandate to protect people with psychiatric disabilities from abuse, neglect, and rights violations, most EDs have never heard of protection and advocacy programs and would be astonished to discover that they operate within the jurisdiction of such programs.

There are three possible ways to solve the dilemmas presented in this book. The first is to recognize the role currently played by EDs in the treatment and control of people with psychiatric disabilities and, solely with regard to that role and function, bring them under the regulatory authority of state mental health agencies. This would also require articulating and increasing the civil rights protections associated with the use of force and deprivation of liberty that take place in EDs every day. This solution would be administratively cumbersome and would be vigorously resisted by hospitals and EDs. While perhaps increasing protection for people with psychiatric disabilities, it would not fundamentally change the fast-paced, dispositionally oriented culture of EDs so inimical to the needs of people in psychiatric crisis.

The second solution is to remove the social control function from EDs altogether, using them for medical clearance and detoxification when an individual's level of intoxication presents serious medical concerns. Psychiatric assessment and resolution of psychiatric crises would simply not be the responsibility of a medical ED, even in rural areas. This suggestion is not the same as utilizing independent evaluation teams to conduct assessments for involuntary commitment, as is the current practice in some states such as Washington, Vermont, Maine, and Oregon and cities such as Boston. Although assessment teams do have more expertise in mental health evaluation and remove the fear of legal liability, this practice does not remove the incentive of secondary utilizers to bring their problem residents, family members, and individuals creating public disturbances to the ED and leave them there. Individuals are still detained involuntarily while they wait for the independent evaluation team to arrive. In addition, when the assessment teams are busy and backed up, individuals wait for hours and sometimes days in ED assessment rooms, and the problems of seclusion, restraint, force, and loss of liberty are not only present, but are often magnified by delay.

This second solution would require re-conceptualizing the nature and function of social reactions to psychiatric crises, and would, as much as possible, attempt to understand and rationally account for the current role of the most common secondary utilizers of psychiatric emergency services: family members, police, mental health service providers, state mental health agencies, and departments of medical assistance.

These secondary utilizers of EDs are not evil or malicious; they are desperate. They use the ED to solve pressing problems for which no other solutions exist in their community. In other words, the availability of EDs has done much to soften social pressures for the development of adequate community mental health resources. (Although it is beyond the scope of this book, the over-utilization of the police in responding to people in psychiatric crisis is a similar response to an underdeveloped, underfunded community mental health system.)

The problem with this solution is that secondary utilizers might turn to the only other available place where they can bring people who are causing problems with the assurance that the person will not be able to leave: jails. Because secondary utilizers are generally well-meaning and not malicious, they might hesitate to use jails as a solution to problems for which the ED presents an attractive solution. And while police are well schooled in being called to arbitrate or resolve interpersonal conflicts, they may refuse to arrest or hold an individual where it is obvious that no crime has been committed. Police departments, after all, are not subject to EMTALA.

The third solution is to make secondary utilizers—especially mental health providers—financially responsible for their use of EDs. Mental health agencies in states such as Wisconsin and Ohio successfully limited over-utilization of state psychiatric facilities decades ago by changing their funding mechanisms so that state hospitalization was no longer free to the communities sending their citizens to state institutions. Communities were given budgets for the care of their psychiatrically disabled citizens, and were charged hospital rates whenever a client of the agency utilized the state facility. Utilization rates at state hospitals dropped dramatically.

There may be a place for such cost-shifting when it comes to utilization of EDs by providers of community mental health services as well. When EDs were accused of dumping patients in the 1980s, federal legislation put an end to this practice. Currently, group homes and other community residences can use EDs to dump their own patients without financial consequence—or any negative consequences. I propose that researchers begin to closely investigate use of EDs by community mental health providers, with root cause analyses performed of a statistically representative sample of cases. Did the individual have inadequate transition planning when he or she was discharged from a state psychiatric institution, and arrive at the community residence without an articulated crisis plan? Are the community provider staff members sufficiently trained in crisis de-escalation?

Ironically, some of the highest users of EDs are community mental health providers who purport to provide crisis services themselves. Are these uses appropriate? Much remains to be investigated in this area.

States that are cutting Medicaid reimbursements to agencies that provide crisis services may not be saving money, but increasing costs in other areas. The precise amount of the cost should at least be transparent to policymakers and taxpayers, who pay for the increased inefficiencies both in their tax dollars and in delays when they visit their EDs. When hospitals and emergency physicians push back and shift from identifying patients as the problem to reimbursement as the problem, then costs can be reallocated more sensibly, and state agencies and managed care organizations can begin to make decisions and utilize crisis alternatives based on the actual costs of ED utilization.

There is currently no fiscal incentive structure in place to discourage secondary utilizers, such as mental health service providers, from bringing their clients to EDs or (less directly) from providing such inadequate services that their clients are driven to access EDs for help that could have been provided far more inexpensively elsewhere. This must be developed by state legislatures. If state mental health agencies and/or their providers have a strong budgetary incentive to investigate the root causes of excess ED use, they can develop solutions. Patients being discharged from hospitals with insufficient transition planning require one solution, while community provider staff with insufficient training to deescalate crises requires another.

Emergency departments must examine their treatment of psychiatric patients far more closely, including the use of seclusion and restraint, force by security guards, minimization of medical complaints, and required disrobing. The standards attached as Appendix A provide a useful framework for assessing and improving practices.

State legislatures should also pass statutes that clearly describe and limit the authority of EDs to involuntarily detain people with psychiatric disabilities who have been triaged but not assessed. Time limits need to be put in place. Patients who are in seclusion or restraints should wait no more than one hour to be assessed; patients in the waiting room or whose movements are not restricted should wait no more than three hours maximum to be assessed. If legislatures do not pass statutes, advocates and attorneys from protection and advocacy agencies should consider litigation to require the establishment of such limits as a matter of due process.

People with psychiatric disabilities have an array of experiences in EDs. Not all are negative. A man recalled being called by a friend of his who lived a lonely and marginal existence on disability benefits. The friend asked if he could come over for Thanksgiving, and the man explained that he would be going out of town to visit relatives. Sighing, the friend responded, "I guess I'll go to the emergency room, then."[3] Emergency departments may be the place where security guards forcibly removed their clothing or the only place where they can be with other people at Thanksgiving. Robert Frost wrote that "home is the place where, when you have to go there, they have to take you in."[4] Robert Frost was not, however, referring to the ED, whose medical mission is becoming distorted as exhausted and underfunded social service providers transform it into a home for their most difficult clients. People in psychiatric crisis need and deserve a better home—a place that has to take them in and will assist them in their distress—beyond the ED, the jail cell, and the grate.

Appendix A

Emergency Department Treatment of People with Psychiatric Disabilities: Findings and Proposed Standards

Values That Should Guide the Treatment of People with Psychiatric Disabilities in Crisis Situations

1. Emergency Department care of people with psychiatric disabilities should be **patient-centered,** that is "care that is respectful of and responsive to individual patient preferences, needs, and values and ensuring that patient values guide all clinical decisions" (Institute of Medicine 2001). Patient-centered care is an independent value, in and of itself, *id*. Patient-centered care includes consciousness of and respect for cultural differences.

2. Emergency Department care of people with psychiatric disabilities should seek to **minimize coercion, increase choice**, and **reduce or eliminate the need for force**.

3. Emergency Department care of people with psychiatric disabilities should be **individualized** and enhance a patient's perception of **safety.** Emergency Departments should not assume that interventions intended to ensure patient safety enhance either patients' perceptions of safety or actual safety.

4. Emergency department treatment of people with psychiatric disabilities should **respect a person's dignity**, including attention to basic needs, such as **food, hydration, and hygiene**.

Restraint

Findings

1. Few data are available on the extent of restraint and seclusion in emergency departments. The data that are available suggests great variation in restraint use between emergency departments. Rationale for restraint includes danger to the patient or others, but patients are also restrained to prevent them from leaving the emergency department. Some hospital policies or forms list "flight risk" among the reasons for restraint, despite the fact that expert consensus considers this a clinically inappropriate rationale for restraint.

2. For decades, research has underscored the detrimental effect that restraint has on most psychiatric patients, both emotional and physical. The federal government, the National Association of State Mental Health Program Directors, and the National Council on Disability all have recommended working toward the abolition of the use of restraint on individuals with psychiatric disabilities (National Association of State Mental Health Program Directors, 1999; United States Department of Health and Human Services, Substance Abuse and Mental Health Services Administration 2003). The Joint Commission on Accreditation of Health Care Organizations has noted that seclusion and restraint constitute "an aversive experience with potential for serious physical and emotional consequences including death. Organizations are required to continually explore ways to decrease and eliminate use through training, leadership commitment, and performance improvement" (JCAHO 2002).

3. People responding to surveys about emergency department experience frequently mentioned restraints as among the most harrowing and painful parts of their experience. A substantial number state that after experiencing restraints, they were unwilling to seek emergency department care voluntarily. Often these complaints reflect the isolation and retraumatization of the restraint process. Although regulations require a person in restraints to be continually observed, in many cases the observer was either not present or refused to speak to the patient:

- "I woke up in restraints soaking wet and no one talked to me for hours."
- "I was strapped down despite my protests—it was so humiliating and degrading."
- "I was restrained for hours and left with a guard with a gun who refused to say one word to me or even look at me when I tried to talk with her. I was not dangerous or in any way threatening anybody—the restraints were because I tried to move the thing I was laying on

out from under a drip holder that I was hallucinating was coming at me."

4. Emergency departments that have made an effort to reduce use of restraints have succeeded in doing so through a wide variety of techniques. The most helpful one appears to be the use of sitters/companions/psychiatric advocates, who stay with the person in psychiatric crisis. One hospital, Baystate Hospital in Springfield, Massachusetts, introduced such a program, with 24/7 coverage, for approximately $22,000 a year.

Standards

1. The use of restraints in emergency departments should be considered a sentinel event, requiring root cause analysis and reporting to the Joint Commission on Accreditation of Health Care Organizations.

2. The use of restraint to prevent a voluntary patient from leaving the emergency department prior to assessment is not justified and should not be permitted. The use of restraints for the purpose of completing a medical evaluation or to hold a patient while completing a competence evaluation is not justified and should not be permitted.

3. The reduction of seclusion and restraint in emergency departments should be a core indicator of performance for purposes of quality assurance and risk assessment.

   a. Hospitals should supplement staff if necessary to comply with JCAHO and CMS requirements regarding in-person monitoring of seclusion and restraint. Models exist such as the one at Baystate Hospital in Springfield that are low cost and effective.
   b. Chart audits of all restrained patients should be conducted to identify compliance with standards, as well as to identify both staff and patients who are repeat users of restraint or seclusion. Individual staff should receive prompt feedback on compliance with standards after a restraint episode.
   c. Forms exist that permit patients to indicate what helps them in a crisis. These forms are often called "restraint reduction forms." Emergency departments should work with patients who present frequently in psychiatric crisis to ensure that a restraint reduction form is in the file of anyone who visits the emergency department because of psychiatric crisis on a regular basis.
   d. Emergency departments should collect data on frequency of seclusion/restraint by sex, race, shift, day of the week, type of restraint, and duration of seclusion/restraint. Emergency departments should follow the protocol of the National Association of State Mental Health Program Directors, which is in the process of being adopted by private

hospitals, in order to ensure uniformity of data for comparison purposes. This data should be published internally and compared to known rates at similar facilities.

e. Emergency departments should debrief staff, and (if possible) the patient, after every episode of restraint, especially when the restraint involves an individual who is known to the emergency department staff. "Debriefing" means an analysis of (1) triggers, (2) antecedent behaviors, (3) alternative behaviors, (4) least restrictive or alternative interventions attempted, (5) deescalation preferences or safety planning measures identified.

4. The use of restraint should be as humane and non-traumatizing as possible under the circumstances.

a. Staff who are assigned to observe and support an individual in restraints should be trained to communicate with individuals in restraints in a supportive and reassuring way, and should do so.
b. Clocks should be securely affixed to the walls of any room used to restraint patients and should be visible to the patient.
c. Patients who need to use the bathroom should be escorted to toilet facilities. Bedpans should not be used.
d. If security guards take any part in restraining patients, they should receive the same training as all ED staff involved in restraint procedures, including non-violent crisis management, deescalation, and training in interactions with people with psychiatric disabilities. At least some of this training should be conducted by people with psychiatric disabilities.

Seclusion

Findings

1. The Center for Medicare and Medicaid Services defines "seclusion" as "the involuntary confinement of a person in a room or an area where the person is physically presented from leaving" (CMS Interpretive Guidance 482.13(f)(1)). The Joint Commission on the Accreditation of Health Care Organizations defines seclusion as involuntary confinement of a person alone in a locked room.

2. For years, research has underscored the detrimental effect that seclusion has on most psychiatric patients. The federal government, the National Association of State Mental Health Program Directors, and the National Council on Disability all have recommended working toward the abolition of the use of seclusion and restraint on individuals with psychiatric disabilities (National Association of State Mental Health Program Directors, 1999;

United States Department of Health and Human Services, Substance Abuse and Mental Health Services Administration 2003). The Joint Commission on the Accreditation of Health Care Organizations finds that seclusion and restraint as "an aversive experience with potential for serious physical and emotional consequences including death. Organization are required to continually explore ways to decrease and eliminate use through training, leadership commitment, and performance improvement" (JCAHO 2002).

3. Patients report that seclusion is one of the worst aspects of their experience in emergency departments. Their comments underscore the adverse emotional consequences of isolation:

- I arrived at Bridgeport Hospital in bad emotional condition but calm and compliant, was not combative or hysterical and still sent to the isolation room . . .
- I felt very isolated in that little room . . .
- The most scary thing for me was being told how lucky I was that my social worker came with me otherwise I would have had to stay in an "isolation room" because they did not have enough staff to watch me.
- All psychiatric patient's rights as human beings not as animals should be respected and not violated by being cooped up in isolation in a filthy urine smelling room . . .
- Don't lock patients in an observation room for many hours without talking to someone professional.
- I was often left alone for hours in a cubicle and terrified, thinking I was in all kinds of evil places.
- Try to avoid putting patients in the little locked room and ignoring them . . .

4. Hospital emergency departments often lock psychiatric patients into assessment rooms while waiting for evaluation. This is particularly true for patients who are subject to involuntary detention petitions, but is also true even for voluntary patients. Some hospitals acknowledge a policy of locking patients in rooms because they do not have sufficient staff to watch them. Although hospitals often do not consider a patient in seclusion unless he or she is in a room denominated as a seclusion room, the practice of locking assessment rooms, or prohibiting patients from leaving assessment rooms, is equally frightening and isolating to patients. Furthermore, because the patient cannot leave the room, this practice legally constitutes seclusion of the patient.

Standards

1. Under federal regulations, locked assessment rooms constitute seclusion. Patients may not be prevented from leaving rooms in which they are alone unless the conditions for seclusion have been met.

2. A patient who is not permitted to leave a room in which he or she is alone must be continuously observed in person for the first hour, as required by federal regulations, with continuous audio-visual monitoring permissible after the first hour, and fifteen minute well-being checks through out this period.

3. The use of seclusion to prevent a voluntary patient from leaving the hospital prior to assessment is not justified and should not be permitted. The use of seclusion for a brief period of time to permit a medical evaluation for the purpose of determining if the individual has a life-threatening condition or is competent is permissible if the period of time is as short as possible under the circumstances, and in no case over one hour.

4. The reduction of seclusion and restraint in emergency departments should be a core indicator of performance for purposes of quality assurance and risk assessment.

a. Hospitals should supplement staff if necessary to comply with JCAHO and CMS requirements regarding in-person monitoring of seclusion and restraint. Models exist such as the one at Bay State Hospital in Springfield that are low cost and effective.

b. Utilize additional staff as sitters/companions/psychiatric advocates. Many hospitals have hired "sitters" or "psychiatric advocates" or use light duty staff or available staff as "sitters." Although the names vary, the function is to sit with a person in psychiatric crisis, to provide comfort and attention and awareness of the individual's needs. This obviates the need for seclusion and often for restraints as well. Hospital personnel monitoring a person in seclusion should be instructed to speak to the patient and attempt to comfort them and discern their needs.

c. Chart audits of all restrained and secluded patients should be conducted to identify compliance with standards, as well as to identify both staff and patients who are repeat users of restraint or seclusion. Individual staff should receive prompt feedback on compliance with standards after a restraint episode.

d. Emergency departments should collect data on frequency of seclusion/restraint by sex, race, shift, day of the week, type of restraint, and duration of seclusion/restraint. Emergency departments should follow the protocol of the National Association of State Mental Health Program Directors, which is in the process of being adopted by private hospitals, in order to ensure uniformity of data for comparison purposes. This data should be published internally and compared to known rates at similar facilities.

5. The use of seclusion should be as humane and non-traumatizing as possible under the circumstances.

a. Staff who are assigned to observe and support an individual in seclusion should be trained to communicate with individuals in seclusion in a supportive and reassuring way, and should do so.

b. Clocks should be securely affixed to the walls of any room used for seclusion purposes. Magazines should be available, as well as material on relaxation techniques.

c. Patients who need to use the bathroom should be escorted to toilet facilities. Bedpans should not be used.

d. If security guards take any part in observing patients in seclusion, they should receive the same training as all ED staff involved in restraint procedures, including non-violent crisis management, deescalation, and training in interactions with people with psychiatric disabilities. At least some of this training should be conducted by people with psychiatric disabilities.

Security Guards

Findings

1. About 15–20% of hospital security guards carry guns. About 20–30% carry pepper spray. The proportion of armed security guards has been steadily decreasing over the past two decades due to increased training of health care security in de-escalation techniques and increasing concern over the health and safety issues involved when hospital security personnel carry weapons (Colling 2004).

2. While the presence of armed security guards may make some medical patients feel safer, many patients with a history of psychiatric disability, and of unpleasant encounters with the police, are made uncomfortable and frightened by the presence of uniformed security guards, especially when armed. For some people with psychiatric disabilities, police uniforms can be extremely intimidating and threatening, increasing the chances of escalation on the part of the individual (Miccio 2005, Colling 2005).

3. The Center for Medicare and Medicaid Services ("CMS") has investigated and disciplined hospitals for using pepper spray on patients, including psychiatric patients. CMS has issued interpretive guidance to its regulations regarding patient's rights that "pepper spray, mace, nightsticks, Tasers, cattle prods, stun guns, pistols and other such devices" are considered weapons, and that "CMS does not consider the use of weapons in the application of restraint as safe appropriate health care interventions . . . CMS does not approve the use of weapons by an hospital staff as a means of subduing a patient to place that patient in patient restraint/seclusion" (Center for Medicare and Medicaid Services, State Operations Manual, Interpretive Guidance to 45 C.F.R. 482.13(f), available at www.cms.hhs.gov/manuals/107_som/som1O7ap_a_hospitals.pdf).

Standards

1. Hospital security guards in emergency departments should not carry guns, pepper spray or Tasers.

2. Security guards should wear distinctive clothing but not full police uniforms.

3. Hospital security guards should receive training in interacting with people with psychiatric disabilities, including training on deescalation and redirection. At least one segment or module of the training should be conducted by an individual with a psychiatric disability, and at least one segment or module of the training should relate to the effect of stereotypes and stigma on perceptions of likely violence and unpredictability of persons with psychiatric disabilities.

Trauma

Findings

1. There is a clear relationship between an individual's experience of severe trauma, such as childhood physical or sexual abuse, and later psychiatric and emotional difficulties, including self-injury. Over 60% of people with serious psychiatric disabilities report a history of childhood sexual or physical abuse. Over 80% of adolescents and children in continuing care inpatient and intensive residential treatment programs in Massachusetts were found to have trauma histories (LeBel and Stromberg 2004).

2. People with trauma histories are frequently the highest users of costly mental health crisis and emergency services (SAMHSA 2004). These patients' trauma histories may greatly affect their presentation to the emergency department, their reactions to various treatment interventions in the emergency department, and appropriate recommendations for treatment. For example, emergency department policies on restraint or removal of clothing may cause serious emotional damage to people with histories of rape or sexual abuse, whether they experience such practices or witness others being restrained or having their clothing removed. In addition, there is evidence that in some cases dissociation or PTSD flashbacks related to trauma may be inappropriately diagnosed as psychosis or schizophrenia (Harris 1994). There is also evidence that people with schizophrenia and longer term psychoses have a high incidence of trauma co-morbidity (Kessler, R.C., Sonnega, A., Bromet, E. et al 1995).

3. State Departments of Mental Health have paid increasing attention to the impact of trauma on individuals in state systems (SAMHSA 2004; National Association of State Mental Health Program Directors 2004). However, emergency department and crisis services have not been as attuned to

this issue. Emergency departments have, however, been sensitized to the treatment of rape victims, and many of these policies could be usefully and positively applied to individuals with psychiatric disabilities who have suffered trauma.

4. A number of emergency department policies specifically impact negatively on people with trauma histories: the requirement that patients disrobe, the use of seclusion and restraints, the utilization of armed and uniformed security guards, and the equation of cutting with suicidality, resulting in seclusion, restraint, or involuntary detention. Patients with trauma histories are particularly vulnerable to harm from these policies, although they also have a negative impact on all patients with psychiatric diagnoses.

Recommendations

1. **Universal screening** is recommended for history of trauma. These questions should be brief and simple, asked in private, and be extensions of assessments already currently required by the Joint Commission on the Accreditation of Health Care Organizations for domestic violence, abuse and neglect (PC 3.10). A number of different models exist for these questions, and are attached.

2. **Universal precautions.** Because not all patients feel comfortable reporting a history of trauma, and because practices that benefit patients with trauma histories benefit all patients, ED staff should adopt trauma-informed practices toward all patients. These practices often involve replicating treatment of rape victims, and include maximizing information given to the patient, maximizing choice wherever possible, assuming a collaborative and respectful stance, and minimizing coercion. Examples of these practices include asking a patient's permission before taking blood or vital signs, or before touching a patient (except in an emergency); addressing a patient by her last name rather than her first, explaining why certain procedures are being followed, and being sensitive to gender preferences in staff-patient interactions.

3. **Requirements for clothing removal.** If a patient refuses to comply with a hospital requirement of clothing removal, and the person in fact has a history of trauma, an individualized determination should be made and documented by a physician that the medical and psychiatric risk involved in forcibly removing the clothing from an individual with a trauma history is outweighed by the benefit of forcibly removing the clothing.

4. **Treatment.** It is important to identify trauma victims, because it highlights the importance of differentiating between hallucinations and post-traumatic flashbacks or dissociation. The medications of individuals diagnosed with a severe mental illness who are the survivors of sexual abuse should be reevaluated in light of the impact of the trauma on the symptoms

and behavior of the individual. In addition, self-injury, a common practice in individuals with trauma histories, requires informed treatment, and treaters should distinguish this from suicidal behavior in their treatment planning.

5. **Disposition.** Emergency Departments should make particular efforts to avoid inpatient admission for people with histories of trauma unless absolutely necessary. Because control is so important for people with trauma histories, inpatient admissions rarely have long-term benefits and should only be used when there is no other means to assure safety in the short term.

6. **Referrals.** If a patient has a trauma history, it is helpful to have information about available resources and books, as well as knowing whether any local agency offers trauma-specific treatment. "Evolution of Trauma-Informed and Trauma-Specific Services in State Mental Health Systems" is available from the Substance Abuse and Mental Health Services Administration in Washington, D.C., or from the Center for Public Representation.

Crisis Plans

Findings

1. One of the major developments in theory and practice relating to the treatment of people with serious psychiatric disabilities is the focus on recovery, as well as the patient's control over his or her own recovery. This focus is supported by the President's New Freedom Commission Report (2003), the Surgeon General's Report on Mental Health (1999), the National Center on Disability's report "From Privileges to Rights" (2000), and the National Association of State Mental Health Program Directors (1999). The Institute of Medicine also indirectly supports this model in its call for health care in general to become more patient-centered (Crossing the Quality Chasm 2001).

2. Emergency departments, perhaps because they primarily see people in psychiatric crisis, have generally not adopted either the person-centered Institute of Medicine approach or the strength-based recovery model increasingly accepted in mental health.

3. For many people with psychiatric disabilities, crises are often both predictable and potentially avoidable. Many people have psychiatric crises around anniversaries of traumatic events, as a result of certain predictably stressful events (court appearances, Social Security reviews, family reunions), or as a predictable response to certain environmental triggers. Planning ahead for responses to these crises can help avoid, alleviate or mitigate the crisis.

4. Many different written models and training manuals exist for cre-

ating crisis plans. The best known of these is Mary Ellen Copeland's WRAP (Wellness Recovery Action Plan). Mary Ellen Copeland's web site also offers a post-crisis plan for those patients who are discharged from a crisis setting back into the environment that helped cause the crisis in the first place.

Standard

1. Training for social workers employed in emergency departments should include orientation to wellness maintenance and crisis plans, e.g. the Wellness Recovery Action Plan (WRAP).

Recommendations

1. Emergency department social workers should make wellness maintenance and crisis plan materials available to patients with psychiatric disabilities upon discharge, along with a referral to any peer operated support groups in their areas.

2. Hospital social workers should maintain a list of peer operated support groups and clubhouses in their area, and work with them to improve emergency department services for people who have psychiatric disabilities. Hospitals which are not aware of the groups in their area can contact their State Department of Mental Health, State Protection and Advocacy agency (list of all State Protection and Advocacy agencies available at www.napas .org).

3. Emergency departments should develop standard forms as part of patient history that includes both specific medications and treatments that have been used in the past, and whether these medications and treatments have proven to be helpful or harmful to the patient's condition. The form should be attached to the chart prominently (first page on medication order section, or inside front cover of chart).

4. Forms exist that permit patients to indicate what helps them in a crisis. These forms are often called "restraint reduction forms." Emergency departments should work with patients who present frequently in psychiatric crisis to ensure that a restraint reduction form is in the file of anyone who visits the emergency department because of psychiatric crisis on a regular basis.

Informed Consent

Findings

1. Legal requirements that patients give informed consent to proposed treatment apply in the emergency department just as they do in other health

care settings (Sanders 1991). These requirements may vary in the case of patients under involuntary detention orders (Stefan 2005).

2. People with psychiatric disabilities rank "being asked about what treatment I want" and "being asked about what treatments were helpful and not helpful to me in the past" as being of primary importance to them in emergency department treatment (Allen, Carpenter, Sheets, Miccio and Ross 2003; Connecticut Protection and Advocacy 1999).

3. Professionals in emergency departments often fail to obtain informed consent from people with psychiatric disabilities. People with psychiatric disabilities report that they are not told the risks and benefits of treatment, including invasive medical treatment, they receive in emergency departments. In one survey, 82% of people with psychiatric disabilities who had received treatment in an emergency department disagreed or disagreed strongly with the statement that the nature of proposed treatment, its risks, benefits and alternative options had been described to them before they were asked to consent to the treatment (Allen, Carpenter, Sheets, Miccio and Ross 2003).

4. Survey results from people with psychiatric disabilities regarding informed consent include

- Nurses and doctors pumped my stomach but I was not told what they were doing . . .
- They put me in a separate room with a guard. I had signed a form for tests—I didn't realize one was putting a long pipe down my throat into my stomach and I said no, I didn't want that—they could give me the paper back. I rescinded my consent. The MD told me to shut up—you're a psych patient, you don't know what's good for you. They put me in restraints and did it anyway.

5. Informed consent is a regulatory and licensing requirement for emergency departments (45 C.F.R. 482.13, JCAHO RI-2.30, RI-2.40). The failure to obtain informed consent from psychiatric patients in emergency department settings has led to substantial damage awards in a number of recent cases.

Standards

A. Existing Standards

1. No assessment procedure or medical test should be performed upon a conscious, competent patient without describing to the patient ahead of time what will be done, and why, and inviting the patient to ask questions about the procedure.

2. A patient's refusal of a procedure or test should be respected, except if a physician determines and documents that the patient is not competent

to make a decision about the procedure or test after being given information in language that he or she can understand about the benefits and drawbacks of the procedure or test. A patient can be informed of the non-medical consequences of refusal (e.g. an inpatient bed in a psychiatric facility may be available only if the patient has undergone a drug screen).

3. No medication should be given to a conscious patient on a non-emergency basis without describing to the patient what the medication is, why it is being given, and inviting the patient to ask questions about the medication.

4. Competent refusals of medications must be respected.

5. Conclusions that a patient is not competent must be made by a physician and the form of examination and basis for the conclusion documented in detail in the patient's chart.

B. Proposed Standards

1. Force, including restraints, may not be used under any circumstances to perform procedures, tests or screens on an unconsenting, unwilling patient without a court order from a court of competent jurisdiction, unless a professional specifically documents that the patient is at risk of death or serious medical injury if the specific test being ordered is not immediately conducted.

2. No procedure should be performed solely at the request of police upon an unconsenting, unwilling patient. The fact that the procedure may be medically justifiable does not, by itself, suffice to overcome the refusal of a competent patient.

3. The fact that a psychiatric hospital or ward requires a toxicology screening in order to admit a patient is not a sufficient medical justification to overcome the refusal of a competent patient.

Disrobement

Findings

1. One of the issues that causes the most complaints by individuals with psychiatric disabilities surveyed about their experiences in emergency department treatment is mandatory disrobing.

- "... the ER nurse instructed me to take off my clothes as she put the shackles on the bed. I have been hospitalized numerous times and have long given up any physical fight."
- "I was immediately strapped down, given two injections, and my clothes were taken. I was given a hospital gown ..."

- "There is a practice in the crisis unit which is particularly degrading and humiliating. Once on the unit, before being seen, they demand your shoes and clothes. This of course puts them in control . . . I refused to give things up and was threatened with the use of physical force and restraint (8 guys showed up)."
- "When a patient arrives, you are forced to take all clothes off!!! Not always necessary."

2. Mandatory disrobement of psychiatric patients is common. In one survey of Connecticut patients, 57% of patients presenting with psychiatric complaints were asked to remove their clothes. Individuals with a history of psychiatric treatment presenting with medical complaints were asked to remove their clothing 40% of the time (State of Connecticut Office of Protection and Advocacy for Persons with Disabilities, Protection and Advocacy for Individuals with Mental Illness, Emergency Room Survey, 1999).

3. Hospital policies vary considerably. Some hospitals require all psychiatric patients under involuntary detention orders to disrobe; others require all psychiatric patients to disrobe; still others require all patients to disrobe. Still others permit patients to keep their clothing after a pat down, or leave requests for disrobing up to the discretion of emergency department staff (Policies on file at Center for Public Representation).

4. Both courts and state licensing agencies have disapproved blanket policies regarding mandatory disrobement without individualized assessments of dangerousness. There is no safety justification for discrepant treatment of psychiatric and medical patients with regard to disrobement policies, and no justification for uniform treatment of psychiatric patients based on flight concerns. There is no policy justification for blanket assumptions about psychiatric patients. Moreover, such blanket assumptions contradict the requirements of the Americans with Disabilities Act (Stefan 2001).

5. Being forced to remove street clothing can be extremely disturbing and feel very unsafe for individuals who have a history of sexual abuse and trauma. These individuals may refuse to remove their clothing and ultimately engage in physical struggles as security guards attempt to strip them, reenacting their former abuse and greatly exacerbating the emotional crisis that brought them to the emergency department in the first place.

Standards

1. Care and treatment in emergency departments should not be conditioned on disrobing, except in extremely limited circumstances where professionally documented assessments specifically weigh the emotional and physical risk to the individual of enforced clothing removal against the immediate medical necessity for such removal to provide treatment, and conclude that the requirement of disrobing is essential.

2. If the professional assessment is made that disrobing is necessary to provide treatments, voluntary patients may leave in lieu of disrobing. No patient may be converted from voluntary to involuntary status on the basis of refusing to disrobe.

3. A hospital policy requiring automatic disrobement solely on the basis that a patient has a psychiatric diagnosis or is seeking psychiatric treatment is clinically unjustified, discriminatory, and illegal.

4. Flight risk is not a sufficient justification for removal of clothing.

Implementation

1. Hospitals should rescind any blanket policies regarding mandatory disrobement or patdowns that apply solely to patients seeking psychiatric treatment or who have psychiatric histories.

2. If a hospital's policy on disrobement applies to all patients, medical or psychiatric, the hospital should modify the policy in ways that make disrobement as minimally intrusive as possible. Hospitals whose policy or practice is to give the patient a choice about disrobing should ensure that the patient is aware that she has this choice.

3. Safety concerns are only a sufficient justification for forcible removal of clothing if an individualized assessment of dangerousness has been made that weighs the safety risk against the risk of emotional and physical harm attendant upon forced disrobing.

4. If a medical examination requires a patient to disrobe, he or she should be required to disrobe only to the extent necessary to conduct the examination, and should not be asked to disrobe until such time as the doctor can reasonably be expected to conduct the examination within one half hour of disrobing. Clothing should be returned as soon as possible.

5. An order of involuntary detention by itself does not constitute an individualized assessment of dangerousness for purposes of requiring patients to disrobe. If the hospital's policy on disrobing applies solely to individuals under involuntary detention orders, disrobing should not be mandatory without an individualized assessment of dangerousness and flight risk that weighs the risk against the risk of emotional and physical harm attendant upon forced disrobing.

Medical Clearance

Findings

1. Emergency department professionals and mental health professionals greatly disagree about what constitutes appropriate medical clearance of a

person presenting with a psychiatric condition. There is also division among emergency department professionals about what constitutes appropriate medical clearance (Stefan 2005).

2. It is undisputed that many medical conditions present with symptoms that may lead to a mistaken psychiatric diagnosis. Thus, ruling out medical causes of behavioral problems is crucial. In addition, many people with psychiatric problems have co-occurring medical problems which may contribute to or appear to exacerbate the psychiatric condition.

3. Many emergency department professionals believe that medical clearance simply means identifying and treating emergency medical conditions, and believe that unreasonably extensive medical clearance requests represent an attempt to shift costs to emergency departments and result in unreasonably lengthy emergency department stays for people with known psychiatric conditions. On the other hand, psychiatric professionals on inpatient units believe that they do not have the expertise or the testing equipment to rule out a variety of medical syndromes that may be causing or contributing to symptomatology that appears to be behaviorally related.

4. These differences of opinion and approach may also implicate legal rights. For example, the need to do toxicology tests including blood tests and urine tests has led to forced catheterizations of psychiatric patients and patients being restrained to draw blood (*Straub v. Kilgore* 2004; *Sullivan v. Bornemann* 2004; *Tinius v. Carroll County Sheriff Dept.* 2004).

Recommendations

1. Uniform medical clearance standards applicable to all patients presenting with psychiatric conditions are inappropriate. For example, individuals presenting with first-time psychiatric crises, elderly people, and children, should receive more thorough medical clearance procedures than individuals who are well known in the emergency department and have been seen recently. People who present with symptoms of psychosis and confusion may need more thorough medical clearance evaluations than people who present with depression.

2. Standard minimum medical clearance procedures for all patients include vital signs, medical history and visual examination (Expert Consensus Guidelines Series 2001). Toxicology screenings should be considered and the professional's decision relating to the screening should be documented.

3. The National Institute of Mental Health should convene an expert panel, which should include representatives of people receiving psychiatric evaluations in emergency department settings, to recommend a nation-wide minimum set of tests, or algorithm, to be followed by emergency departments in their medical clearance procedures.

Inappropriate Assessment and Treatment
of Medical Complaints

Findings

1. Medical reports, treatises, testimony to Congress and patient surveys all concur that people with known psychiatric histories or diagnoses are frequently not given appropriate assessments for medical complaints because it is assumed that their reported problems are psychiatric in nature (Stefan 2005).

2. Testimony before Congress when it was considering the Americans with Disabilities Act included an account of a woman with a psychiatric disability miscarrying and hemorrhaging in the street after an emergency room assumed her report that she was pregnant was a delusion (A&P Comm.Print 1990 28B *1251). Among the complaints of survey respondents:

- [patient went in] "for stomach pains, which they kept saying was all in my mind. So they sent me over to the Crisis where they didn't believe me either when all this time it was a bleeding ulcer which I just found out now."
- [patient went in for] "severe back numbness . . . 9 1/2 hours nobody ever looked at my back instead did psych eval."
- "I am a 36-year-old, divorced Mom working full time and raising 2 children. I felt like I was treated like a 'hysterical female,' the way doctors hooked women on valium in the 60s. . . ."
- "It seemed that my symptoms of a possible heart attack were ignored by the doctors, especially my own, since I had a bipolar diagnosis, even though my blood pressure was high. I was treated as though I had an anxiety attack which I did not. I was stigmatized as soon as they heard my diagnosis."
- "Had a cut cornea and was crying. Intake took down my psychiatric meds. The doctor came in to treat me for emotional upset. I'm crying because my eye needs to be fixed."

Recommendations

1. Hospital risk management and/or quality assurance committees should investigate how the hospital's emergency department treats medical complaints made by patients with known psychiatric histories.

2. Hospitals should conduct trainings of all emergency department staff, including physicians and nurses, which emphasize that minimizing medical complaints of psychiatric patients is poor medical practice, may endanger lives, and may also constitute both medical malpractice and a violation of

the Americans with Disabilities Act. An important component of the trainings should be addressing the doctor's own stereotypes about people with psychiatric disabilities, and how those stereotypes interfere with good medical practice. At least some of these trainings should be led by people with psychiatric disabilities.

3. Teaching hospitals should ensure that the principles of these trainings are incorporated into every day teaching rounds.

Advance Directives

Findings

1. All states have statutes permitting individuals to create advance directives, which must be honored by emergency departments. A substantial number of those states have statutes specifically recognizing psychiatric advance directives. A number of Web sites exist which contain sample advance directive forms specifically oriented to the needs of individuals with psychiatric disabilities (see, e.g. Bazelon Center for Mental Health Law Web site, www.bazelon.org).

2. Few individuals with psychiatric disabilities have advance directives. This is true of people who visit emergency departments in general. Although the American College of Emergency Medicine recommends that patients bring advance directives to the emergency department, even people who already have advance directives often do not bring them to emergency departments. Emergency departments are more familiar with the concept of "DNR"s ("do not resuscitate") orders or patient "codes" than they are with advance directives, and it is probable that most emergency department staff will be completely unfamiliar with psychiatric advance directives (Stefan 2005).

3. Some individuals with psychiatric disabilities who have advance directives report that the emergency departments would not honor their advance directives (State of Connecticut Office of Protection and Advocacy for Individuals with Mental Illness Emergency Room Survey 1999).

4. Both the Joint Commission on the Accreditation of Health Care Organizations and the Center for Medicare and Medicaid Services require emergency departments to document the existence of advance directives in patient charts and to honor advance directives (42 C.F.R. 482.13(b)(2) and (b)(3), State Operations Manual, Hospital Interpretive Guidelines; JCAHO Standards RI-1.2.4, IM 7.2).

Recommendation

1. Hospitals should ensure that emergency department staff are aware of and respect the advance directives of people with psychiatric disabilities. A psychiatric disability does not preclude an individual from executing an advance directive, and the advance directive may contain directions regarding psychiatric treatment (*Hargrave v. Vermont* 2003).

2. The Joint Commission on the Accreditation of Health Care Organizations and the Center for Medicare and Medicaid Services should enforce their requirements regarding advance directives with respect to psychiatric advance directives in emergency departments.

Accompaniment

Findings

1. About one third of people with psychiatric disabilities who visit emergency departments are accompanied by family members or friends. The American College of Emergency Physicians encourages patients to bring a family member or friend to "be at the bedside" ("The Emergency Department: What to Expect," www.acep.org/1,241,0.html).

2. However, many hospital emergency departments refuse to permit friends, relatives or advocates to accompany people with psychiatric disabilities when they are sent back to the assessment room or area. This is true even if the individual requests accompaniment, and even when the hospital permits such accompaniment for medical patients. In some hospitals, this refusal is articulated in a hospital policy prohibiting such accompaniment for psychiatric patients, or patients under orders of involuntary detention. In others it is left to staff discretion, and accompaniment becomes a matter of which staff are on duty (Stefan 2005).

3. Surveys of individuals with psychiatric disabilities indicate that waiting alone in an assessment room often exacerbates anxiety, depression or panic which created the psychiatric emergency in the first place. The presence of a *desired* other—friend, advocate, or family member—is seen as extremely important. At the same time, if there is any element of involuntariness to the ER visit, they may not want to be accompanied or assessed in the presence of a relative or other individual whom they view as being responsible for bringing them or causing them to be brought to the emergency department (Office of Protection and Advocacy of the State of Connecticut 1999).

4. Among the reasons cited by emergency departments for the policy or practice of prohibiting accompaniment of patients with psychiatric dis-

abilities to assessing areas are concerns for the safety of the accompanying individual and/or the patient's safety; clinical concerns regarding the exacerbation of the patient's condition; discomfort with the presence of a peer advocate, and the fact that if psychiatric patients are locked in rooms, the emergency department does not want to lock a non-patient in the room (Stefan 2005).

5. Although neither the Center for Medicare and Medicaid Services nor the Joint Commission on Accreditation of Health Care Organizations have standards directly addressing this issue, both underscore the importance of respecting the individual's requests, involving the individual in decisions regarding care, as well as involving family members when appropriate (RI 1.2, 42 C.F.R. 482.13(b)).

Standard

Individuals with psychiatric disabilities are entitled to accompaniment in emergency departments, if desired by the patient, unless doing so would create a documented risk of immediate danger to the patient or others.

Implementation

1. Hospital emergency departments should adopt policies that accompaniment by a family member, friend, or advocate while the individual awaits assessment is presumptively permitted, if desired by the patient, unless doing so would create a risk of immediate danger.

2. The desires of the individual as to accompaniment should be ascertained privately. This can be accomplished at triage or in any other way appropriate to the individual emergency department setting.

3. The assessment that accompaniment would create a risk of immediate danger must be made by a qualified professional, be specific, and be documented in the individual's chart.

4. The hospital may limit the number of persons accompanying the individual to one.

5. Emergency departments should comply with federal and JCAHO standards prohibiting the utilization of individuals accompanying patients as a substitute for the presence of hospital staff when required by law (e.g. observation of a patient in restraints) or other persons required by law (e.g. interpreters for patients who are deaf or do not speak English).

Maximum Hours of Involuntary Detention in Emergency Departments Prior to Assessment: Involuntary Patients

Findings

1. A number of patients are brought to emergency departments for assessments on legally executed certificates permitting their involuntary detention.

2. Research on the proportion of psychiatric patients brought to emergency departments under orders of involuntary detention varies from location to location, and ranges from 17% to over 50% of patients.

3. The fact that people arrive at emergency departments with certificates indicating probable cause to believe that they are mentally ill and dangerous to themselves or others should indicate a high level of urgency in assessment, placement and treatment.

4. Some states have statutes which regulate the maximum time a person who is already under a legal order of involuntary detention because of dangerousness findings (e.g., by the police) may be forced to wait for an evaluation in an emergency department. The most common statutory maximum is six hours, N.Y. Mental Hygiene Law 9.40; Md Health Gen. Code Ann. 10-624(b)(2).

5. Often a patient who arrives with an involuntary certificate is placed in seclusion or restraint upon arrival at the hospital emergency room.

Proposed Standards

1. No person under an order of involuntary detention should wait more than three hours to be assessed and evaluated, resulting in a disposition decision or treatment plan.

2. No person in seclusion or restraints should wait more than one hour for assessment and evaluation resulting in a decision regarding disposition or treatment plan.

If a person is secluded or restrained, the Center for Medicare and Medicaid Services one-hour rule requires that a physician assess the individual in person within one hour. This assessment should include the required evaluation, so that no person in restraints should wait more than one hour for an evaluation.

Notes

CHAPTER 1

1. Letter on file with the Center for Public Representation; reproduced with permission of the author.

2. "Upsurge in people with mental illness seeking treatment in emergency departments is taking toll on patient care," News-Medical.Net, April 27, 2004, www.news-medical.net/?id=890 (Survey by the American College of Emergency Physicians, the American Psychiatric Association, the National Alliance for the Mentally Ill, and the National Mental Health Association finds "psychiatric patients board in hospital emergency departments more than twice as long as other patients. And, emergency physicians say their staff spends more than twice as long looking for beds for psychiatric patients than for non-psychiatric patients."); Mark Moran, "As Insurance Coverage Wanes, Psychiatric ERs get Busier," 39 *Psychiatric News* No. 21, p. 12 (2004). (Dr. Michael Allen, emergency department psychiatrist and author, states that "health insurance comes with such poor mental health benefits that it would be more accurate to count many people as effectively uninsured.")

3. G. A. Barker, "Emergency Room 'Repeaters,' " in James Randolph Hilliard, *Manual of Clinical Emergency Psychiatry* (American Psychiatric Press 1990) at p. 344.

4. Douglas A. Rund, "Suicide Attempts," in Michael Callaham, ed., *Current Practice of Emergency Medicine* (2d ed.) (Philadelphia: B.C. Decker 1991).

5. Cynthia A. Claassen, Carroll W. Hughes, Saundra Gilfillan, Don McIntire, Ann Roose, et al., "Towards a Redefinition of Psychiatric Emergency," 35 *Health Services Research* 735 (2000).

6. APA Task Force on Psychiatric Emergency Services, Report and Recommendations Regarding Psychiatric Emergency and Crisis Services: A Review and Model Program Descriptions, American Psychiatric Association 5 (2002); Glenn

Currier and Michael Allen, "Physical and Chemical Restraint in the Psychiatric Emergency Service," 51 *Psychiatric Services* 717–718 (2000) ("there is a remarkable lack of consensus about the scope of emergency assessment . . .").

7. APA Task Force on Psychiatric Emergency Services, Report and Recommendations Regarding Psychiatric Emergency and Crisis Services: A Review and Model Program Descriptions, American Psychiatric Association 5 (2002); Michael J. Bresler and Robert S. Hoffman, "General Approach to Behavioral Emergencies," in Michael L. Callaham, *Current Practice of Emergency Medicine,* 2d ed., (Philadelphia: B.C. Decker 1991) lists over 50 conditions in nine distinct categories from metabolic disorders, endocrine disorders and infectious diseases to drug reactions and drug abuse that mimic psychiatric disabilities. These are listed and discussed further at p. 43 and p. 62, n. 11, *infra.*

8. APA Task Force on Psychiatric Emergency Services, Report and Recommendations Regarding Psychiatric Emergency and Crisis Services: A Review and Model Program Descriptions, American Psychiatric Association 5 (2002).

9. Michael Allen, Glenn W. Currier, Douglas W. Hughes, et al, "Treatment of Behavioral Emergencies: A Summary of the Expert Consensus Guidelines," 9 *Journal of Psychiatric Practice* 16 (January 2003). This article summarizes the Expert Consensus Guidelines, which are published in full as "The Expert Consensus Guidelines Series: Treatment of Behavioral Emergencies, A Postgraduate Medicine Special Report" (May 2001).

10. The Joint Commission's new standard under the category of "Leadership," LD 3.10.10, "Managing Patient Flow," took effect on January 1, 2005. It states "The leaders develop and implement plans to identify and mitigate impediment to efficient patient flow throughout the hospital." The rationale for this standard states, "The Emergency Department is particularly vulnerable to experiencing negative effects of inefficiency in the management of this process." See www.ed-qual.com/Emergency_Medicine_News/JCAHO_Patient_Flow _Standard.htm, site visited 4/20/05.

CHAPTER 2

1. Lorna A. Rhodes, *Emptying Beds: The Work of an Emergency Psychiatric Unit* (University of California Press 1991). For another intriguing anthropological study of psychiatry, which contains trenchant observation of the role of residents in assessing psychiatric clients in the emergency department, see T. M. Luhrmann, *Of Two Minds: The Growing Disorder in American Psychiatry* (Knopf 2000). See also Sue Estroff's classic *Making It Crazy* (University of California Press 1981).

2. Samuel Gerson and Ellen Bassuk, "Psychiatric Emergencies: An Overview," 137 *American Journal of Psychiatry* 1, 3–4 (1980).

3. M. H. Allen, P. Forster, J. Zealberg, and G. Currier, APA Task Force on Psychiatric Emergency Services. Washington D.C.: American Psychiatric Association, August 2002, p. 10.

4. G. A. Barker, "Emergency Room 'Repeaters' " in James Randolph Hillard, ed., *Manual of Clinical Emergency Psychiatry* (American Psychiatric Press 1990) at 344.

5. Interview with Ann Maynard, Bay State Medical Center, Feb. 18, 2005.

6. M. H. Allen, P. Forster, J. Zealberg, and G. Currier, APA Task Force on Psychiatric Emergency Services, August 2002, p. 5.

7. Joint Commission Resources, *Accreditation Issues for Emergency Departments* (Joint Commission Resources: Oakbrook Terrace Illinois 2003) at 5.

8. *Cook v. Oschner Foundation Hospital*, 319 F.Supp. 603 (E.D.La. 1971).

9. www.cmmc.org/pc-em-history.html (accessed on January 31, 2005).

10. Leonard S. Powers, "Hospital Emergency Services and the Open Door," 66 *Michigan Law Review* 1455, 1462–1464 (1968).

11. Joint Commission on Accreditation of Health Care Organizations, Accreditation Issues for Emergency Departments (Oakbrook Terrace, Ill. 2003) at 5.

12. Michael J. Sateia, David H. Gustafson, and Sandra W. Johnson, "Quality Assurance for Psychiatric Emergencies: An Analysis of Assessment and Feedback Methodologies," 13 *Psychiatric Clinics of North America* 35, 37 (1990).

13. Karen Auge, "Cuts Squeeze Treatment of Mentally Ill," *Denver Post*, Dec. 16, 2002. The counselor testified in deposition, "I have never seen an ER doctor read the psych notes even though they sign every one of them. They just don't have the time."

14. R. Reinhold, "Crisis in Emergency Rooms: More Symptoms than Cures," *New York Times*, July 28, 1988, A-1, col. 1.

15. Ricardo Mendoza, "The Vicissitudes of Emergency Psychiatry: A Service Systems Perspective," in Glenn Currier, ed., *New Developments in Emergency Psychiatry: Medical, Legal and Economic* (New Directions for Mental Health Services, San Francisco: Jossey Bass 1999) p. 4.

16. New York State Commission on the Quality of Care for the Mentally Disabled, "Psychiatric Emergency Room Overcrowding: A Case Study," (May 1989) (on file at the Center for Public Representation).

17. "Woman in Florida Shot in Back, Waits 13 Hours for Surgery," *New York Times*, Aug. 9, 1987, A-21.

18. The Lewin Group, Emergency Department Overload: A Growing Crisis: The Results of the AHA Survey of Emergency Department (ED) and Hospital Capacity, April 2002, at p. 18 (when asked to name the "top three hardest specialties to fill," 20.3% of hospitals included neurosurgeons, 7.7% of hospitals reported difficulty meeting need for surgeons, 4% named OB/Gyn, but only 1.6% named emergency medicine, and only 1.5% named psychiatry/psychology).

19. *Id.*, at p. 17 ("Hospitals Experiencing ED Diversions Have Higher RN Vacancy Rates"). It should be noted that the relationship between nurse vacancy rates and diversions reflected in the report appears weak; hospitals with no diversion time reported a nurse vacancy rate of about 13%, while hospitals spending 20% or more time on diversion had a nurse vacancy rate of about 16–17%).

20. Ole J. Thienhaus, "Academic Issues in Emergency Psychiatry," in Michael Allen, ed., *The Growth and Specialization of Emergency Psychiatry* (New Directions for Mental Health Services, San Francisco: Jossey Bass 1995) at 110.

21. Paul Starr, *The Social Transformation of American Medicine* (Basic Books 1982) at 438. The hospital remains liable for negligence by its ED, even when it has entirely contracted out the operation, *Richmond County Hospital Authority v. Brown*, 361 S.E.2d 153 (Va. 1987).

22. Joint Commission Resources, *Accreditation Issues for Emergency Departments* (Oakbrook Terrace, Ill. 2003) at 5.

23. The Joint Commission's new standard under the category of "Leadership," LD 3.10.10, Managing Patient Flow, took effect on January 1, 2005, see www.jcaho.org. The wording of the new standard and its rationale can be found at note 10 to the Introduction (chapter 1) of this book.

24. Ross Koppel, Joshua P. Metlay, Abigail Cohen, Brian Abaluck, et al., "The Role of Computerized Physician Order Entry Systems in Facilitating Medication Errors," 293 *Journal of the American Medical Association* 1197, 1198 (March 9, 2005).

25. For accounts by and about each of these actors, see T. M. Luhrmann, *Of Two Minds: The Growing Disorder in American Psychiatry* (Knopf 2000) (psychiatric residents).

26. Scott Plantz, Lance Kreplick, Edward Panacek, Tejas Mehta, et al., "A National Survey of Board Certified Emergency Physicians: Quality of Care and Practice Structure Issues," *American Journal of Emergency Medicine*, Jan. 1988.

27. Id.

28. American Nurses Association, "Survey of 76,000 Nurses Probes Elements of Job Satisfaction," April 1, 2005, www.nursingworld.org/pressrel/2005/pr0401.html

29. Id.

30. Laura Browning and Martin Greenberg, "Cross-Sectional Survey of Burnout in Emergency and Non-Emergency Nurses," 29 *Journal of Emergency Nursing* 408 (2003). See also Vicki A. Keough, Rita S. Schlomer, and Barbara W. Bollenberg, "Serendipitous Finding from an Illinois ED Nursing Educational Survey Reflect a Crisis in Emergency Nursing," 29 *Journal of Emergency Nursing* 17 (2003) (attempt to survey 900 emergency nurses on their educational needs revealed nurses were "overburdened and frustrated").

31. The American College of Surgeons developed a classification system to describe the kinds of resources available at hospitals and emergency departments designated as Levels I–IV Trauma Centers. Level I, the highest, has a full range of specialists available 24 hours a day and serves as a comprehensive regional resource. Level I Trauma Centers admit a minimum required annual volume of severely injured patients.

32. Interview with Amy Gremillion, R. N., March 22, 2005.

33. Ricardo Mendoza, "The Vicissitudes of Emergency Psychiatry: A Service Systems Perspective," in Glenn Currier, ed., *New Developments in Emergency Psychiatry: Medical, Legal and Economic* (New Directions for Mental Health Services, San Francisco: Jossey Bass 1999) at 4.

34. Michael H. Allen, P. Forster, J. Zealberg, and G. Currier, APA Task Force on Psychiatric Emergency Services (Washington, D.C.: American Psychiatric Association, August 2002) p. 9.

35. Internal Revenue Service, Revenue Ruling 69–545 (1969), requiring all hospitals wishing to retain their tax-exempt status to provide "community benefit," including the offering of 24-hour emergency service open to the community served by the hospital. Because this ruling also contained a more limiting interpretation of the hospitals' obligation to provide free care to the poor, it was challenged by an organization representing poor people. In *Simon v. Eastern Kentucky Welfare Rights Organization*, 426 U.S. 26 (1976), the Supreme Court held that the organization did not have standing to challenge the ruling. In 1983, the IRS broadened the grounds on which hospitals could claim charitable

tax exemption, Internal Revenue Service, Revenue Ruling 83-157, thus reducing the pressure on hospitals to maintain 24-hour emergency departments.

36. Alexander C. Tsai, Joshua H. Tamayo-Sarver, Rita K. Cydulka, and David W. Baker, "Declining Payments for Emergency Department Care 1996–1998," 41 *Ann. Emerg. Med.* 319–320 (2003).

37. *Id.*

38. P.L. 88–164 (1963).

39. P.L. 93–154 (1973).

40. Ellen L. Bassuk and R. Apsler, "Managing the Chronic Patient in an Acute Care Setting," 6 *Psychosocial Rehabilitation Journal* 20–21 (1982). Ellen L. Bassuk and Ann W. Birk, *Emergency Psychiatry: Concepts Methods and Practices* (New York: Plenum Press 1986).

41. M. H. Allen, P. Forster, J. Zealberg, and G. Currier, APA Task Force on Psychiatric Emergency Services, August 2002, p. 7.

42. *Id.*

43. *Id.*, at 4.

44. Samuel Gerson and Ellen Bassuk, "Psychiatric Emergencies: An Overview," 137 *American Journal of Psychiatry* 1 (1980).

45. *Id.*, at 3–4.

46. A Historical Review of the Madison Model of Community Care, 41 *Hospital and Community Psychiatry* 625 (June 1990).

47. Stephen M. Soreff, *Management of the Psychiatric Emergency* (Wiley 1981).

48. See Norman Siegal and Robert Levy, "Koch's Mishandling of the Homeless," *New York Times*, Sept. 17, 1987, A-35.

49. Ricardo Mendoza, "The Vicissitudes of Emergency Psychiatry: A Service Systems Perspective," in Glenn Currier, ed., *New Developments in Emergency Psychiatry: Medical, Legal and Economic* (New Directions for Mental Health Services, San Francisco: Jossey Bass 1999) at 4.

50. Editorial, "This is Nuts—Fix It Now," *Los Angeles Times*, July 3, 2001, p. 12.

51. Charles Ornstein, "Use of Taser Spurs Change: King/Drew, threatened with funding cuts after stun gun incident, plans to call on mental health workers instead of police to calm patients," *Los Angeles Times*, Dec. 24, 2004, B-1.

52. John Petrila and Noel Mazade et al., "Mediation as an Alternative Dispute Resolution Device in Managed Behavioral Health Care," *Behavioral Healthcare Tomorrow* 26–32. (1997); Noel Mazade, Andrea Blanch, and John Petrila, "Mediation as a New Technique for Resolving Disputes in the Mental Health System, 21 *Administration and Policy in Mental Health* 431 (May 1994) [special issue on mental health and the law].

53. P. Micheels, L. F. Cuoco, F. Lipton, and A. J. Anderson, "Criteria Based Voluntary and Involuntary Psychiatric Admissions Modeling," 2 *International Journal of Psychosocial Rehabilitation* 176 (1998); S. P. Segal, T. A. Laurie and M. J. Segal, "Factors in the Use of Coercive Retention in Civil Commitment Evaluations in Psychiatric Emergency Services," 52 *Psychiatric Services* 514 (2001). See also A. L. Lincoln and M. H. Allen, "The Influence of Collateral Informants on Psychiatric Emergency Service Disposition Decisions and Access to Inpatient Care, 6 *International Journal of Psychosocial Rehabilitation* 99 (2002).

54. P. Micheels, L. F. Cuoco, F. Lipton, and A. J. Anderson, "Criteria Based

Voluntary and Involuntary Psychiatric Admissions Modeling," 2 *International Journal of Psychosocial Rehabilitation* 176 (1998).

55. Robert M. Factor and Ronald J. Diamond, "Emergency Psychiatry and Conflict Resolution," in J. V. Vaccarro and G. H. Clark, Jr., eds., *Practicing Psychiatry in the Community: A Manual* (American Psychiatric Association Press 1996), 54.

56. *Id.*

57. Marcia Linehan, *Skills Training Manual for Treating Borderline Personality Disorder* (New York: Guildford Press 1993). David Dawson and Harriet MacMillan, *Relationship Management of the Borderline Patient: From Understanding to Treatment* (New York: Brunner/Mazel 1992).

58. Mark Moran, "As Insurance Coverage Wanes, Psychiatric ERs get Busier," 39 *Psychiatric News*, no. 21, p. 12, Nov. 5, 2004.

59. www.hospitals.unm.edu/UNMPC/PsychiatricEmergencyServices.shtml, last accessed on April 18, 2005. See also R. Muller, *Psych ER: Psychiatric Patients Come to the Emergency Room* (Hillsdale, NJ: The Analytic Press 2003), in which the author discusses a difficult patient sent to the emergency room by a therapist who wanted the patient committed in order to give herself (the therapist) a vacation from the patient.

60. www.hospitals.unm.edu/UNMPC/PsychiatricEmergencyServices.shtml, last accessed on April 18, 2005.

61. Ricardo Mendoza, "The Vicissitudes of Emergency Psychiatry: A Service Systems Perspective," in Glenn Currier, ed., *New Developments in Emergency Psychiatry: Medical, Legal and Economic* (New Directions for Mental Health Services, San Francisco: Jossey Bass 1999) at 5–6.

62. *Id.* at 5.

63. P. L. Forster and L. H. Wu, "Assessment and Treatment of Suicidal Patients in an Emergency Setting," in Michael Allen, ed., *Emergency Psychiatry* (Washington, D.C.: American Psychiatric Association Press 2002) ("Just as suicide has markedly shaped the practice of emergency psychiatry, the threat of malpractice has a profound impact on how we treat suicidal patients").

64. R. Muller, *Psych ER: Patients Come to the Emergency Room* (Hillsdale, N.J.: The Analytic Press 2003) at 34.

65. Michael T. Lambert, "Seven Year Outcomes of Patients Evaluated for Suicidality," 53 *Psychiatric Services* 92 (2002) (of 45 patients judged to be contingently suicidal, that is, who threatened to commit suicide if they were not admitted, of 92 non-contingently suicidal patients, ten were apparent suicide victims); Anna Fitzgerald, "Assessing Risk: Getting Beyond 'Suicidal Ideation, Will Not Contract for Safety,'" Presentation, Psychiatric Emergencies: The Case for Diversionary Care, Boston University School Medicine, Cambridge, Massachusetts, Nov. 5, 2004.

66. S. V. McCrary, J. Swanson, H. S. Perkins, and W. J. Winslade, "Treatment Decisions for Terminally Ill Patients: Physicians' Legal Defensiveness and Knowledge of Medical Law," 20 *Medicine and Health Care* 364 (1992). See also B. A. Liang, "Medical Malpractice: Do Physicians Have the Knowledge of Legal Standards and Assess Cases as Juries Do?" *University of Chicago Roundtable* 59 (1996).

67. M. H. Allen, P. Forster, J. Zealberg, and G. Currier: APA Task Force on Psychiatric Emergency Services. August 2002.

68. Centers for Disease Control, "Visits to the Emergency Department Increase Nationwide," April 22, 2002, www.cdc.gov/od/oc/media/pressrel/r020422 .html; Centers for Disease Control and Prevention, 2000 Emergency Department Summary, April 30, 2002; http://www.hospitalmanagement.net/informer/ breakthroughs/break142, June 5, 2002; American College of Emergency Physicians, "The Emergency Department: What to Expect," http://www.acep.org/ 1,241,0.html, April 8, 2002.

69. American College of Emergency Physicians, Care of Children in the Emergency Department: Guidelines for Preparedness, Sept. 2000. www.acep.org/ 1,2669,0.html.

70. "Number of ED Visits Continues to Trend Higher," *American College of Emergency Physicians News* (October 2003) p. 2.

71. Alisa Lincoln and Michael Allen, "The Influence of Collateral Information on Access to Inpatient Psychiatric Services," 6 *International Journal of Psychosocial Rehabilitation* 99 (2002). See more information about psychiatric emergency services at Section II(B).

72. Linda McCaig and Catharine W. Burt, "National Hospital Ambulatory Medical Care Survey: 2002 Emergency Department Summary," *Advance Data from Vital and Health Statistics*, No. 340 (Hyattsville, Maryland: National Center for Health Statistics, 2004).

73. Linda McCaig and Catharine W. Burt, "National Hospital Ambulatory Medical Care Survey: 2001 Emergency Department Summary," *Advance Data from Vital and Health Statistics*, No. 335 (Hyattsville, Maryland: National Center for Health Statistics, 2003).

74. L. F. McCaig and N. Ly, "National Hospital Ambulatory Care Survey: 2000 Emergency Department Summary," *Advance Data from Vital and Health Statistics*, No. 326 (Hyattsville, Maryland, National Center for Health Statistics, 2002).

75. Linda McCaig and Catharine W. Burt, "National Hospital Ambulatory Medical Care Survey: 2002 Emergency Department Summary," (2004) at n. 71, and Linda McCraig and Catharine W. Burt, 2001 Emergency Department Summary at n. 72.

76. *Id.*

77. *Id.*

78. *Id.*

79. *Id.*

80. K. Yamane, "Hospital Emergency Departments: Crowded Conditions Vary Among Hospitals and Communities," General Accounting Office Report 03-460 (Washington, D.C.: General Accounting Office 2003).

81. "Upsurge in People with Mental Illness Seeking Treatment in Emergency Departments is Taking Toll on Patient Care," News-Medical.Net, April 27, 2004 (70% of emergency physicians report with mental illness "boarding"); Jonathan M. Mansbach, Elizabeth Wharff, S. Bryn Austin, Katherine Ginnis, and Elizabeth R. Woods, "Which Psychiatric Patients Board on the Medical Service?" 111 *Pediatrics* 693 (2003).

82. L. F. McCraig and N. Ly, 2000 Emergency Department Summary at n.73.

83. Linda McCraig and Catharine Burt, 2002 Emergency Department Summary, at n. 71, table 1.

84. *Id.*

85. L. F. McCraig and N. Ly, "National Hospital Ambulatory Care Survey: 2000 Emergency Department Summary," at n. 73, table 79 (2003).

86. J. Hornberger, H. Itakura, S. R. Wilson, "Bridging Language and cultural barriers between physicians and patients," 112 *Public Health Report* 410 (1997); A. Manson, "Language Concordance as a Determinant of Patient Compliance and ER Use in Patients with Asthma," 26 *Med Care* 1919 (1988); see generally Institute of Medicine, "Unequal Treatment: Confronting Racialized Ethnic Disparities in Health Care," National Academies Press 2002.

87. Xuemi Luo, Gordon Liu, Karen Frush, and Lloyd A. Hey, "Children's Health Insurance Status and Emergency Department Utilization," 112 *Pediatrics* 314 (August 2003) (finding black and Hispanic children less likely to have ED visit and less likely to have non-urgent ED visit).

88. National Center for Health Statistics, *Health, United States, 2002*, table 79 (2003).

89. MB Kushel, S. Perry, D. Bangsberg, R. Clark, and AR Moss, "Emergency Department Use Among the Homeless and Marginally Housed: Results from a Community-Based Study," 92 *American Journal of Public Health* 778 (2002).

90. Linda McCraig and Catharine W. Burt, 2002 Emergency Department Summary, n. 71, table 3; Linda McCraig and Catharine Burt, 2001 Emergency Department Summary at n. 72.

91. *Id.*

92. Linda McCraig and Catharine W. Burt, 2002 Emergency Department Summary at n. 71, table 3.

93. S. Pilossoph-Gelb, W. R. Mower, I. Ajaelo, and S. C. Yang, "Psychosocial Difficulties and Emergency Department Use," 4 *Academic Emergency Medicine* 589 (1997).

94. *Id.* For example, individuals who were homeless or alcoholic had emergent problems 62% of the time, compared to 54% and 53% emergent visits for people who did not fall into those categories.

95. Linda T. Krohn, et al., eds., *To Err Is Human: Building a Safer Health System* (Washington, D.C.: Government Printing Office 2000).

96. *Id.* See also R. L. Wears and L. L. Leape, "Human Error in Emergency Medicine," 34 *Annals of Emergency Medicine* 370 (1999).

97. Andrew S. Kaufman, "Outside Counsel: An Introduction to Hospital Emergency Room Litigation," 230 *New York Law Journal* 4 (July 31, 2003).

98. *John Jordan v. Thomas Jefferson University Hospital*, 23 Phila. 434, 1992 Phila.Cty.Rptr. LEXIS 4 (January 10, 1992) (jury award of no compensatory damages and $50,000 in punitive damages upheld); *Peter Rogers v. Thomas Jefferson University Hospital* 23 Phila. 632, 1992 Phila.Cty. Rptr. LEXIS 34 (Feb. 21, 1992) (jury award of $100,000 for malicious prosecution, $67,000 for negligence and $98,162 for soft tissue injuries upheld). Cases against hospital security guards are also are discussed in chapter 5.

99. Linda McCaig and Catharine Burt, 2002 Emergency Department Summary, n. 71, table 5. The proportion of ED visits attributable to psychiatric symptoms vary widely between EDs. In the early 1980s, Bassuk, Winter, and Apsler estimated that 10% of visits to emergency departments were for psychiatric symptoms; see E. Bassuk, L. Winter, and R. Apsler, "Cross-Cultural Com-

parison of British and American Psychiatric Emergencies," 140 *American Journal of Psychiatry* 183 (1983).

100. *Id.*, table 8.

101. American Association for Emergency Psychiatry, Newsletter, Spring 2003, available online at www.emergencypsychiatry.org.

102. This is true at the University of Cincinnati's Psychiatric Emergency Service, www.Psychiatry.uc.edu./care/pes.shtml. The Comprehensive Psychiatric Emergency Program at Bellevue Hospital has 6000 visits per year. Allisa Lincoln and Michael Allen, "The Influence of Collateral Informants on Psychiatric Emergency Service Disposition Decisions and Access to Inpatient Psychiatric Care," 6 *International Journal of Psychosocial Rehabilitation* 99–100 (2002).

103. Linda McCraig and Catharine W. Burt, 2002 Emergency Department Summary, n. 71.

104. Unpublished study on file at the Center for Public Representation.

105. Linda McCraig and Catharine W. Burt at n. 71, table 7.

106. D. M. Dhossche, "Suicidal behavior in Psychiatric Emergency Room Patients," 93 *South Med. J.* 310 (2000).

107. "Nonfatal Self-Inflicted Injuries Treated in Hospital Emergency Departments," 51 MMWR Weekly (Center for Disease Control, May 24, 2002) (264,108 self-inflicted injuries, of which 60% were "probably" and 10% "possibly" suicide attempts as determined by examination of the treatment charts).

108. Richard E. Breslow, "Structure and Function of Psychiatric Emergency Services," in Michael H. Allen, ed., *Emergency Psychiatry* (APA Press 2002) at 2; D. Wingerson, J. Russo, R. Reis, et al., "Use of Psychiatric Emergency Services and Enrollment Status in a Public Managed Mental Health Care Plan," 52 *Psychiatric Services* 1494 (2001) (studying presentations to a crisis triage unit).

109. R. E. Breslow, B. I. Klinger and B. J. Erickson, "Acute Intoxication and Substance Abuse Among Patients Presenting to a Psychiatric Emergency Service," 18 *General Hospital Psychiatry* 183 (1996).

110. Cynthia A. Claassen, Carroll W. Hughes, Saundra Gilfillan, Don McIntire, Ann Roose, et al., "Towards a Redefinition of Psychiatric Emergency," 35 *Health Services Research* 735 (2000).

111. Bryan Yates, Carol R. Nordquist, and R. Andrew Schultz-Ross, "Feigned Psychiatric Symptoms in the Emergency Room," 47 *Psychiatric Services* 998 (Sept. 1996).

112. Lonnie Snowden and Jane Holschuh, "Ethnic Differences in Emergency Psychiatric Care and Hospitalization in a Program for the Severely Mentally Ill," 28 *Community Mental Health Journal* 281 (1992).

113. S. Rosenfeld, "Race differences in involuntary hospitalization: psychiatric v. labeling perspectives," 25 *Journal of Health and Social Behavior* 14 (1984).

114. L. W. Reinish and R. Ciccone, "Involuntary Hospitalization and Police Referrals to a Psychiatric Emergency Department," 23 *Bulletin of the American Academy of Psychiatry and Law* 289 (1995). Obviously, this shifts rather than resolves the question of possible race discrimination.

115. Alisa Lincoln and Michael Allen, "The Influence of Collateral Information on Psychiatric Emergency Service Disposition Decisions and Access to Inpatient Psychiatric Care," 6 *International Journal of Psychosocial Rehabilitation* 99 (2002).

116. Michael Allen, Daniel Carpenter, John L. Sheets, Steven Miccio, and Ruth Ross, "What Do Consumers Say They Want and Need During a Psychiatric Emergency?" 9 *Journal of Psychiatric Practice* 39, 44 (2003) (7% of survey respondents were African-American, 9% were Hispanic).

117. Joint Commission on the Accreditation of Health Care Organizations, "The Emergency Department Overcrowding Symposium: Condition Critical: Meeting the Challenge of ED Overcrowding," Feb. 24–26, 2003, Boston Massachusetts.

118. Jonathan M. Mansbach, Elizabeth Wharff, Bryn Austin, Katherine Ginnis et al., "Which Psychiatric Patients Board on the Medical Service," 111 *Pediatrics* 1426 (June 2003).

119. *Lizotte v. New York City Health and Hospitals Corporation*, 1992 U.S.Dist.LEXIS 10976 (S.D.N.Y. July 16, 1992) (approving settlement of case).

120. "Police Interactions with Individuals in Psychiatric Crisis: A Briefing Prepared for Michael A. Cardozo, Corporation Counsel of the City of New York" (Urban Justice Center 2002) at p. 4.

121. Michael Allen and Glen Currier, "American Association for Emergency Psychiatry Survey: I. Psychiatric Emergency Service Structure and Function," presented at the Institute on Psychiatric Services, New Orleans, Oct. 29–Nov. 2, 1999. In another national survey in which individuals with psychiatric disabilities who had experienced ED treatment were asked to pick one incident of treatment and answer questions about it, approximately half reported on voluntary visits and half reported on involuntary visits, Michael H. Allen, Daniel Carpenter, John Sheets, Steven Miccio, and Ruth Ross, "What Kinds of Help do Consumers Want and Need During a Psychiatric Emergency?" 9 *Journal of Psychiatric Practice* 1, 7 (January 2003).

122. Charles W. Lidz, Edward P. Mulvey, Robert P. Arnold, Nancy S. Bennett, and Brenda L. Kirsch, "Coercive Interactions in a Psychiatric Emergency Room," 11 *Behavioral Sciences and the Law* 269 (1993); Cynthia A. Claassen, Carroll W. Hughes, Saundra Gilfillian, Don McIntire, Ann Roose and Monica Basco, "The Nature of Help-Seeking During Psychiatric Emergency Service Visits by a Patient and Accompanying Adult," 51 *Psychiatric Services* 924–925 (2000).

123. Survey No. 5, on file at the Center for Public Representation.

124. Cynthia A. Claassen, Carroll W. Hughes, Saundra Gilfillian, et al., "The Nature of Help-Seeking During Psychiatric Emergency Service Visits by a Patients and Accompanying Adult," 51 *Psychiatric Services* 924–925 (July 2000) (48.2% of adult visits to ER were accompanied by family member or friend); Michael H. Allen, Daniel Carpenter, John Sheets, Steven Miccio and Ruth Ross, "What Kinds of Help do Consumers Want and Need During a Psychiatric Emergency?" 9 *Journal of Psychiatric Practice* 1, 7 (January 2003) (national survey of consumers who had experiences in EDs; participants were asked to pick a particular incident and describe it. Results showed 30% brought by a family member or friend, 25% brought by police, 11% by mobile crisis unit, and 5% accompanied by mental health professional); D. M. Dhossche and S. O. Ghani, "Who brings patients to the psychiatric emergency room? Psychosocial and psychiatric correlates," 20 *General Hospital Psychiatry* 235 (1999); R. C. Rosenberg and M. Kessellman, "The Therapeutic Alliance and the Psychiatric Emergency Room," 44 *Hospital and Community Psychiatry* 78 (1993).

125. Cynthia A. Claassen, Carroll W. Hughes, Saundra Gifillan, Don McIntire, Ann Roose, et al., "Toward a Redefinition of Psychiatric Emergency," 35 *Health Services Research* 735 (2000) (25% of people brought by police to Parkland Hospital's psychiatric emergency room in Dallas hospitalized); G. N. Sales, "A Comparison of Referrals by Police and Other Sources to a Psychiatric Emergency Service," 42 *Hospital and Community Psychiatry* 950 (1991) (50% of individuals brought by police to Cincinnati emergency room hospitalized); R. E. Breslow, B. J. Erickson and K. C. Cavanaugh, "The Psychiatric Emergency Service: Where We've Been and Where We're Going," 71 *Psychiatric Quarterly* 101, 115 (2000) (49% of people who come to psychiatric emergency service are hospitalized); Gordon Strauss, Mark Glenn, Padma Reddi, Irfan Afaq et al., "Psychiatric Disposition of Patients Brought in by Crisis Intervention Team Police Officers," 41 *Community Mental Health Journal* 223 (2005) (one-third of people who self-referred to the ED for psychiatric treatment were hospitalized, while 71.6% of people who were brought pursuant to a "mental inquest warrant" for evaluation of dangerousness were hospitalized).

126. David H. Gustafson, Francois Sainfort, Sandra W. Johnson, Michael Sateia, "Measuring Quality of Care in Psychiatric Emergencies: Construction and Evaluation of a Baysian Index," 28 *Health Services Research* 131, 132–33 (June 1993).

127. Charles W. Lidz, Phyllis D. Coontz, and Edward P. Mulvey, "The 'Pass-Through' Model of Psychiatric Emergency Room Assessment," 23 *International Journal of Law and Psychiatry* 43, 47 (2000) (51.3% of people accompanied by police, ambulance, or other persons with a formal relationship with the patient were involuntarily committed, compared to 8.4% of self-referred individuals); Breslow, Erickson, and Cavanaugh, *supra* at n. 124 (noting that people brought in by police are hospitalized at a much higher rate without quantifying).

128. Gordon Strauss, Mark Glenn, Padma Reddi, Irfan Afaq et al., "Psychiatric Disposition of Patients Brought in by Crisis Intervention Team Police Officers," 41 *Community Mental Health Journal* 223 (2005).

129. *Id.*

130. Charles W. Lidz, Edward P. Mulvey, et al., note 121 (22% of patients brought to emergency room eventually involuntarily hospitalized); Ed Dwyer-O'Connor, David M. Wertheimer, Boston Triage Consultation, April 16, 2003 (half of those hospitalized voluntarily, half involuntarily).

131. David H. Gustafson, Francois Sainfort, Sandra W. Johnson, and Michael Sateia, "Measuring Quality of Care in Psychiatric Emergencies: Construction and Evaluation of a Bayesian Index," 28 *Health Services Research* 131 (1993).

132. *Id.*

133. Charles Ornstein, "Use of Taser Spurs Change: King/Drew, threatened with funding cuts after stun gun incident, plans to call on mental health workers instead of police to calm patients," *Los Angeles Times*, Dec. 24, 2004, B-1.

CHAPTER 3

1. This survey was a paper survey designed and distributed by Susan Werboff, director of the Protection and Advocacy for Individuals with Mental Ill-

ness (PAIMI) program of the State of Connecticut Office of Protection and Advocacy for Persons with Disabilities. A report based on the surveys was released on April 12, 1999. A total of 64 surveys were completed. The survey and report are on file both with the author and at the State of Connecticut Office of Protection and Advocacy for Persons with Disabilities in Hartford, Connecticut.

2. This survey was the result of four Emergency Service Forums held in Poughkeepsie, New York; Syracuse, New York; Los Angeles, California; and Marshalltown, Iowa, with a total of 56 participants, and asked about lifetime experience with emergency services. A complete description of the survey and results can be found in Micheal H. Allen, D. Carpenter, John Sheets, Steven Miccio, and J. Ross, "What Do Consumers Want and Need During a Psychiatric Emergency," 9 *Journal of Psychiatric Practice* 39 (January 2003).

3. The Center for Public Representation's survey is national in scope and asks about ED experience in the past year. It has utilized both an on-line survey and an identical paper survey that has received 316 responses so far. The paper survey has been distributed at conferences and by consumer self-help groups in a number of states, including Massachusetts, Texas, and Connecticut.

4. *John Jordan v. Thomas Jefferson University Hospital*, 23 Phila. 434, 1992 Phila.Cty.Rptr.LEXIS 4 (Common Pleas Court Philadelphia County January 10, 1992); *Peter F. Rogers v. Thomas Jefferson University Hospital*, 23 Phila. 632, 1992 Phila.Cty.Rptr. LEXIS 34 (Common Pleas Court Philadelphia County Feb. 21, 1992); *Straub v. Kilgore*, 100 Fed.Appx. 379, 2004 U.S.App.LEXIS 10668 (6th Cir. May 27, 2004); *Payton v. Rush-Presbyterian-St. Luke's Medical Center*, 184 F.3d 623 (7th Cir. 1999); *Rowe v. Children's Hospital of Michigan*, 1997 Mich.App.LEXIS 1238 (Michigan Court of Appeals Jan. 10, 1997); *Owens v. City of Fort Lauderdale*, 174 F.Supp.2d 1298 (S.D.Fla. 2001). Many more cases involve security guards than are reported; some are settled prior to trial; see Susan Jaffe, "Family of Dead Man Settles Negligence Suit," *Cleveland Plain Dealer*, Feb. 19, 2000, p. 4-B. Others are settled subject to confidentiality agreements; the author knows of at least two such cases in a six-month period.

5. *Owens v. City of Fort Lauderdale*, 174 F.Supp.2d 1298 (S.D.Fla. 2001). See case referred to at note 6, *infra*.

6. Susan Jaffe, "Family of Dead Man Settles Negligence Suit," *Cleveland Plain Dealer*, Feb. 19, 2000, p. 4-B.

7. Carolyn Knight, "Night Sticks or Needles? Use of Force in the Emergency Room," Ohio Legal Rights Service, www.state.oh.us/olrs/nitestik.htm

8. *Id.*

9. Interpretive Guidance to 45 C.F.R. 482.13(f), available online at www.cms.hhs.gov/manuals/107_som/som107ap_a_hospitals.pdf

10. *Collins v. First Unknown Security Officer et al*, 2002 Conn.Super.LEXIS 3419 (Conn. Super. Oct. 24, 2002).

11. Charles Lidz, Edward P. Mulvey, Robert Arnold, et al, "Coercive Interventions in a Psychiatric Emergency Room," 11 *Behavioral Sciences and the Law* 269, 276 (1993).

12. Joint Commission on Accreditation of Health Care Organizations, *Comprehensive Accreditation Manual for Hospitals*, Management of the Environment of Care (EC) Standards (Oakbrook Terrace, Ill., 2004).

13. American Psychiatric Association, Task Force on Emergency Psychiatry, p. 10.

14. *Owens v. City of Fort Lauderdale*, 174 F.Supp.2d 1298 (S.D.Fla. 2001).

15. Russell Colling, *Hospital and Health Care Security* 133 (4th ed. 2001).

16. Survey No. 1, Center for Public Representation, on file at the Center for Public Representation.

17. Recommendations for Creating a Crisis Triage Units for People with Psychiatric Disabilities and Substance Abuse Problems," David Wertheimer, Kelly Point.

18. Carolyn Knight, "Night Sticks or Needles? Use of Force in the Emergency Room," Ohio Legal Rights Service, www.state.oh.us/olrs/nitestik.htm.

19. Personal Communication, Russell Colling, November 8, 2004.

20. R. Rosenheck, "From conflict to collaboration: Psychiatry and the Hospital Police," 48 *Psychiatry* 254 (1985).

21. Russell Colling, *Hospital and Health Care Security* (4th ed. 2001) at 181.

22. *Id.* at 184.

23. Allan Anderson, A. Y. Ghali, and Rakesh K. Bansil, "Weapon Carrying Among Patients in a Psychiatric Emergency Room," 40 *Hospital and Community Psychiatry* 845 (1989) (24 of 287 patients entering ER and judged to need inpatient admission were carrying some form of weapon in psychiatric ER serving inner city neighborhood in Newark).

24. Lyda Longe, "Guard Shoots Man at Grady," *Atlanta Journal and Constitution*, August 3, 1999, p. A-1. The details in this story are few, but apparently the man was a patient about to be admitted and the security guard believed he was carrying a gun. The man was shot twice and was in critical condition at the time of the story. "Wounding Charges in Rampage Certified," *Richmond Times Dispatch*, Nov. 5, 1996, discusses an off duty police officer who worked as a security guard shooting a woman in the leg who tried to shoot two people as they waited in a cubicle.

25. Letter from Dr. Woodhall Stopford to the Consumer Product Safety Commission, on file at the Center for Public Representation.

26. Kenton Robinson, "Backus Psychiatric Care Criticized in State Reviews," *The Day*, Dec. 14, 2003, p. A-1.

27. Interpretive Guidance to 45 C.F.R. 482.13(f), available online at www .cms.hhs.gov/manuals/107_som/som107ap_a_hospitals.pdf.

28. Case filed under seal (D.Conn. filed Sept. 19, 2003).

29. *Id.*

30. Interview with Dr. Robert Factor, January 2004.

31. *John Jordan v. Thomas Jefferson University Hospital*, 23 Phila. 434, 1992 Phila.Cty.Rptr. LEXIS 4 (Jan. 10, 1992).

32. *Id.* at 189.

33. 45 C.F.R. 482.13(f), Interpretive Guidance, State Operations Manual, available online at www.cms.gov/manuals/107_som/som107ap_a_hospitals.pdf.

34. *Id.*

35. See, e.g., *Doby v. Decrescenzo*, 171 F.3d 858 (7th Cir. 1999) (handcuffing reasonable to prevent flight); *Hidalgo v. Gonzalez*, 2004 Tex.App.LEXIS 1853 (Tex.Ct.App. Feb. 26, 2004); *Thielman v. Leean*, 659 N.W.2d 73 (Wisc.App. 2003) (no individualized assessment required before transporting civilly committed sexually dangerous persons in full restraints).

36. JCAHO, "Accreditation Issues for Emergency Departments," p. 44.

37. "Md. Urges Action Against Hospital for Restraining Patient; Man was Tied Down for 11 Days in ER," *Washington Post*, Feb. 1, 2003, p. B2.

38. *Id.*

39. Glenn W. Currier and Michael Allen, "Physical and Chemical Restraint in the Psychiatric Emergency Service," 51 *Psychiatric Services* 717 (June 2000).

40. See, e.g., *Freeman v. St. Clare's Hospital and Health Center*, 156 A.D.2d 300 (N.Y.Sup.Ct. 1989) (patient raped while in restraints in emergency room); *Boles v. Milwaukee County*, 443 N.W.2d 679 (Wisc.App. 1989) (patient in restraints escaped and was run over after leaving hospital); *Schorr v. Borough of Lemoyne*, 265 F.Supp.2d 188 (M.D.Pa. 2003) (man who was locked in seclusion room escaped, was tracked to his house by police and shot there; both the police and the hospital were sued).

41. See Case filed under seal, discussed *supra* at p. 37.

42. See, e.g., *Schorr v. Borough of Lemoyne*, 265 F.Supp.2d 188 (M.D.Pa. 2003) (the court notes that immediately after being brought to the emergency room by police, "Schorr was locked in a seclusion room, where he became agitated and threatening").

43. 42 C.F.R. 482.13(f)(1) (West 2003).

44. 42 C.F.R. 482.13(f)(1) and (2) (emphasis added) (West 2003).

45. Office of Protection and Advocacy for the State of Connecticut, Report of PAIMI Survey of Consumers ER Experiences, April 12, 1999, p. 1.

46. Interview with Laura Cain of the Maryland Disability Law Center, October 20, 2003.

47. *Scherer v. Waterbury Hospital et al.*, 2000 Conn.Super.LEXIS 481 (Conn.Super.Ct. 2000).

48. *Threlkeld v. White Castle Systems*, 127 F.Supp.2d 986 (N.D.Ill. 2001); *Shine v. Vega*, 429 Mass. 456, 709 N.E.2d 58 (1999).

49. *Barker v. Netcare Corp.*, 768 N.E.2d 698, 147 Ohio App.3d 1 (Ohio App. 2001).

50. Testimony of Patricia Deegan, Hearing on H.R. 4498, Subcommittee on Select Education of the House Committee on Education and Labor, Boston, Lafayette Hotel, October 24, 1988. This testimony is recorded in Arnold and Porter Committee Print 1990 (28B) at 1251, and reproduced in Susan Stefan, *Unequal Rights: Discrimination Against People with Mental Disabilities and the Americans with Disabilities Act* (American Psychological Association Press 2001) at p. 195.

51. It is true that in a few cases requests for medical care are a part of psychiatric symptomatology. On the rare occasions that this is true, emergency rooms have different ways of responding to this situation. One respondent in our survey—who was extremely satisfied with the care that she received at a Portland, Oregon, emergency room—acknowledged that she is a "hypochondriac" who goes to emergency rooms for "reassurance." Survey No. 207.

52. Survey No. 1.

53. Office of Protection and Advocacy of the State of Connecticut, Report of PAIMI Survey of Consumers ER Experiences, April 12, 1999, p. 2.

54. *Id.*

55. Survey No. 224.

56. For a more extensive discussion of which screening tests should be routine when a person presents with a psychiatric disability, see chapter 4, *infra.*

57. Michael J. Bresler and Robert S. Hoffman, "Behavioral Emergencies," in Michael L. Callaham, ed., *Current Practice of Emergency Medicine* (2d Ed) (Philadelphia: Decker 1991) at 354.

58. See, e.g., *Thomas v. Christ Hospital and Medical Center*, 2003 U.S.App.LEXIS 7921 (7th Cir. Feb. 25, 2003).

59. Richard Hall, Earl R. Gardner, Michael K. Popkin et al., "Unrecognized Physical Illness Prompting Psychiatric Admission: A Prospective Study," 138 *American Journal of Psychiatry* 629, 630 (1981).

60. *Id.*

61. *Id.* at 629.

62. Glenn Currier, Michael Allen, Mark R. Serper, Adam J. Trenton, and Marc L Copersino, "Medical, Psychiatric and Cognitive Assessment in the Psychiatric Emergency Service," in Michael H. Allen, ed., *Emergency Psychiatry* 21 *Review of Psychiatry*, (American Psychiatric Association Press 2002) vol. 3, p. 38.

63. P. L. Henneman and R. J. Mendoza, "Prospective evaluation of emergency department medical clearance," 24 *Annals of Emergency Medicine* 672 (1994).

64. J. J. Caro, A. Ward, C. Levinton, and K. Robinson, "The risk of diabetes during olanzapine use compared with risperidone use: a retrospective data base analysis," 63 *Journal of Clinical Psychiatry* 1135 (2002); K. Melkersson, A-L Hulting, and K. Brismar, "Elevated levels of insulin, leptin and blood lipids in olanzapine-treated patients with schizophrenia or related psychoses," 61 *Journal of Clinical Psychiatry* 742 (2000).

65. In April 2003, the FDA warned of "cerebrovascular adverse events including fatalities" in patients treated with risperidone for demetia-induced psychoses. Tese results were "significantly higher" than patients treated with placebo (www.fda.gov/medwatch/SAFETY/2003/risperdal.htm, last accessed Nov. 7, 2005). The Canadian government had issued a similar warning six months earlier (www.hc-sc.gc.ca/hpfb-dgpsa/tpd-dpt/risperdal1e.html, last accessed Nov. 7, 2005). These warnings were based on several studies, including H. Brodety, D. Ames, J. Snowden, M. Woodward, et al., "A Randomized Placebo Controlled Trial of Risperidone for the Treatment of Aggression, Agitation, and Psychoses in Dementia," 64 *J. Clin. Psych.* 134–43 (2003).

66. Glenn Currier, Michael Allen, Mark R. Serper, et al., note 62 at p. 36.

67. *Jackson v. East Bay Hospital*, 246 F.3d 1248 (9th Cir. 2001).

68. Interview with Beckie Child, patients' rights advocate, Portland, Oregon, Jan. 31, 2005.

69. Survey No. 265.

70. *Id.*

71. Richard E. Breslow, "Structure and Function of Psychiatric Emergency Services," in Michael H. Allen, ed., *Emergency Psychiatry*, 21 *Review of Psychiatry* no. 3 (2002) p. 7.

72. M. Weissburg, "Open Forum: Chained in the Emergency Department: The New Asylum for the Poor," 42 *Hospital and Community Psychiatry* 317 (1991).

73. Samuel Gerson and Ellen Bassuk, "Psychiatric Emergencies: An Overview," 137 *American Journal of Psychiatry* 1, 7–8 (1980).

74. Stephen M. Soreff, *Management of the Psychiatric Emergency* (Wiley 1981) at p. 7.

75. JCAHO, "Accreditation Issues for Emergency Departments," p. 39.

76. Interpretive Guidelines, Hospital Conditions of Participation for Patients' Rights, interpreting 42 C.F.R. 482.13(c)(1), which states "The patient has the right to personal privacy" (May 23, 2000).

77. *Id.*

78. *Id.* at 47.

79. *Id.* at 59–60.

80. *Id.*

81. As of June 6, 2005, the JCAHO Web site continues to state that a White Paper on Emergency Department Overcrowding will be issued "in late 2004." www.jcaho.org.

82. Survey No. 224.

83. Hospital Management Net, Center for Disease Control and Prevention: 2000 Emergency Department Summary, April 30, 2002. Accessible online at http://hospitalmanagement.net/informer/breakthroughs/break142/.

84. National Center for Health Statistics, Ambulatory Care Statistics Branch, "Advance Data from Vital and Health Statistics No. 340," March 18, 2004, p. 10.

85. JCAHO, Accreditation Issues for Emergency Departments, p. 107.

86. Joelle Babula, "Emergency Rooms: Experts pose changes for LV Hospitals," *Las Vegas Review Journal*, Sept. 21, 2000, p. 1-A ("People think the ER experience is one to two hours, but it usually ends up being eight or nine").

87. Interview with Dr. Niels Rathlav, Boston Medical Center, May 2004.

88. *Lizotte v. New York City Health and Hospitals Corporation et al.*, 1992 U.S.Dist.LEXIS 10976 (S.D.N.Y. July 16, 1992).

89. *In re C.W.*, 53 P.3d 979, 147 Wash.2d 259 (2002).

90. Lynne Richardson, M.D., "America's Health Care Safety Net: Intact or Unraveling?" Academic Emergency Medicine Consensus Conference, Society for Academic Emergency Medicine, May 9, 2001, available online at www.saem.org/newsltr/2001/march.april/amsafnet.htm.

91. 42 U.S.C. 12181(7)(F) specifically lists hospitals as a public accommodation.

92. 28 C.F.R. 36.303(c).

93. 28 C.F.R. 36.303(b)(1).

94. *DeVinney v. Maine Medical Center*, consent decree available online at www.doj.gov; *Connecticut Association for the Deaf v. Middlesex Memorial Hospital*, consent decree available online at www. doj.gov.

95. *Aikins v. St. Helena Hospital*, 843 F.Supp. 1329 (N.D.Ca. 1994); *Schroedel v. New York University Medical Center*, 885 F.Supp. 594 (S.D.N.Y. 1995); *Daviton v. Columbia/HCA Healthcare Corp.*, 241 F3d 1131 (9th Cir. 2001).

96. 42 C.F.R. 489.10(b)(2)("provider must meet the applicable civil rights requirements of . . . Section 504 of the Rehabilitation Act").

97. See "Hospital Conditions of Participation for Patients' Rights," Interpretive Guidelines, 482.13(a), (Tag number A 751), p. A-171, available online at www.cms.hhs.gov/manuals/pm_trans/R17SOM.pdf.

98. *Id.*

99. Standards of Accreditation for Hospitals, RI.2.100 (2004).

100. RI 2.100(3).

101. RI 2.100(4)

102. J. Lebel and Nan Stromberg, "State Initiative to Reduce the Use of Restraint and Seclusion and Promote Strength-Based Care" (Boston: Massachusetts Department of Mental Health 2004) (over 80% of adolescents and children in continuing care inpatient and intensive residential treatment programs in Massachusetts were found to have trauma histories).

103. Ann Jennings, Models for Developing Trauma-Informed Behavioral Health Systems and Trauma-Specific Services (National Association of State Mental Health Program Directors/SAMHSA 2004), www.annafoundation.org/ MDT.pdf, last accessed Nov. 7, 2005.

104. Ronald C. Rosenberg and Kerry Sulkowicz, "Psychosocial Interventions in the Psychiatric Emergency Service: A Skills Approach," in Michael Allen, ed., *Emergency Psychiatry* (American Psychiatric Association Press) at 174.

105. "What to Expect in the Emergency Department" can be found online at www.crystal.palace.net/-llama/selfinjury/er.html.

106. Cara Baruzzi and Bree J. Schuette, "Proposed Massachusetts law would require translator in emergency rooms," *Daily Free Press,* April 12, 1999.

107. JCAHO, Accreditation Issues for Emergency Departments, p. 55.

108. *Id.* at p. 61.

109. United States Department of Health and Human Services, Office of Minority Health, Standards for Culturally and Linguistically Appropriate Services in Health, Standard 4.

110. *Id.* Standard 5.

111. *Id.* Standard 6.

112. U.S.C. 1396b(v)(1) excludes undocumented aliens, but 42 U.S.C. 1396b(v)(2)(a) permits hospitals to be reimbursed for treating "emergency medical conditions."

113. *Greenery Rehabilitation Group v. Hammon,* 150 F.3d 226, 232 (2nd Cir. 1998).

114. *Scottsdale Healthcare v. Arizona Health Care Cost Containment Systems,* 75 P.3d 91 (Ariz. 2003). The three adverse conditions include a condition that would place the individual's health in serious jeopardy, a condition that would result in serious impairment to bodily function, and a condition that would result in serious dysfunction of any organ or body part. See also *Mercy Healthcare v. Arizona Health Care,* 181 Ariz. 95, 887 P.2d 625 (App.Div. 1994) (Arizona Medicaid program must provide emergency Medicaid coverage to an undocumented alien after he no longer requires acute care).

115. *Greenery Rehabilitation Group,* 150 F.3d 226 at 232 (2nd Cir. 1998) (emphasis added).

116. These facilities do not receive Medicaid payments in any event because Medicaid excludes payments to those in "IMD" (institutions for mental disorders).

117. 28 C.F.R.36.302(c)(1) provides that "[g]enerally, a public accommodation shall modify policies, practices or procedures to permit the use of a service animal by a person with a disability."

118. See, e.g. *Branson v. West,* 1999 WL 1186420 (N.D. Ill. 1999).

119. *Pool v. Riverside Health Service,* 1995 WL 519129 (D.Kan. 1995).

120. Cynthia A. Claasen, Carroll W. Hughes, Saundra Gilfillian, Don Mc-

Intire, Ann Roose, et al., "The Nature of Help-Seeking During Psychiatric Emergency Service Visits by a Patient and an Accompanying Adult," 51 *Psychiatric Services* 924, 925 (2000).

121. *Id.*

122. Michael Allen, Daniel Carpenter, John Sheets, Steven Miccio, and Ruth Ross, "What Kinds of Help Do Consumers Want and Need During a Psychiatric Emergency?" 9 *Journal of Psychiatric Practice* 1, 9, 11, 12 (2003).

123. See The American College of Emergency Physicians, Fact Sheet on Family Presence in Emergency Departments, online at www.acep.org.

124. Civista Medical Center Emergency Department, Policy "Management of Psychiatric Emergencies," on file, Center for Public Representation. Although the hospital policy defines psychiatric emergencies, the policy itself is devoted, by turn, to patients on emergency petition, "all psychiatric patients," and patients on emergency petition.

CHAPTER 4

1. Lorna A. Rhodes, *Emptying Beds: The Work of an Emergency Psychiatric Unit,* (University of California Press 1991) p. 1.

2. *Id.*

3. Dr. Robert Factor and Dr. Ronald Diamond, "Emergency Psychiatry and Crisis Resolution," in J. V. Vaccarro and G. H. Clark, eds., *Practicing Psychiatry in the Community: A Manual* 55, 59 (American Psychiatric Press 1996).

4. See, e.g. *Tewksbury v. Dowling,* 169 F.Supp. 103, 107 (E.D.N.Y. 2001) (defendant admits spending only five minutes assessing plaintiff); *Kulak v. City of New York,* 88 F.3d 63, 67 (2nd Cir. 1996)(five minute interview); *Marion v. La Fargue,* 2004 U.S.Dist.LEXIS 2601 (S.D.N.Y. 2004) (one psychiatrist interviewed for "5–10 minutes, or maybe 10–15 minutes"; the other simply observed plaintiff through a plate glass window); *Ruhlmann v. Ulster County Department of Social Services,* 234 F.Supp.2d 140, 150 (N.D.N.Y. 2002) (evaluation by one individual took 15 minutes; another recommended retention without evaluation); *DeMarco v. Sadiker,* 952 F.Supp.134, 137 (E.D.N.Y. 1996) (doctor admits signing the involuntary detention form after approximately one minute of reading other doctor's note, observing patient, and asking him how he is doing; doctor claims that after signing the form he conducted a more thorough examination) *rev'd on other grounds* 199 F.3d 1321 (table case), 1999 U.S.App.LEXIS 36136 (2nd Cir. Nov. 8, 1999); *Riffe v. Armstrong,* 197 W.Va. 626, 477 S.E.2d 535 (1996) (finding jury issue of false imprisonment where doctor signed certificate after observing patient across a room); *Rubenstein v. Benedictine Hospital,* 790 F.Supp. 396, 410 (N.D.N.Y. 1992) (plaintiff alleges doctor spent less than one minute examining her). Interestingly, a recent article in a professional journal of emergency medicine stated that it would take five to seven minutes just to fill out the paperwork for involuntary commitment *after* conducting an appropriate examination, Roy R. Reeves, Harold B. Pinkofsky, and Lee Stevens, "Medicolegal Errors in the ED Related to the Involuntary Confinement of Psychiatric Patients," 16 *American Journal of Emergency Medicine* 631, 633 (Nov. 1998) (finding that 4.2% of involuntary detention forms reflected errors significant enough to invalidate the form, ranging from "lack of indication of the le-

gal grounds for involuntary confinement" to one form that reflected that the patient had not been examined at all.)

5. *Ruhlmann v. Ulster County Department of Social Services*, 234 F.Supp.2d 140, 150 (N.D.N.Y. 2002); *Lubera v. Jewish Association for Services for the Aged*, 1996 U.S.Dist.LEXIS 10771 at *28-30 (S.D.N.Y. July 30, 1996).

6. *Marion v. LaFargue*, 2004 U.S.Dist.LEXIS 2601 (S.D.N.Y. 2004) (court affirms liability but reduces damages to $181,000); *Ruhlmann v. Smith*, 323 F.Supp.2d 356 (N.D.N.Y. 2004) (jury awards 1 million dollars, and $75,000 in punitive damages; court reduces one million dollar award to $450,000 and affirms $75,000 punitive award); *Roy Lund v. Northwest Medical Center*, No. Civ. 1805-95 (Ct. Common Pleas, Venango Cty, Pa June 16, 2003), Jury verdict forms for $750,000 compensatory damages and $425,000 in punitive damages on file with the Center for Public Representation.

7. Glenn Currier and Michael Allen, "Physical and Chemical Restraint in the Psychiatric Emergency Service; Glenn W. Currier, Michael Allen, Mark R. Serper, Adam J. Trenton and Marc L. Copersino, "Medical, Psychiatric and Cognitive Assessment in the Psychiatric Emergency Service," in Michael Allen, ed., *Emergency Psychiatry* at p. 61.

8. Michael H. Allen, Glenn W. Currier, Douglas W. Hughes, et al., "Treatment of Behavioral Emergencies: A Summary of the Expert Consensus Guidelines," 9 *Journal of Psychiatric Practice* 16 (2003); APA Task Force on Psychiatric Emergency Services, Report and Recommendations Regarding Psychiatric Emergency and Crisis Services: A Review and Model Program Descriptions (American Psychiatric Association 2002) and cases referred to at n. 4.

9. John Monahan, Henry J. Steadman, Paul S. Appelbuam, Thomas Grisso, Edward P. Mulvey, Loren H. Roth, Pamela Clark Robbins, Steven Banks, and Eric Silver, Classification of Violence Risk Instrument, available from Psychological Assessment Resources, 16204 N. Florida Ave., Lutz, Florida 33549. See discussion at text and notes, pp. 71–72.

10. Michael H. Allen, Glenn W. Currier, Douglas W. Hughes, et al., "Treatment of Behavioral Emergencies: A Summary of the Expert Consensus Guidelines," 9 *Journal of Psychiatric Practice* 16, 17 (January 2003) summarizes the Expert Consensus Guidelines, which are published in full as "The Expert Consensus Guidelines Series: Treatment of Behavioral Emergencies, A Postgraduate Medicine Special Report" (May 2001). These will be referred to hereafter as "Expert Consensus Guidelines."

11. American College of Emergency Physicians, Policy Statement on Civil Commitment, Approved March 1997, reaffirmed December 2001 ("When participating in commitment procedures, the emergency physicians should perform an appropriate history and physical examination, with special attention not only to the psychiatric evaluation but also to the possibility of causative underlying medical problems").

12. A relatively unhelpful mnemonic (in the sense that it is entirely unmemorable) for life-threatening and treatable causes of acute mental status changes is WWHHHHIMPS, which stands for withdrawal from barbituates, Wernicke's encephalopathy, hypoxia/hypoperfusion of the brain, hypertensive crisis, hypoglycemia, hyper/hypothermia, intracranial bleeding, meningitis, poisoning, and status epilepticus. A more easily recalled acronym for organic causes of mental status changes is "VINDICTIVE MAD" which includes vascular, infectious, neo-

plastic, degenerative, intoxication, congenital, traumatic, intraventricular, vitamin deficiency, endocrine-metabolic, medications and metals, anoxia, and depression-other. Trude Kleinschmidt and Kathy Sanders, "Psychiatric Triage, Crisis Intervention, and Disposition," in Lloyd Sederer and Anthony Rothschild, *Acute Care Psychiatry: Diagnosis and Treatment* (Williams and Wilkins 1997) at p. 55.

13. Kerry Broderick, E. Brooke Lerner, John D. McCourt, Emily Fraser, and Killian Salerno, "Emergency Physician Practices and Requirements Regarding the Medical Screening Examination of Psychiatric Patients," 9 *Academic Emergency Medicine* 88, 89 (2002); see also Glenn Currier, Michael Allen, Mark Serper, et al., "Medical, Psychiatric and Cognitive Assessment in the Psychiatric Emergency Service," in Michael Allen, ed., *Emergency Psychiatry* (Washington D.C.: American Psychiatric Association Press 2002) at p. 41–43.

14. E. Koller, S. Malozowski, and P. M. Doraiswamy, "Atypical Antipsychotic Drugs and Hyperglycemia in Adolescents," 286 *Journal of the American Medical Association* 2547–48, no. 20, Nov. 28, 2001; J. J. Caro, A. Ward, C. Levinton, and K. Robinson, "The risk of diabetes during olanzapine use compared with risperidone use: a retrospective data base analysis," 63 *Journal of Clinical Psychiatry* 1135 (2002); K. Melkersson, A-L Hulting, and K. Brismar, "Elevated levels of insulin, leptin and blood lipids in olanzapine-treated patients with schizophrenia or related psychoses," 61 *Journal of Clinical Psychiatry* 742 (2000).

15. Trude Kleinschmidt and Kathy Sanders, "Psychiatric Triage, Crisis Intervention, and Disposition," in Lloyd Sederer and Anthony Rothschild, *Acute Care Psychiatry: Diagnosis and Treatment* (Williams and Wilkins 1997) at p. 55.

16. Michael H. Allen, Glenn W. Currier, Douglas W. Hughes, et al., The Expert Consensus Guideline Series, "Treatment of Behavioral Emergencies," May 2001 at p. 9 (urine toxicology screen "key assessment to perform"); Douglas Hughes, "Risk Assessment—Violence," in Lloyd Sederer and Anthony Rothschild, eds, *Acute Care Psychiatry: Diagnosis and Treatment* (Williams and Wilkins 1997) at p. 35.

17. J. S. Olshaker, B. Browne, D. A. Jerrard, et al., "Medical Clearance and Screening of Patients in the Emergency Department," 4 *Academic Emergency Medicine* 124 (1997); John D. McCourt, James P. Weller, and Kerry B. Broderick, "Mandatory Laboratory Testing for the Emergency Department Psychiatric Medical Screening Exam: Useful or Useless?" 8 *Academic Emergency Medicine* 572 (2001).

18. Richard C. W. Hall, Earl R. Gardner, Michael K. Popkin, et al., "Unrecognized Physical Illness Prompting Psychiatric Admission: A Prospective Study," 5 *Am. J. Psychiatry* 629, 632 (1981).

19. Philip L. Henneman, Ricardo Mendoza, and Roger J. Lewis, "Prospective Evaluation of Emergency Department Medical Clearance," 24 *Annals of Emergency Medicine* 672, 676 (1994).

20. J. S. Olshaker, B. Browne, D. A. Jerrard, H. Prendergast, et al., "Medical clearance and screening of psychiatric patients in the emergency department," 4 *Academic Emergency Medicine* 124 (1997) (.05%).

21. Kerry Broderick, E. Brooke Lerner et al., at note 13.

22. *Id.*

23. Laura J. Fochtman, "Psychiatric Perspectives on Medical Screening of Psychiatric Patients," 9 *Academic Emergency Medicine* 963-64 (2002).

24. *Id.* (citations omitted).

25. Kerry Broderick, Brooke Lerner, John D. McCourt, et al., "In Reply," 9 *Academic Emergency Medicine* 963 (2002).

26. Expert Consensus Guidelines at 23.

27. *Genevieve McGraw v. UCSD Medical Center, et al.,* Case No. 625598 (San Diego Cty. Superior Ct., Feb. 28, 1992), available on LEXIS in the Jury Verdicts directory and on file with the author.

28. Tufts University School of Medicine, Department of Psychiatry, "The Mini-Mental State Examination," available online at www.nemc.org/psych/mmse .asp.

29. Expert Consensus Guidelines at 22.

30. Trude Kleinschmidt and Kathy Sanders, "Psychiatric Triage, Crisis Intervention, and Disposition," in Lloyd Sederer and Anthony Rothschild, eds., *Acute Care Psychiatry: Diagnosis and Treatment* (Williams and Wilkins 1997) at p. 53 ("there is no formula for medical clearance").

31. Glenn Currier, Michael Allen, Mark R. Serper, Adam J. Trenton and Marc L. Copersino, "Medical, Psychiatric and Cognitive Assessment in the Psychiatric Emergency Service," in Michael Allen, ed., *Emergency Psychiatry* (American Psychiatric Press 2002) at p. 67, 61.

32. *Id.*

33. Sharon S. Dawes and Anthony M. Creswell, *Report of the Field Test to Evaluate a Decision Support Tool for Psychiatric Assessments in Emergency Rooms* (Center for Technology in Government, University at Albany/SUNY, 1995) available online athttp://www.ctg.albany.edu/publications/reports/field_test.

34. *Id.* at 8.

35. Expert Consensus Guidelines at p. 23.

36. Of course, this allocation raises issues of its own regarding liability. For example, one court held that such as assessment team could not be sued for malpractice because no doctor-patient relationship existed, *Garcia v. City of Boston and Boston Emergency Services Team,* 115 F.Supp.2d 74 (D.Mass. 2000).

37. In *re C.W.,* 147 Wn.2d 259, 53 P.3d 979 (Washington 2003).

38. *Rodriguez v. City of New York,* 72 F.3d at 1062-63 (2nd Cir. 1995). *Jensen v. Lane County,* 312 F.3d 1145, 1147 (9th Cir. 2002) (adopting *Rodriguez* standard).

39. *Id.*

40. James Holstein, *Court-Ordered Insanity: Interpretive Practice and Involuntary Commitment* (Aldyne de Gruter 1993); Joe Sharkey, *Bedlam: Greed, Profiteering and Fraud in a Mental Health System Gone Crazy* (St. Martin's Press 1994) (describing involuntary detention tactics of private hospitals to inflate profits, which ultimately generated some of the largest civil fraud fines in American history).

41. *Marion v. LaFargue,* 2004 U.S.Dist.LEXIS 2601 (S.D.N.Y. 2004) at *6.

42. *Mertz v. Temple University,* 25 Pa. D&C4th 541, 1995 Pa. D. & C. LEXIS 202 (Pa. Ct. Common Pleas July 25, 1995); Alisa Lincoln and Michael Allen, "The Influence of Collateral Informants on Psychiatric Emergency Service Disposition Decisions and Access to Inpatient Care," 6 *International Journal of Psychosocial Rehabilitation* 99–100 (2002).

43. D. E. McNiel, R. S. Myers, H. K. Zeiner, et al., "The Role of Violence in Decisions About Hospitalization from the Psychiatric Emergency Room," 149

American Journal of Psychiatry 207 (1992) (violence less important than diagnosis and overall severity of psychiatric impairment in predicting hospitalization).

44. In *Tewksbury v. Dowling,* 169 F.Supp. 103, 114 (E.D.N.Y. 2001), attorney Bill Brooks offered the affidavit of a psychiatric nurse who had worked over the years at many different psychiatric hospitals, and who swore that financial considerations played a major role in decisions of whether or not to admit patients. This allegation is supported by discussions in ED books and treatises; see, e.g., Trude Kleinschmidt and Kathy Sanders, "Psychiatric Triage, Crisis Intervention, and Disposition," in Lloyd Sederer and Anthony Rothschild, eds, *Acute Care Psychiatry: Diagnosis and Treatment* (Williams and Wilkins 1997) at p. 58 (listing the "central factors in disposition" as "dangerousness, severity of psychiatric and medical pathology, substance abuse, compliance, liability, resources and insurance coverage").

45. Alisa Lincoln and Michael H. Allen, "The Influence of Collateral Information on Psychiatric Emergency Service Disposition Decisions and Access to Inpatient Psychiatric Care," 6 *International Journal of Psychosocial Rehabilitation* 99 (2002).

46. *Gregory B. Monaco and the Mental Disability Law Clinic v. James Stone, et al.* No. CV-98-3386 (E.D.N.Y. filed May 5, 1998).

47. L. Rubin and M. Mills, "Behavioral precipitants to civil commitment," 140 *American Journal of Psychiatry* 603 (1983) (the overwhelming majority of patients' behavior characterized as "harmful acts" were either threats or acts that caused no harm to the victim).

48. Charles W. Lidz, et al., "The Accuracy of Predictions of Violence to Others," 269 *Journal of the American Medical Association* 1007, 1009 (1993).

49. John Monahan and Henry Steadman, "Toward a Rejuvenation of Risk Assessment Research," in John Monahan and Henry Steadman, eds., *Violence and Mental Disorder: Developments in Risk Assessment* (Chicago: University of Chicago Press 1994).

50. Charles W. Lidz, et al., "The Accuracy of Predictions of Violence to Others," 269 *Journal of the American Medical Association* 1007, 1009 (1993).

51. *Marion v. LaFargue,* 2004 U.S.Dist.LEXIS 2601 (S.D.N.Y. 2004) at *6.

52. *James v. Grand Lake Mental Health Center,* 1998 U.S.App.LEXIS 23916 (10th Cir. Sept. 24, 1998).

53. For a thorough analysis of this problem, see John Monahan, "Violence Risk Assessment: Scientific Validity and Evidentiary Admissibility," 57 *Washington and Lee Law Review* 901 (2000), and Erica Beecher-Monas and Edgar Garcia-Rill "Danger at the Edge of Chaos: Predicting Violent Behavior in a Post-*Daubert* World," 24 *Cardozo Law Review* 1845 (2003). See also, Charles W. Lidz et al., "The Accuracy of Predictions of Violence to Others," 269 *Journal of the American Medical Association* 1007, 1009 (1993); Douglas Mossman, "Assessing Predictions of Violence: Being Accurate about Accuracy," 62 *Journal of Cons. and Clinical Psych.* 783 (1994).

54. *Barefoot v. Estelle,* 463 U.S. 880, 920 (1983). An American Psychiatric Association Fact Sheet produced in 1994 emphasized that psychiatric predictions of dangerousness were in error two out of three times, American Psychiatric Association, "Violence and Mental Illness," Fact Sheet, Nov. 1994.

55. Charles W. Lidz, et al., *id.* at note 50.

56. *Id.*

57. Daniel Shuman and Bruce Sales at 1228-1229; Vernon L. Quinsey, et al., *Violent Offenders: Appraising and Managing Risk* 62 (1998) (experts and lay-persons have few differences of opinion about assessments of dangerousness, and neither are very accurate).

58. Virginia Hiday and Lynne Smith, "Effects of the Dangerousness Standard in Civil Commitment," 15 *Journal of Psychiatry and Law* 443, 449 (1987).

59. Bruce B. Way, Michael H. Allen, Jeryl L. Mumpower, Thomas R. Stewart, and Steven M. Banks, "Interrater Agreement Among Psychiatrists in Psychiatric Emergency Assessments," 155 *American Journal of Psychiatry* 1423 (1998).

60. Alisa Lincoln and Michael Allen, "The Influence of Collateral Information on Psychiatric Emergency Service Disposition Decisions and Access to Inpatient Psychiatric Care," 6 *International Journal of Psychosocial Rehabilitation* 99 (2002).

61. Both case law and research confirm that this is the case. In *Marion v. LaFargue*, the plaintiff was interviewed by a medical student. 2004 U.S.Dist.LEXIS 2601 at *7.

62. C. G. Fichtner and J. A. Flaherty, "Decisions to Hospitalize: A Longitudinal Study of Psychiatric Residents," 17 *Academic Psychiatry* 130 (1993). This of course raises the question of whether residents should be making these decisions at all, as opposed to doing initial evaluations and making recommendations to the physicians who should actually be responsible for these decisions.

63. Dr. Ron Roesch, personal communication, May 24, 2005. Dr. Roesch is an expert in the field of risk assessment and author of the principal texts on competency to stand trial over the last 25 years, e.g., Ronald Roesch and Steven L. Golding, *Competency to Stand Trial* (1980); R. Roesch, J. R. P. Ogloff, and Steven L. Golding, "Competency to Stand Trial: Legal and Clinical Issues," 2 *Applied and Preventative Psychology* 43 (1993); and T. L. Nicholls, R. Roesch, M. C. Olley, J. R. P. Ogloff, and J. F. Hemphill, "Jail Screening Assessment Tool (JSAT): Guidelines for Mental Health Screening in Jails" (Burnaby, B.C.: Mental Health, Law and Policy Institute, Simon Fraser University 2005).

64. I am grateful to Dr. Ron Roesch for suggesting the structure and a great deal of the content expressed in the summary of risk assessment.

65. Gary Melton, John Petrila, Norman Poythress, and Christopher Slobogin, *Psychological Evaluation for the Courts,* 2d ed. (New York: Guilford Press 1997) 284.

66. Thomas R. Litwack, "Actuarial v. Clinical Assessments of Dangerousness," 7 *Psychology, Public Policy and Law* 409, 412 (2001).

67. 509 U.S. 579 (1993). *Daubert* holds that in order to be admissible, expert testimony must be both relevant and reliable, and looked to four factors for a court to consider in determining reliability: (1) whether the expert's theory or method is falsifiable and has been tested; (2) its reliability and potential rate of error; (3) whether it has been subject to peer review; and (4) whether the expert's methods and reasoning enjoy general acceptance in the relevant scientific community.

68. 526 U.S. 137 (1999). In *Kumho Tire*, the Supreme Court held that *Daubert* standards applied to expert testimony involving social science and elaborated on how lower courts were to apply *Daubert*.

69. 522 U.S. 136 (1997) (holding that expert conclusions must be based on scientifically accepted methodology).

70. Daniel Shuman and Bruce Sales, "The Admissibility of Expert Testimony Based Upon Clinical Judgment and Scientific Research," 4 *Psychology, Public Policy and the Law* (1998) 1226, 1228.

71. *United States v. Barnette*, 211 F.3d 803 (4th Cir. 2000).

72. Personal Communication from Dr. John Monahan, June 8, 2005.

73. Charles W. Lidz, et al., *supra* at n. 48; Douglas W. Mossman, "Assessing Predictions of Violence: Being Accurate about Accuracy," 62 *Journal of Cons. and Clinical Psych.* 783 (1994).

74. Douglas W. Mossman, "Assessing Predictions of Violence: Being Accurate about Accuracy," 62 *Journal of Cons. and Clinical Psych.* 783 (1994).

75. Thomas Gutheil and Paul Appelbaum, et al., *Clinical Handbook of Psychiatry and the Law* (3rd ed. 2000) 68; Dale McNeil, "Empirically Based Clinical Evaluation and Management of the Potentially Violent Patient," in P. Kleespies, ed., *Emergencies in Mental Health Practice: Evaluation and Management* 95, 96 (1998).

76. Robert Menzies and Christopher D. Webster, "Construction and Validation of Risk Assessments in a Six-Year Follow-up of Forensic Patients: A Tri-Dimensional Analysis," 63 *Journal of Consulting and Clinical Psychology* 766 (1995); Vernon L. Quinsey, et al., *Violent Offenders: Appraising and Managing Risk* 62 (1998).

77. The TRIAD, for instance, is a checklist designed to describe the factors that clinicians use in determining dangerousness, but it consists of three lists of 88 questions. The VRAG can take days to complete and was normed against a forensic population in any event. It is unlikely that physicians or psychiatrists in emergency room settings will perceive themselves as having the time to use either of these tests.

78. South Dakota changed its imminence requirement in 2000 from "the very near future" to "the near future," S.D. Codified Laws 27A-1-1 (Michie 2001). Minnesota removed its "imminence" requirement in 2002, and Maryland removed its imminence requirement in 2003. Md.Code.Ann., Health-Gen., §10-622a (2004). The Wisconsin Supreme Court upheld the commitability of individuals who, if left untreated, will lose their "ability to function independently in the community," *State v. Dennis H.*, 647 N.W.2d 851 (Wisc. 2002).

79. D. E. McNiel and R. I. Binder, "Predictive Validity of Judgments of Dangerousness in Emergency Civil Commitment," 144 *American Journal of Psychiatry* 197 (1987); see also D. E. McNiel, D. A. Sandberg, and R. L. Binder, "The Relationship Between Confidence and Accuracy in Clinical Assessments of Psychiatric Patients' Potential for Violence," 22 *Law and Human Behavior* 655 (1998).

80. L. J. Apperson, E. P. Mulvey, and C. W. Lidz, "Short term clinical prediction of assaultive behavior: artifacts of research methods," 150 *American Journal of Psychiatry* 1374 (1993).

81. Douglas Hughes, "Can the Clinician Predict Suicide?" 46 *Psychiatric Services* 449 (1995); A. D. Pokorney, "Prediction of suicide in psychiatric patients: report of a prospective study," 40 *Archives of General Psychiatry* 249 (1983).

82. Andrew Lazarus, "Dumping Psychiatric Patients in the Managed Care Sector," 45 *Hospital and Community Psychiatry* 529–30 (1994).

83. See *Taylor v. Johnson*, No. Civ.98-1382 JC/DJS (D.N.M., second

amended complaint filed April 19, 2000), charging the State of New Mexico and the HMOs with which it contracted to provide mental health services to children with violations of the Medicaid Act and of federal anti-discrimination law. The case was settled on August 2, 2001.

84. Richard E. Breslow, "Structure and Function of Psychiatric Emergency Services," see note 27, p. 21.

85. 42 C.F.R. 438.114(a).

86. 42 C.F.R. 438. 114.

87. 42 C.F.R. 422.13.

88. Ga. Code Ann. 31-11-81.

89. Ga. Code Ann. 31-11-82(b). Ariz.Rev.Stat. 20-2803(A).

90. Ariz. Rev.Stat. Ann. 20-2803(B).

91. Ariz. Rev.Stat.Ann. 20-2803(H).

92. Ariz.Rev.Stat. 20-2803(I).

93. Ariz.Rev.Stat. 20-2803(E).

94. Ariz.Rev.Stat. 20-2803(D).

95. Joelle Babula, "Emergency Rooms: Experts pose changes for LV Hospitals," *Las Vegas Review Journal* (Sept. 21, 2000) 1-A.

96. David Feifel, "Psychopharmacology in the Acute Setting: Review and Proposed Guidelines," 18 *Psychiatric Times* (May 2001). Available online at www .psychiatrictimes.com/p010537.html.

97. Center for Public Representation Survey No. 6.

98. Lorna A. Rhodes, *Emptying Beds: The Work of an Emergency Psychiatric Unit* (University of California Press 1991) at 13, 14, 101, 117-121, 125–126, 145, 153–155.

99. Margot Kushel, S. Perry, D. Bangsberg, R. Clark, and A. R. Moss, "Emergency Department Use Among the Homeless and Marginally Housed: Results From a Community Based-Study," 92 *American Journal of Public Health* 778 (2002).

100. Stephen M. Soreff, *Management of the Psychiatric Emergency* (Wiley 1981) 10. ("When one patient came to the ED for the eighth time in two month, staff totally ignored her for several hours.")

101. G. A. Barker, "Emergency Room 'Repeaters,'" in James Randolph Hilliard, ed., *Manual of Clinical Emergency Psychiatry* (Washington: American Psychiatric Association Press 1990) 351.

102. *Id.*

103. *Barker v. Netcare Corp.*, 768 N.E.2d 698, 147 Ohio App.3d 1 (Ohio App. 2001).

104. *Id.*

105. Karen Auge, "Cuts Squeeze Treatment of Mentally Ill," *Denver Post* Dec. 16, 2002, p. B-1. The counselor testified, "I have never seen an ER doctor read the psych notes even though they sign every one of them. They just don't have the time."

CHAPTER 5

1. An individual can sue to enforce a federal statute that establishes rights under one of three circumstances. First, Congress could have written language

in the statute permitting private citizens to enforce rights created by the statute, such as it did in the ADA. This is called a "private right of action." Second, Congress could have written the statute in such as way as to demonstrate that it intended individuals to be able to enforce their rights. This is called "an implied private right of action." Third, the statute could create a federal right enforceable under 42 U.S.C. 1983, which is a statute that permits an individual to file suit when a state actor violates his or her federal rights. An individual can sue to enforce rights created by a regulation if the regulation does not exceed Congressional intent reflected in the statute, and if Congress intended for the statute to create a private right of action, *Alexander v. Sandoval*, 532 U.S. 275 (2001).

2. 42 U.S.C. 10801 (West 2004).

3. 42 U.S.C. 10804-10806 (West 2004).

4. *Rockwell v. Cape Cod Hospital*, 26 F.3d 254, 257-258 (1st Circuit 1994); *Donald Benn v. Universal Health System*, 371 F.3d 165 (3rd Cir. 2004); *S.P. v. City of Takoma*, 134 F.3d 260 (4th Cir. 1998); *Bass v. Parkwood Hospital*, 180 F.3d 234 (5th Cir. 1999); *Spencer v. Lee*, 864 F.2d 1376, 1380-81 (7th Cir. 1989); *Pino v. Higgs*, 75 F.3d 1461 (10th Cir. 1996); *Harvey v. Harvey*, 949 F.2d 1127, 1131 (11th Cir. 1992); but see *Rubenstein v. Benedictine Hospital*, 790 F.Supp. 396 (N.D.N.Y. 1992).

5. *Jensen v. Lane County*, 222 F.3d 570, 575 (9th Cir. 2000); *Schorr v. Borough of Lemoyne*, 265 F.Supp.2d 488 (M.D. Pa. 2003); *C.K. v. Northwestern Human Services*, 255 F.Supp.2d 447 (E.D.Pa. 2003); *Ruhlmann v. Ulster County Dept. of Social Services*, 234 F.Supp.2d 140 (N.D.N.Y. 2002); *Tewksbury v. Dowling*, 169 F.Supp.2d 103 (E.D.N.Y. 2001).

6. *Straub v. Kilgore*, 2004 U.S.App.LEXIS 10668 (6th Cir. May 27, 2004) (hospital personnel who forcibly catheterized individual brought in by police officers not acting as agents of the state).

7. *Ellison v. University Hospital Mobile Crisis Team*, 2004 U.S.App.LEXIS 13772 (6th Cir. June 30, 2004).

8. *Payton v. Rush-Presbyterian-St. Luke's Medical* Center, 184 F.3d 623 (7th Cir. 1999); *Owens v. City of Fort Lauderdale*, 174 F.Supp.2d 1282 (S.D.Fla. 2001); *Stokes v. Northwestern Memorial Hospital*, 1989 U.S.Dist.LEXIS 8543 (N.D.Ill. July 20, 1989).

9. *McCabe v. Life-Line Ambulance Service*, 77 F.3d 540, 544 (1st Cir. 1996).

10. *Ahern v. O'Donnell*, 109 F.3d 809 (1st Cir. 1997).

11. *Ferguson v. City of Charleston*, 532 U.S. 67 (2001).

12. *Ahern v. O'Donnell*, 109 F.3d 809 (1st Cir. 1997).

13. 339 F.3d 129 (2nd Cir. 2003).

14. *Id.* at 142. See *Ferguson v. City of Charleston*, 532 U.S. 67, 76-80 (2001).

15. Interview with Beckie Child, advocate, Portland, Oregon, January 31, 2005.

16. Thomas Grisso and Paul Appelbaum, *Assessing Competence to Consent to Treatment* (New York: Oxford University Press 1998).

17. I am indebted to Professors Bruce Winick, Michael Perlin, Elyn Saks, Dr. Joel Dvoskin, and Ira Burnim, Esq., for their assistance in understanding the application of *Zinermon* to the emergency room setting.

18. See, e.g., *Green v. City of New York*, 2004 U.S.Dist.LEXIS 5 (S.D.N.Y. Jan. 5, 2004) (man who could not speak and his wife indicated that he did not

want to be taken to the hospital; in light of the fact that his breathing apparatus had malfunctioned and his daughter called 911, the court concluded that "the crisis atmosphere would reasonably have caused the officers to conclude that this was not a setting in which Walter Green could make an informed and competent decision"); *Taylor v. University Medical Center*, 2005 U.S.Dist. LEXIS 7269 (W.D.Ky. April 26, 2005) (rejecting claim of patient that he had not given informed consent to the treatment he received in light of his apparent need for treatment and his highly intoxicated state).

19. *Doby v. DeCrescenzo*, 171 F.3d 858, 870 (3rd Cir. 1999).

20. *Benn v. Universal Health System, Inc.*, 371 F.3d 165, 174 (3rd Cir. 2004).

21. *Heater v. Southwood Psychiatric Center, et al.*, 42 Cal.App.4th 1068 (1996).

22. 53 P.3d 979, 147 Wash.2d 259 (2002).

23. Washington Revised Code 71.05.050 (2001).

24. *In re C.W.*, 53 P.3d 979, 988, 147 Wash.2d 259, 279 (2002).

25. *Id.* at 283, 990.

26. *Lizotte v. New York City Health and Hospitals Corporation et al*, 1992 U.S.Dist.LEXIS 10976 (S.D.N.Y. July 16, 1992).

27. See Norman Siegal and Robert Levy, "Koch's Mishandling of the Homeless," *New York Times*, Sept. 17, 1987, A-35.

28. *Lizotte v. New York City Health and Hospital Corporations*, 1992 U.S.Dist.LEXIS 10976 (S.D.N.Y. July 16, 1992).

29. 42 U.S.C. 12181 et seq. (West 2004).

30. 42 U.S.C. 12181(7)(F) (covering "professional office of a health care provider") (West 2004).

31. 42 U.S.C. 12182(a); 28 C.F.R. 35.201(a) (individuals may be liable under Title III if they "own, lease, or operate" a place of public accommodation); see *Howe v. Hull*, 874 F.Supp. 779 (N.D.Ohio 1994) (doctor subject to individual liability under Title III); *Sharrow v. Bailey*, 910 F.Supp. 187 (M.D.Pa. 1995) (doctor subject to individual liability under Title III); *United States v. Morvant*, 843 F.Supp. 1092 (E.D.La. 1994) (dentist subject to individual liability under Title III).

32. 42 U.S.C. 12188 (a)(1) and (2) (West 2004).

33. 42 U.S.C. 12188(b)(2)(B) and (C); 28 C.F.R. 36.503(a) and (b) (West 2004).

34. See Section IV(G)(1), *supra*.

35. *Simenson v. Hoffman*, 1995 U.S.Dist.LEXIS 15777(N.D.Ill. 1995).

36. *Blake v. Southcoast*, 145 F.Supp.2d 126 (D.Mass. 2001), *aff'd in part, vac. and remanded sub nom. Blake v. Pellegrino*, 329 F.3d 43 (1st Cir. 2003).

37. *Aikins v. St. Helena Hospital*, 843 F.Supp. 1329 (N.D.Ca. 1994); *Schroedel v. New York University Medical Center*, 885 F.Supp. 594 (S.D.N.Y. 1995).

38. *Pool v. Riverside Health Services*, 1995 U.S.Dist.LEXIS 12724 (D.Kan. 1995).

39. *Scherer v. Waterbury Hospital*, 2000 Conn.Super.LEXIS 481 (Conn.Super. Feb. 22, 2000).

40. 28 C.F.R. 36.202(c)(West 2003).

41. 28 C.F.R. 36.203(b)(West 2003).

42. 29 U.S.C. 1101 (West 2004).

43. See Web site www.appealsolutions.com/tal for assistance in crafting letters appealing denials of insurance coverage.

44. Section 502(a)(1)(b) of ERISA, codified at 29 U.S.C. §1132 (West 2003).

45. Section 502(a)(2) of ERISA.

46. 29 U.S.C. 1144 a (West 2003).

47. A number of courts followed the U.S. Supreme Court's lead in *Pegram v. Herdrich,* 530 U.S. 211 (2000).

48. *Aetna Health Inc. v. Davila,* 542 U.S. 200, 124 S.Ct. 2488, 159 L.Ed.2d 312 (2004).

49. 29 U.S.C. 1104 (West 2003).

50. 48 F.3d 937 (6th Cir. 1995).

51. *Andrews-Clarke v. Traveler's Insurance Company,* 984 F.Supp. 49 (D.Mass. 1997).

52. *Id.*

53. *Id.*

54. *Huss v. Green Spring Health Services, Inc.,* 1999 U.S.Dist.LEXIS 10014 (E.D.Pa. June 30, 1999); *Andrews-Clarke, supra* at n. 51, *Clark v. Humana Kansas City,* 975 F.Supp. 1283 (D.Kan. 1997).

55. *Rubin-Schneiderman v. Merit Behavioral Care Corp,* 165 F.Supp.2d 277 (S.D.N.Y. 2001), *dismissed by* 2001 U.S.Dist.LEXIS 18527 (S.D.N.Y. Nov. 13, 2001), *vac.* 2003 U.S.App.LEXIS 7413 (2nd Cir. April 18, 2003), *on remand,* 2003 U.S.Dist.LEXIS 14811 (S.D.N.Y. Aug. 2, 2003); *Huss, supra* n. 54; *Clark, supra* at n. 54.

56. *Danca v. Private Health Care Systems, Inc.,* 185 F.3d 1 (1st Cir. 1999); *Huss, supra* note 54, *Andrews, supra* at note 51.

57. *Andrews, supra* at note 51.

58. *Huss, supra* at note 54.

59. *Danca, supra* at note 56; *Rubin-Schneiderman, supra* at note 55.

60. 42 U.S.C. 1395dd (2003). Regulations can be found at 42 C.F.R. 489.24. The Bush administration enacted new EMTALA regulations on September 4, 2003, and updated its interpretive guidelines on May 13, 2004; see New EMTALA Instructions for Site Reviewers, State Operations Manual, Appendix V, Responsibilities of Medicare Participating Hospitals in Emergency Cases, available online at www.cms.hhs.gov/medicaid/survey_cert/sco434.pdf. To the extent that these regulations impact on the treatment of people with psychiatric disabilities, they are discussed below.

61. *Baber v Hospital Corporation of America,* 977 F.2d 872 (4th Cir. 1992); *Gatewood v. Washington Healthcare Corporation,* 933 F.2d 1037, 1040, n. 1 (D.C. Cir. 1991); *Eberhardt v. City of Los Angeles,* 62 F.3d 1253 (9th Cir. 1995).

62. 42 U.S.C. 1395dd(d)(2)(A)(West 2004).

63. Psychiatric conditions are included by regulation, 42 C.F.R. 489.24(b)(1), see also HCFA State Operations Manual, Appendix V, V-22, available online at www.hcfa.gov/pubforms/progman.htm

64. "A specially equipped and staffed area of the hospital that is used a significant portion of the time for the initial evaluation and treatment of outpatients for emergency medical conditions." 42 C.F.R. 489.24(b) (West 2004).

65. Appendix V, Interpretive Guidelines: Responsibilities of Medicare Par-

ticipating Hospitals in Emergency Cases, available online at www.cms.hhs.gov/medicaid/survey_cert/sco434.pdf, (May 13, 2004) at p. 4.

66. *Roberts v. Galen of Virginia Inc.*, 525 U.S. 249 (1999).

67. *Pettyjohn v. Mission St. Joseph's Health System*, 2001 U.S.App. LEXIS 23423 (4th Cir. Oct. 30, 2001); *Gerber v. Northwest Hospital Center*, 943 F.Supp. 571 (D.Md. 1996).

68. *Arrington v. Wong*, 237 F.3d 1066 (9th Cir. 2001) (EMTALA is triggered if hospital is contacted by ambulance en route to the hospital).

69. 42 C.F.R. 489.24(b)(West 2004).

70. *Tolton v. American Biodyne*, 48 F.3d 937 (6th Cir. 1995) (more than one month after discharge); *Pettyjohn v. Mission St. Joseph's Health System*, 2001 U.S.App. LEXIS 23423 (4th Cir. Oct. 30, 2001) (six days after discharge); *Gerber v. Northwest Hospital Center*, 943 F.Supp. 571 (D.Md. 1996) (two days after discharge); *Gossling v. Hays Medical Center*, 1995 U.S.Dist.LEXIS 5765 (D.Kansas April 21, 1995) (3 days after discharge); *Baker v. Adventist Health*, 260 F.3d 987 (9th Cir. 2001) (2 days after discharge); see also *Eberhardt v. City of Los Angeles*, 62 F.3d 1253 (9th Cir. 1995) (man who was shot by police 30 hours after being discharged from emergency room was shot "well after" his discharge).

71. *Ward v. Presbyterian Hospital*, 72 F.Supp.2d 1285 (D.N.M. 1999).

72. *Tinius v. Carroll County Sheriff Dept*, 321 F.Supp.2d 1064 (N.D. Iowa 2004).

73. *Correa v. Hospital San Francisco*, 69 F.3d 1184 (1st Cir. 1995).

74. *Tolton v. American Biodyne*, 48 F.3d 937 (6th Cir. 1995) (more than one month after discharge); *Pettyjohn v. Mission St. Joseph's Health System*, 2001 U.S.App. LEXIS 23423 (4th Cir. Oct. 30, 2001) (six days after discharge); *Gerber v. Northwest Hospital Center*, 943 F.Supp. 571 (D.Md. 1996) (two days after discharge); *Gossling v. Hays Medical Center*, 1995 U.S.Dist.LEXIS 5765 (D.Kansas April 21, 1995) (3 days after discharge); *Baker v. Adventist Health*, 260 F.3d 987 (9th Cir. 2001) (2 days after discharge); see also *Eberhardt v. City of Los Angeles*, 62 F.3d 1253 (9th Cir. 1995) (man who was shot by police 30 hours after being discharged from emergency room was shot "well after" his discharge).

75. State Operations Manual, Interpretive Guidelines to 489.24(d)(2)(i) (May 13, 2004).

76. *Fleming v. HCA Health Services*, 691 So.2d 1216 (La. 1997).

77. *Eberhardt v. City of Los Angeles, supra* at n. 310; *Gerber v. Northwest Hospital Center*, 943 F.Supp. 571 (D.Md. 1996).

78. *Thomas v. Christ Hospital and Medical Center*, 328 F.3d 890 (7th Cir. 2003).

79. 42 C.F.R. 489.24(c)(2).

80. *Thomas v. Christ Hospital and Medical Center, supra* at n. 296.

81. *Tinius v. Carroll County Sheriff Department*, 321 F.Supp.2d 1064 (N.D. Iowa 2004); *Straub v. Kilgore*, 2004 U.S.App.LEXIS 10668 (6th Cir. May 27, 2004).

82. 42 C.F.R. 489.24(c)(1).

83. *Thomas v. Christ Hospital and Medical Center*, 2003 U.S.App.LEXIS 7921 (7th Circuit Feb. 25, 2003).

84. Appendix V, Interpretive Guidelines: Responsibilities of Medicare Participating Hospitals in Emergency Cases, available online at www.cms.hhs.gov/medicaid/survey_cert/sco434.pdf, (May 13, 2004) at p. 40.

85. *Baker v. Adventist Health*, 260 F.3d 987 (9th Cir. 2001).

86. 42 C.F.R. 489.24(c)(i).

87. Public Law 104-191.

88. 45 C.F.R. 160.306(a) and (b)(3).

89. 45 C.F.R. 164.520 (prison inmates do not have this right).

90. 45 C.F.R. 164.522.

91. 45 C.F.R. 164.524.

92. 45 C.F.R. 164.526.

93. 45 C.F.R. 164. 528.

94. C.F.R.164.524(a)(1).

95. 65 Fed.Reg. 82554 (Dec. 28, 2000).

96. 65 Fed.Reg. 82556 (Dec. 28, 2000).

97. This act is found at 42 U.S.C. 263a. (West 2003).

98. 42 C.F.R.493.3(a)(2). The Clinical Laboratory Improvement Amendments is an act that forbids laboratories doing tests on human specimens to disclose the results to anyone except the individual or entity who requested the lab tests. The commentary acknowledges that this could result in an individual being unable to obtain his or her own test results, but leaves these rules governing laboratories in place.

99. 45 C.F.R. 164.508(a)(3)(iv)(A)(West 2004).

100. *Id.*

101. 65 Fed.Reg. 82555 (Dec. 28, 2000).

102. 45 C.F.R. 164.524(a)(2) (West 2004).

103. 45 C.F.R. 164.524(a)(2)(ii) (West 2004).

104. 45 C.F.R. 164.524(a)(2)(iii).

105. 5 U.S.C. 552a (West 2004).

106. 45 C.F.R. 164.524(a)(2)(v).

107. 45 C.F.R. 164.524(a)(3)(i).

108. 65 Fed.Reg. 82555 (Dec. 28, 2000).

109. *Id.*

110. 45 C.F.R. 164.524(a)(3)(ii).

111. 45 C.F.R. 164.524(a)(3)(iii).

112. 65 Fed.Reg. 82555 (Dec. 28, 2000).

113. 45 C.F.R. 164.524(d)(1).

114. 45 C.F.R. 164.524(d)(2)(iii).

115. 45 C.F.R. 164.524(b)(2)(iii)(B).

116. 45 C.F.R. 164.524(c)(2)(ii)(A).

117. 45 C.F.R. 164.524(c)(4).

118. 45 C.F.R. 164.524(c)(2)(i).

119. 45 C.F.R. 164.524(d)(4).

120. 65 Fed.Reg. 82556 (Dec. 28, 2000).

121. This case involved the Whiting Forensic facility in Middletown, Connecticut. For further information contact the Connecticut Legal Rights Project in Middletown at 860-262-5030.

122. Ellen Barry, "Breakdown in Care: Embracing Change, Vermont Neglected its Mental Hospital; Neglect Cited in Vermont State Hospital," *Boston Globe*, Oct. 20, 2003.

123. *Alexander v. Sandoval*, 532 U.S. 275 (2001).

124. 42 C.F.R. 482.13(a)(1)(West 2004).

125. 42 C.F.R. 482.13(a)(2)(West 2004).

126. 42 C.F.R. 482.13(d)(West 2004).

127. 42 C.F.R. 482.13(c)(2)(West 2004).

128. See "Hospital Conditions of Participation for Patients' Rights," Interpretive Guidelines, 482.13(a), (Tag number A 751), p. A-171, *id.*

129. *Id.*

130. *Id.*

131. 42 C.F.R. 482.13(a)(2)(i),(ii), and (iii) (West 2004).

132. Interpretive Guidance to 482.13(a)(2)(iii) (West 2004).

133. C.F.R. 482.13(c)(2) (West 2004).

134. 42 C.F.R. 482.11(a) (West 2004).

135. The manual can be found online at www.cms.hhs .gov/manuals/pub07pdf/AP-a.pdf. Note that although the page number in the hard copy of the manual is A-171, in the electronic version this material is on p. 167.

136. 42 C.F.R. 489.10(b)(2) ("provider must meet the applicable civil rights requirements of . . . Section 504 of the Rehabilitation Act").

137. 42 C.F.R. 482.13(f)(3)(ii)C) (West 2004).

138. Center for Medicare and Medicaid Services, State Operations Manual, 5240A (Rev. 5-21-04) (available online at www.cms.hhs.gov/manuals/107_som/som107index.asp), p. A-0082.

139. *Id.*

140. *National Association of Psychiatric Health Systems v. Shalala*, 120 F.Supp.2d 33 (D.D.C. 2000).

141. 42 C.F.R. 482.13(f)(1) (West 2004).

142. 42 C.F.R. 482.13(f)(3)(i) (West 2004).

143. CMS State Operations Manual, *supra* at note 378.

144. 42 C.F.R. 482.13(f)(3)(vi).

145. 42 C.F.R. 482.13(f)(3)(ii)(D).

146. CMS State Operations Manual at p. A-0082.

147. Interpretive Guidance to 42 C.F.R. 482.13(f), available online at www .cms.gov/manuals/107_som/som107ap_a_hospitals.pdf.

148. 42 C.F.R. 482.13(d)(2).

149. CMS, State Operations Manual, A-0061.

150. CMS, State Operations Manual A-0061. Note possible conflict with HIPAA, which provides that hospitals which have concerns about patients' representatives may refuse those representatives access to the patients' records; see text at p. 95, *supra.* This decision is subject to appeal by the patient's representative, *id.*

151. 42 C.F.R. 164.524(c)(3).

152. CMS, State Operations Manual, A-0061.

153. 42 C.F.R. 482.13(b)(1).

154. 42 C.F.R. 482.13(b)(2).

155. 42 C.F.R. 482.13(b)(2).

156. 42 C.F.R. 482.13(b)(2)

157. 42 C.F.R. 482.13(b)(3).

158. Breslow (2001).

159. 42 U.S.C. 1395cc(f) and 1396a(w) (1994).

160. 42 U.S.C. 1983 is a statute that creates no rights of its own but per-

mits individuals who believe state employees have violated their federal rights to sue in federal court.

161. See *Gonzaga v. Doe*, 536 U.S. 273 (2002).

162. Elizabeth M. Gallagher, "Advance Directive Instruments for Mental Health Treatment: Advance Directives for Psychiatric Care: A Theoretical and Practical Overview for Legal Professionals," 4 *Psych. Pub. Pol. and L.* 746, 769 (1998).

163. *Id.*

164. *Id.* at n. 113.

165. Revised Code of Washington 71.05.050 (2001).

166. Md. Health General Code Ann. 10-624(b)(2).

167. Md. Health General Code Ann. 10-624(b)(4).

168. 50 Pa.Stat.Ann. 7302(b).

169. 34B Maine Revised Statutes Annotated 3863(B). This limit is subject to certain exceptions.

170. 34B Maine Revised Statutes Annotated 3861(1) and 3861(2)(A).

171. Bellevue policy, on file at the Center for Public Representation.

172. For example, Connecticut courts have held that the patient bill of rights applies to the treatment psychiatric patients receive in emergency rooms, *Scherer v. Waterbury Hospital*, 2000 Conn.Super.LEXIS 481 (Conn.Super. Feb. 22, 2000).

173. Wisconsin does not require emergency departments to comply with patients' rights statutes, Wisc.Stat. 51.61(1), see *Sherry v. Salvo*, 555 N.W.2d 402 (Wisc.App. 1996).

174. *Scherer v. Waterbury Hospital*, 2000 Conn.Super.LEXIS 481 (Conn.Super. Feb. 22, 2000).

175. This case is filed under seal in federal district court in Connecticut.

176. *Wilmington General Hospital v. Manlove*, 54 Del. 15 (1961).

177. 237 Ill.2d 326 (1966).

178. Paul Appelbaum, "*Tarasoff* and the Clinician: Problems in Fulfilling the Duty to Protect," 142 *American Journal of Psychiatry* 425, 428 (1985) (man who threatened to kill his wife was transferred to an inpatient facility in his catchment area and staff there were warned of his threat). See, however, *Ewing v. Northridge Hospital Medical Center*, 120 Cal.App.4th 1289 (Cal.App. 2004) (when patient's father told therapist that patient had threatened to kill the new boyfriend of the patient's ex-girlfriend, the fact that the father was not a patient of the therapist's was not relevant to the duty to warn. No expert testimony was needed on the standard of care for the duty to warn.

179. *Arthur v. Lutheran General Hospital, et al*, 692 N.E.2d 1238 (Ill.App. 1998); *Riffe v. Armstrong*, 197 W.Va. 626 (1996).

180. *Scherer v. Waterbury Hospital*, 2000 Conn.Super.LEXIS 481 (Conn.Super. Feb. 22, 2000).

181. *Fair Oaks Hospital v. Pocrass*, 628 A.2d 829 (N.J.App. 1993).

182. *Mawhirt v. Ahmed*, 86 F.Supp.2d 81 (E.D.N.Y. 2000).

183. *Rodriguez v. City of New York*, 72 F.3d 1051 (2nd Cir. 1995).

184. *Tarlecki v. Mercy Fitzgerald Hospital*, 2002 U.S.Dist.LEXIS 12937 (E.D.Pa. July 15, 2002).

185. *Collins v. First Unknown Security Officer*, 2002 Conn.Super.LEXIS 3419 (Conn.Super. Oct. 24, 2002).

186. *Threlkeld v. White Castle Systems,* 127 F.Supp.2d 986 (N.D.Ill. 2001).

187. *Pastorello v. City of New York,* 2001 U.S.Dist.LEXIS 19919 (S.D.N.Y. Dec. 4, 2001).

188. *Tarlecki v. Mercy Fitzgerald Hospital,* 2002 U.S.Dist.LEXIS 12937 (E.D.Pa. July 15, 2002).

189. *Straub v. Kilgore,* 2004 U.S.App.LEXIS 10668 (6th Cir. May 27, 2004); *Tinius v. Carroll County Sheriff Department,* 321 F.Supp.2d 1064 (N.D. Iowa 2004).

190. *Atamian v. Hawk,* 842 A.2d 654 (De.Super. 2003).

191. *Tarlecki v. Mercy Fitzgerald Hospital,* 2002 U.S.Dist.LEXIS 12937 (E.D.Pa. July 15, 2002); *Payton v. Rush-Presbyterian-St.Luke's Medical Center,* 184 F.3d 623 (7th Cir. 1999); *John Jordan v. Thomas Jefferson University Hospital,* 23 Phila. 434, 1992 Phila.Cty.Rptr. LEXIS 4 (Common Pleas Court of Philadelphia County, January 10, 1992).

192. See *Williams v. Guzzardi,* 875 F.2d 46, 52 (3d Cir. 1989).

193. S.W.2d 236 (Tex.App. 1997).

194. *Id.* at 8.

195. *Id.*

196. *Id.* at 25.

197. 342 Pa. Super. 375, 492 A.2d 1382 (Pa. Super. Ct. 1985).

198. *Freeman v. St. Clare's Hospital and Health Center,* 156 A.D.2d 300 (N.Y.App. 1989) (patient raped in emergency room while she was in restraints; verdict of $125,000 against hospital).

199. *Garcia v. City of Boston and Boston Emergency Services Team,* 115 F.Supp.2d 74 (D.Mass. 2000).

200. Fla.Stat.Ann. 768.13(2)(b)1.

201. Ca.Stat.Ch. 1246; Fla.Stat.Ann. 766.102(6)(a), *Goss v. Permenter,* 827 So.2d 285, 289 (Fla.App.2002), *Barrio v. Wilson,* 779 So.2d 413 (Fla.App. 2000).

202. *Sheron v. Lutheran Medical Center,* 18 P.2d 796 (Colo.App. 2000) (defendant had "duty to exercise that degree of skill and knowledge ordinarily possessed by practicing psychiatrist in arriving at an informed and realistic assessment of the patient's medical condition"); *Bates v. Denny,* 563 So.2d 298 (La.App. 1990); *Mertz v. Temple University Hospital,* 29 Phila. 467, 1995 Phila.Cty.Rptr.LEXIS 33 (Common Pleas Ct. 1995); see also *Emergency Medicine Malpractice* 2.02(B) ("in a case against an emergency room specialist, the plaintiff generally must establish that the emergency department physician did not exercise the degree of skill and care ordinarily exercised by physicians within the same medical specialty to which he belongs.")

203. *Brown v. Carolina Emergency Physicians,* 560 S.E.2d 624 (S.C.App. 2001).

204. *Williams v. Shelby County Health Care Corp. Et al,* 803 F.Supp. 1306 (W.D.Tenn. 1992).

205. For an EMTALA case with a similar profile, see *Thomas v. Christ Hospital,* 328 F.3d 890 (7th Cir. 2003).

206. *Beattie v. Bristol Hospital,* No. CV-01-0508467S (New Britain, Ct. Oct. 24, 2003), available on LEXIS through Jury Verdicts directory and on file with the author.

207. *Jinkins v. Lee,* 807 N.E.2d 411 (Ill. 2004).

208. *Bates v. Denny,* 563 So.2d 298 (La.App. 1990).

209. *Id.*

210. *Mertz v. Temple University*, 25 Pa. D&C 4th 541, (Pa.Common Pleas 1995).

211. *Kassen v. Hatley and Johnson*, 887 S.W.2d 4 (Tx. 1994); *Jinkins v. Lee*, 807 N.E.2d 411 (Ill. 2004).

212. See, e.g., N.J.Stat.Ann.30:4-27.7 ("those acting in good faith pursuant to this act who take reasonable steps to assess, take custody of, detain or transport an individual for the purposes of mental health assessment are immune from civil and criminal liability").

213. *Shine v. Vega*, 429 Mass. 456, 709 N.E.2d 58 (1999).

214. *Scherer v. Waterbury Hospital*, 2000 Conn.Super.LEXIS 481 (Conn.Super. Feb. 22, 2000);

215. *Haynes v. Yale New Haven Hospital*, 699 A.2d 964 (Conn. 1997).

216. *Scherer v. Waterbury Hospital, id.* at n. 446.

217. See Restraint and Seclusion Q&A, online at www.jcaho.org/accredited+organizations/behavioral+health+care/standards/faqs/. The site was last revised on January 1, 2004.

218. Only PC 12.60, PC 12.70, PC 12.90, PC 12.100, PC. 12.110, PC 12.130, and PC 12.140 apply outside psychiatric units, *id.*

219. JCAHO, "Accreditation Issues for Emergency Departments," (2003), p. 97.

220. *Id.*

221. Comprehensive Accreditation Manual for Behavioral Health Care (2004).

222. PC 12.60.

223. PC 12.80.

224. PC 12.140.

225. PC 12.50. Joint Commission on Accreditation of Health Care Organizations, Restraint and Seclusion Standards for Behavioral Health. See also Introduction to Behavioral Health Care Restraint and Seclusion Standards, found online at www.jcaho.org/standard/restraint/restraint_stds.html.

226. PC 12.20.

227. American College of Emergency Physicians, Policy No. 400119, approved June 2000, available online at www.acep.org/library/index.cfm/id/680.

228. 9 *Journal of Psychiatric Practice* 16, 25 (January 2003).

CHAPTER 6

1. Information about Baystate Hospital and its response to Linda Stalker's complaint was derived from Fidela S. J. Blank, Marjorie Keyes, Ann M. Maynard, Deborah Provost, and John P. Santoro, "A Humane ED Seclusion/Restraint: Legal Requirements, a New Policy, Procedure, 'Psychiatric Advocate' Role," 30 *Journal of Emergency Nursing* (2004), and interviews with Deborah Provost and Ann Maynard on February 18, 2005.

2. Interview with Ann Maynard, Feb. 18, 2005.

3. Personal communication from Linda Stalker, April 19, 2005.

4. Michael J. Satein, David H. Gustafson, and Sandra Johnson, "Quality Assurance for Psychiatric Emergencies: An Analysis of Assessment and Feedback Methodologies," 13 *Psychiatric Clinics of North America* 35, 36 (1990).

5. David Dawson and Harriet MacMillan, *Relationship Management of the Borderline Patient: From Understanding to Treatment* (New York: Brunner/Mazell 1993).

6. Rose Ries, "A Foolproof Method of Quality Assurance in the Psychiatric Emergency Service," 48 *Psychiatric Services* 1515, 1516 (1997).

7. *Id.*

8. David F. Gustafson, et al., "Measuring Quality of Care in Psychiatric Emergencies: Construction and Evaluation of a Bayseian Index," *Health Services Research*, June 1993.

9. APA Task Force on Psychiatric Emergency Services, Report and Recommendations Regarding Psychiatric Emergency and Crisis Services: A Review and Model Program Descriptions (American Psychiatric Association 2002).

10. Ries, at note 6. This article only considers the appropriate use of seclusion and restraint, not reduction in rates of seclusion and restraint or duration of restraint and seclusion episodes.

11. APA Task Force on Psychiatric Emergency Services, at 93.

12. Developing alternatives to the current system has been one of the major recommendations in every survey of people who have used the emergency room for psychiatric crisis.

13. Ed Dwyer-O'Connor, David M. Wertheimer, Boston Triage Consultation, April 16, 2003 (location of triage unit relative to police station determined successful utilization of the unit).

14. The National Suicide Prevention Lifeline, 1-800-273-TALK, the only federally funded suicide prevention and intervention hot line, was initiated on January 3, 2005. Information is available online at www.suicidepreventionlifeline .org.

15. Interview with Ann Jennings, April 23, 2003.

16. Communication from Mark Joyce, Disability Rights Center of Maine, Feb. 17, 2005.

17. J. Geller, W. H. Fisher, and M. McDermeit, "A National Survey of Mobile Crisis Services and Their Evaluation," 46 *Psychiatric Services* 893 (1995).

18. W. H. Fisher, J. L. Geller, and J. Wirth-Cauchon, "Empirically Assessing the Impact of Mobile Crisis Capacity on State Hospital Admission," 26 *Community Mental Health Journal* 245 (1990).

19. G. R. Reding and M. Raphelson, "Around-the-clock mobile psychiatric crisis intervention," 31 *Community Mental Health Journal* 179 (1995).

20. K. Leaman, "A Hospital Alternative for Patients in Crisis," 38 *Hospital and Community Psychiatry* 1221 (1987).

21. *Id.*

22. *Id.*

23. The description of the START program is taken from William B. Hawthorne, Elizabeth E. Green, James B. Lohr, Richard Hough, and Peggy Smith, "Comparison of Outcomes of Acute Care in Short-Term Residential Treatment and Psychiatric Hospital Settings," 50 *Psychiatric Services* 401, 405 (1999), "APA Achievement Awards: Gold Award: A Community-Based Program Providing A Successful Alternative to Acute Psychiatric Hospitalization," 52 Psychiatric Services 1383 (2001).

24. *Id.*

25. Lorna Rhodes, *Emptying Beds* (University of California Press 1991) at 1.

26. *Id.* at 13.

27. Michael Stoll, "Homeless Overrun San Francisco General Hospital," *San Francisco Examiner*, July 5, 2002.

28. Loren Mosher and Lorenzo Burti, *Community Mental Health: A Practical Guide* (W.W. Norton 1994) at 45.

29. Institute of Medicine, *Crossing the Quality Chasm* (Washington, D.C.: National Academies of the Sciences 2001).

30. *Id.*

31. In *re Rosa M.*, 597 NYS2d 544 (N.Y.Sup.Ct. 1991).

32. *Vermont v. Hargrave*, 340 F.3d 27 (2nd Cir. 2003).

33. In *re Rosa M.*, 597 NYS2d 544 (N.Y.Sup.Ct. 1991).

34. *Vermont v. Hargrave*, 340 F.3d 27 (2nd Cir. 2003).

35. The Bazelon Center for Mental Health Law's Web site is www.bazelon .org.

36. Communication from J. Rock Johnson, April 20, 2005.

37. Personal Communication from Steven Miccio, April 20, 2005.

38. Trauma Conference, Fletcher Allen Hospital, Burlington Vermont, December 5, 2004.

39. Richard E. Breslow, "Structure and Function of Psychiatric Emergency Services," in Michael Allen et al., eds., *Emergency Psychiatry*, (Washington, D.C.: American Psychiatric Association 2002) at 24.

40. Review of Best Practices in Mental Health Reform, p. 30. Richard E. Breslow, "Structure and Function of Psychiatric Emergency Services," in Michael Allen et al., eds., *Emergency Psychiatry* (Washington, D.C.: American Psychiatric Association 2002) p. 24.

41. Personal communication from Dr. Michael Lambert, Dec. 20, 2004.

42. William B. Hawthorne, Elizabeth E. Green, James B. Lohr, Richard Hough, and Peggy Smith, "Comparison of Outcomes of Acute Care in Short-Term Residential Treatment and Psychiatric Hospital Settings," 50 *Psychiatric Services* 401, 405 (1999).

CHAPTER 7

1. Joint Commission on the Accreditation of Health Care Organizations, "The Emergency Department Overcrowding Symposium: Condition Critical: Meeting the Challenge of ED Overcrowding," Feb. 24–26, 2003, Sheraton Boston Hotel, Boston, Massachusetts.

2. Institute of Medicine, "Crossing the Quality Chasm: A New Health System for the 21st Century," Washington D.C.: National Academies of Science (2001).

3. Personal communication from Dr. William Anthony of the Boston University Center for Psychosocial Research, May 20, 2005.

4. "Death of the Hired Man," in Robert Frost, *Complete Poems of Robert Frost* (New York: Holt, Rinehart and Winston 1961), p. 53.

Index